# CUT, PASTE,
# KILL

## BY MARSHALL KARP

*For details and sample chapters
please visit* www.karpkills.com

# CUT, PASTE,
# KILL

## A Lomax and Biggs Mystery

# Marshall Karp

ISBN 978-1-7363792-0-2

Jacket design by Dennis Woloch
Book design by Kathleen Otis
Author photo by Fran Gormley

For information, email contact@karpkills.com.

In memory of

Uncle Icky,

Staff Sergeant Irving Ziffer,

an American hero

and

Jett,

my shadow, my friend

# CHAPTER 1

SHE SCRAPED THE salmon croquettes from her dinner plate into the cats' bowl.

Dizzy, the overweight tiger-striped tabby, took one lady-like nibble of the reheated, three-day-old fish, and walked off. Wayne, the black-and-white longhair, was curled up nose to tail in his favorite spot on the window seat. He didn't even pretend to be interested.

"At least try it," she said. "It's got omega-3. It's good for you."

Wayne yawned, the cat equivalent of giving her the finger.

"I know," she said. "If it's so damn healthy, how come I didn't eat it?"

She poured herself a cup of chai, stirred in five packets of Equal, added a splash of nonfat milk, and took a satisfying sip. Coffee gave her the jitters—definitely a handicap when you've got a pair of razor-sharp scissors in your hand. But the black tea had just enough caffeine to give her the kick she needed to work on her scrapbooks long into the night.

She opened a kitchen cabinet and pulled out a three-quart Tupperware storage bowl. Wayne bolted up.

"I figured this would get your testosterone going," she said, laughing.

The lid was opaque, but the kiwi-colored bowl was transparent enough to see what was inside.

1

Ping-Pong balls.

Three weeks ago there were twenty. Each one carefully numbered with a fine-point Sharpie.

Numbers six and fifteen had already been pulled.

That left eighteen Ping-Pong balls. Eighteen possible victims.

She swirled the bowl around, and four cat ears went on point as the balls skittered softly against the sides.

"Lotto time," she announced, as if the two smartest cats in Los Angeles needed any further explanation.

Then she shook the bowl vigorously. The little white celluloid spheres ricocheted against the polycarbonate container like a rattlesnake attacking a roll of bubble wrap.

Dizzy and Wayne were at her feet, swiping at her skirt, yowling for her to make her next move.

"Not so catatonic anymore, are we?" she said, trotting out the same old joke the kitties never seemed to get tired of hearing.

She pried off the top of the Tupperware and flung the contents against the kitchen wall.

The cats went batshit.

Dizzy waddled under the kitchen table in hot pursuit of a trio of balls. Wayne headed the other way, pounced on number 14, and sent it scooting under the stove.

Lotto night was traditionally a fish night, and since she had tossed the salmon, she decided to treat herself to some dessert. Ben & Jerry's Phish Food ice cream. She took a pint from the freezer and put it in the microwave for thirty seconds to get it nice and soft.

As soon as the timer dinged, she grabbed a spoon and began digging into the carton of creamy chocolate that was laced with caramel swirls, gooey marshmallows, and little fudge fish.

She sat down at the table, just as both cats, chasing the same ball, collided head-on.

It was a total hoot, and she only wished she could tape it and post it on YouTube. Look everybody . . . here are my two cats helping me pick a murder victim. I call it *Feline Felons*.

It took three minutes before Wayne nosed one ball into a corner and sank his teeth into it.

"We have a winner," she called out to the invisible crowd.

Wayne knew the drill. He hopped up on her lap, unclenched his teeth, and loudly demanded his reward.

"Number eleven," she said, examining the ball.

She lifted the cat from her lap, went back to the cabinet, and removed a Ziploc bag filled with leaves and stems.

"Game, set, match," she said to Dizzy, who was still too busy chasing Ping-Pong balls to know that the contest was over. "*Nepeta cataria* for everyone."

She opened the bag, grabbed a small fistful of catnip, and sprinkled it on the kitchen floor. Both cats dove in.

She put on a clean pair of white cotton gloves, went to the bedroom, opened her closet, and twisted the dial on the four-hundred-and-seventy-pound AMSEC safe that protected her precious scrapbooks from fire, water, and nosy Parkers.

Each scrapbook was sealed in its own numbered manila envelope. She felt giddy as she removed number eleven from the safe's plush velour interior. Although she had crafted every page of every scrapbook to perfection, she didn't know which book was in which envelope.

That was the whole idea. Random selection. Each scrapbook went into an identical envelope, then the envelopes were shuffled and numbered.

Dizzy and Wayne chose the winner.

Or in this case, the loser.

She closed the four-inch-thick steel door, yanked the handle and listened as the dead bar clanked into the belly of the safe. She twirled the chrome-plated dial and carried the Lotto-winning envelope to the kitchen.

Sitting down at the table, she scraped up the dregs of the ice cream and sucked the spoon dry. "Would you like to see who you picked?" she asked.

But Dizzy and Wayne were too busy licking themselves, licking each other, and rolling around in the intoxicating weed.

She laughed as she tore open the manila envelope. "Stoners," she said.

# CHAPTER 2

**"SO, MIKE, HOW'S** it going?" my father asked, tears streaming down his face. Granted, he was chopping onions, but still, there's something unnerving about watching a grown man cry.

And Big Jim Lomax is a man full grown. Six-foot-four, which is easy enough to verify, and three hundred pounds, which isn't. He's been claiming that same perfect bowling score weight since the Clinton administration, but I'm betting his scale simply ran out of numbers.

"It's going pretty good," I responded. "Terry and I just wrapped up that gangbanger homicide, and we—"

"I don't mean cop stuff. I'm your father, not Internal Affairs. I meant how's your life going?"

"Diana and I have been in the new house for six months. We finally got the painting done, and—"

"Mike, I've seen the house. I've been there fifty times."

"And two of those times you were actually invited."

He ignored the dig. "Okay, so you and Diana feel good about the house," he said. "How do you feel about everything else?"

Considering the fact that I'm a detective, you would think I'd have picked up on the obvious. When Big Jim asks how it's going, he's worse than Internal Affairs. "It" means my relationship with Diana.

I sidestepped the question. "The message you left on my answering machine said 'lunch at one.' It's 1:15, and we haven't been fed yet."

"Great artistry takes time," he said, giving the last onion a final chop. He put the knife down, wiped his eyes with a dish towel, and cleared his nasal passages with a loud wet snort.

"Very appetizing," I said. "You're lucky I work for LAPD and not the Board of Health."

He turned his attention to a bowl that was heaped with raw chopped meat. "So," he said in that tone of voice that lets you know he's tired of waiting for an answer, "how's it going?"

I deflected the question a second time. "And the rest of your message said there would be an announcement of major proportion. The only thing I've seen of major proportion is a pile of ground round the size of a bowling ball. Do you really need that much red meat for six people?"

"Hey, these aren't dinky-ass McDonald's burgers. These are Big Jim's Famous Cajun Cows on a Bun. The recipe calls for one pound per person."

"I hate to put a crimp in your artistry, but Diana and I can't handle your version of spicy," I said.

"What's wrong with it?"

"The last time I ate one of your burgers it burned the hair right off my chest. From the inside. Hold the Cajun on ours."

"Your loss," he said, digging into the bowl and scooping out a mound of beef. He plopped it into a smaller bowl.

"And hold the cow. We'll each have a dinky-ass burger."

"Hold the Cajun, hold the cow, what next, Mike? Hold the bun?"

"The bun is fine," I said, "but I'd be eternally grateful if you'd hold the transparent questions about my love life."

"*Moi?*" The three-hundred-pound cherub grinned. "Transparent? I was trying to be subtle, but that never works with you. So here's the question in five words. How's it going with Diana?"

"And here's the answer in five words: none of your business."

"That's four words."

"Do you really need the fifth word? Here's a hint. It starts with an F."

"You guys have a great relationship. I'm just curious if you have any plans to, like, maybe permanentize it?"

"Yeah. We're reading *Permanentizing for Dummies*. I'll keep you posted."

He started working the onions into the beef. "Diana isn't getting any younger, you know," he said. "Her biological clock is spinning like a windmill in a hurricane. And, for the record, so is mine. Your son needs a grandfather who can teach him to play ball, fly a plane, and take apart an engine. Or would you rather he just visit me when I'm in the nursing home, crapping in my diapers and drooling in my oatmeal?"

"I don't have a son," I said.

"That's my point, Mike. You should. It's time."

"Has it escaped you that Diana and I aren't even married?"

"Your mother and I weren't married either, and I got her pregnant."

"Once again, I fail to live up to your legacy."

The kitchen door opened, and Angel came in. Jim married her a few years after my mother died. My mom was a movie stunt-woman, tall and athletic, with red hair, fair skin, and classic Irish features. Angel is tiny, and her features are classic South of the Border: black hair, dark eyes, and caramel skin.

She walked up to Jim, her head barely reaching his chest. "Are you going to come outside and grill the hamburgers, or are you going to stay in here and grill your son?"

"You're way off base," he said. "We're just having a pleasant father-son chat."

She smiled at me. "He was sticking his nose into your personal life again, wasn't he, Mike?"

"Again? You mean still. And it wasn't just his nose. He was digging with all fours like a prairie dog with an obsessive-compulsive disorder."

She wagged a finger at him. "If we had more time I'd give you the lecture on personal boundaries again, but Marilyn and Terry are here and we're all hungry."

"Terry's here?" Jim said. "Good. At least I'll have someone to talk to who actually likes me."

The truth is, everyone likes my father. It's his style that can drive people a little nuts. His goal is to make people happy. The problem is Big Jim Lomax never bothers to ask *what* would make you happy. He decides for you. If he sees an old lady standing on a corner, he'll stop traffic and carry her across the street. It doesn't matter if she's screaming, "Put me down, you overgrown idiot. I was waiting for a bus."

He's all heart and no tact. I love him, but since I'm the one whose life he most enjoys trying to fix, I spend a lot of time trying to keep him at bay.

Jim, Angel, and I carried the food out to the backyard. It was late spring, so the place smelled of bougainvilleas and diesel fuel.

The flowers change with the seasons. The oil smell is year-round.

Jim is a trucker. He started out working for the movie studios as a driver. Early on, he realized that the people who rented out the cars and trucks to the film crews made more money than the people who drove them. Today he owns more than fifty equipment trucks, star trailers, and limos. At any given time, a lot of them are scattered over his four-acre spread in Riverside.

I put the food on the table, said hello to Terry and Marilyn, then headed over to Diana.

She looked spectacular—blond, tan, and at forty-three, totally hot. When my wife, Joanie, died I couldn't imagine ever loving another woman. I was wrong. I wanted to spend the rest of my life with Diana Trantanella. I was about to put my arm around her when my cell phone rang.

There are only four people who would call my cell on a Sunday. Three of them were here. That left Brendan Kilcullen, my boss.

I answered. "It's a beautiful Sunday afternoon, Lieutenant. I'd have thought you'd be out on the golf course."

"I was," he said. "Until the watch commander called. That's the thing about homicide, Lomax. It hunts you down, even when you're about to birdie the seventh hole. A woman was stabbed to death at The Afton Gardens Hotel. I need you and your partner on the case now. Do you know where he is?"

"Yes sir. Detective Biggs is ten feet away, contemplating suicide."

"I'm not in the mood for comedy," Kilcullen said. "Tell him to put his gun down, and—"

"It's not a gun," I said. "It's a cholesterol bomb. Should I tell him to cancel his lunch plans?"

"Lunch, dinner, Christmas, Easter. You two don't eat till you solve it. From what the watch commander tells me, this one is high profile."

"They're all high profile, boss. In Hollywood, even the murder victims are celebrities. What's the dead woman's claim to fame? Big screen, small screen, or straight-to-DVD?"

"None of the above. She's more of an O. J. Simpson type."

"She's a sports star?"

"No," Kilcullen said. "She killed someone last year and got away with it."

# CHAPTER 3

**"LUNCH WILL HAVE** to wait," I said. "That was Kilcullen. Terry and I have a date with a hot chick, and she's getting colder by the minute."

The three women took it in stride. Marilyn and Diana, because they're used to having their plans sandbagged by a homicide call, and Angel, because living with Big Jim is like training for the Who-Knows-What-The-Hell-Will-Happen-Next Olympics.

"We can go to Riverside Plaza," Angel said. "Chico's has some cute new summer tops."

"I'm game," Marilyn said.

"What about those of us who already have all the cute new summer tops we need?" Big Jim asked. "What am I supposed to do with six pounds of raw meat?"

"Knowing you, it won't go to waste," I said. "But Terry and I will take one car and be back as soon as we can for dinner and our womenfolk."

"And your father's big surprise," Diana said, putting her arm around as much of Jim's size XXXXX-L back as she could.

Jim softened. "At least somebody cares about my feelings. The problem with—"

Terry was already in the car, with the Kojak light flashing. He hit the siren and cut Jim off.

"Can't hear you, Dad. Gotta run." I jumped in the car.

"What have we got?" Terry asked as we peeled out.

"Woman stabbed to death at The Afton Gardens Hotel."

"That's the little hotel a few blocks from our office," Terry said.

"Yeah, it would have been incredibly convenient if we were at work, instead of an hour away, about to eat lunch."

"Forty minutes with lights and sirens," Terry said. "As for lunch, open these." He handed me a large bag of sour-cream-and-cheddar potato chips.

I flipped the bag over to look at the nutritional chart. "Wow, only a hundred and sixty calories and ten grams of yummy fat per ounce."

"Hey, I knew we were going to go hungry, so I grabbed it off the table. It was the healthiest snack he had."

"One three-hundred-pound Lomax is enough," I said, rolling down the window and flipping the bag onto the highway. "You can order room service when we get to the hotel."

"I don't think I can afford it. The Afton Gardens is pretty la-di-freaking-dah," he said. "We've had to send a couple of units out there for the occasional Drunk and Disorderly, but it's not the kind of hotel where you get a homicide."

"Kilcullen said we're dealing with a high-profile victim."

"That narrows it down to everyone in show business," he said. "Including Oprah's hairdresser."

"According to Kilcullen this woman's not in the biz."

"How else do you get to be high profile in LA?"

"She killed someone."

"Well, there's your motive," he said. "Who did she kill?"

"He didn't give me any details. You know Kilcullen. He just wants you to think this is the biggest case you ever caught."

"I'm hoping it'll be the fastest. Those burgers your father was whipping up looked like a meal and a half."

"The burgers weren't all he was whipping. Before you and Marilyn got there he was on my case about his new favorite subject."

"Ah yes . . . dropping little hints about grandkids?"

"He's done with hints. He brought out the big guns. He made it clear that Diana's biological clock is running out of juice, and that the bus that's taking him to the nursing home is double-parked outside."

"Knowing your father the way I do, I'd say that borders on subtlety," Terry said. "So what's this big announcement he's going to lay on us? Marilyn thinks he's going to retire."

"Fat chance. Big Jim has been renting and driving film trucks for forty years. It's the cushiest job in the world. He drives to a location, sits around doing nothing all day, then when the crew wraps, he drives back. If he retired, he would still sit around doing nothing; only he wouldn't get paid for it."

"So what do you think this big announcement is?"

"I don't know, but if I'm lucky, there's one thing he can say that would make me deliriously happy.

"What's that?"

"'Great news, everybody—I've decided to take a vow of silence.'"

# CHAPTER 4

CRIME SCENES ARE like football games. A lot of the people only show up for the tailgate party.

Terry and I got to The Afton Gardens Hotel, pumped up for the game. But the rest of the crowd—the media, the paparazzi, and the gawkers of every stripe—were there for the festivities.

Cop cars, CSU vans, and a morgue transport wagon were parked at cockeyed angles on both sides of the street, but there was a clear pathway that led right to the front canopy of the hotel. Terry took it.

"Good thing we're the lead detectives," he said, "or we'd never find parking."

There were dozens of people milling around on the business side of the yellow tape, but one guy stood out—a tall, young uniformed cop who smiled and waved like a game show hostess when we pulled up.

"Oh, look," Terry said. "It's Bobby Boy Scout. How much do you want to bet he's the first responder, and today is the day he lost his homicide virginity?"

We got out of the car, and the cop walked toward us smartly. "Detectives?" he said, taking a pad from his back pocket.

Terry nodded. "Mike Lomax and Terry Biggs. What have we got, Officer?"

"Officer Hector DeJean, sir. Just a second, sir." He turned to a cluster of blue uniforms who were working crowd control. "Yo, Tara, the detectives are here."

A female cop sauntered over. "Officer Tara Cibelli," she said. "Me and Hector, we were first on the scene."

"We've been here over an hour," DeJean said, "so we've already done a lot of legwork."

"Sorry we were late," Terry said. "My partner and I were under the misconception that Sunday was a day of rest. Just curious, Officer Legwork, is this your first homicide?"

"In real life, yes," DeJean said, "but I've fantasized about it hundreds of times."

"None of my business," Terry said, "but having done this a while I'd suggest you find a healthier fantasy. Like world peace, or winning the lottery, or getting naked with the starting lineup of your favorite women's basketball team. Tell us what you've got."

"Okay," he said, looking down at his notes. "The dead woman is Eleanor Crump."

"Eleanor Bellingham-Crump," Cibelli said.

DeJean looked at her. "Do we really need her middle name?"

"There's a hyphen," Cibelli said. "Bellingham-Crump is her last name."

DeJean turned back to us and twirled his finger in the air, like his partner was way too focused on the small stuff. "Fine," he said. "So there's a random hyphen in her name. Eleanor *Bellingham*-Crump. She's a British citizen. Her husband, Edward, is a diplomat with the British Embassy here in LA." He looked back at Cibelli. "Have I got it right so far?"

"It's the British Consulate," she said, "but no big deal. We have the address."

DeJean handed her the pad. "Here, you do it."

Cibelli took it, but she didn't look at it. "They live in Brentwood," she said. "They went to mass this morning at St. Mary of the Angels Anglican Church. After services he went off to play golf, and she and three women friends came to the hotel dining room for lunch. They ordered a round of cocktails, at which point the victim left the table and went to the ladies room. Drinks arrived, but Mrs. Bellingham-Crump didn't come back, so after ten minutes one of the friends checked on her. She was dead on the floor, stabbed."

"Good background, officers," I said. "Was she robbed or raped?"

DeJean jumped backed in, "No, sir," he said. "She left her purse at the table with the other women, and she's still wearing a whole bunch of expensive-looking jewelry, so I'd eliminate robbery. And there's no sign of sexual assault. It looks more like Murder One to me. According to the other women, coming to this hotel is kind of a regular Sunday ritual with them, so the killer must've known she'd be here. That's why I'm going with Murder One."

"Let me guess," Terry said. "You're studying for the Detective's Exam."

DeJean stood tall again and beamed. "Day and night, sir."

"Well, study the part where it tells you not to draw conclusions in the first five minutes."

DeJean's shoulders slumped. His partner just stood there looking bored.

"Officer Cibelli," Terry said. "I'm guessing you're not nearly as excited about catching a homicide as your partner here."

"Not unless the department is paying me extra," she said. "But I'm happy for Hector. This is a dream come true for him."

"I think we're all happy for Hector," Terry said. "Has the victim's husband been notified yet?"

"No, sir," Hector said, perking up again. "Do you want us to do it?"

"Definitely not," Terry said. "We like to see the look on the husband's face when we tell him his wife has been murdered."

"Smart," Hector said. "Get the husband's reaction firsthand.

15

Do you think he did it?"

Terry shook his head. "My partner and I just got here. According to the Detectives Manual we can't jump to conclusions till we've been on the scene a good solid twenty minutes."

"Well, it would be a bummer if the husband did do it," Cibelli said.

"And why's that, Officer?" Terry asked.

"He's a foreign diplomat working on American soil," she said. "So even if you found him standing over the body with the murder weapon in his hand and blood on his clothes, you still couldn't arrest him. The guy's got total diplomatic immunity."

"Good observation," Terry said. "Are you studying for the Detective's Exam, too?"

She frowned. "Not remotely."

"You should," Terry said. "I like the way you think."

# CHAPTER 5

THE LOBBY OF The Afton Gardens was elegant, understated, and completely devoid of Southern California glitz. More like nineteenth-century London, than twenty-first-century Hollywood.

Officer Cibelli was happy to be released, but DeJean insisted on escorting us to the crime scene.

"Move it, move it," he announced, parting the sea of busy criminalists, bored cops, and nervous hotel employees. "Lead detectives coming through." An aging bellman didn't move fast enough, and DeJean almost bowled him over.

"They'd get out of the way faster if you had the band play 'Hail to the Chief,'" Terry said.

"That's the dining room over there," DeJean said, pointing. "The victim is in the ladies room. This way." He turned left.

"This guy's like a bloodhound," Terry said. "I never would've seen that sign that said RESTROOMS."

Twenty feet later, we arrived at the yellow tape. "The scene of the crime," DeJean said triumphantly.

"Thanks," Terry said. "Finding the body is the second toughest part of our job."

"Do you mind if I hang around and watch?"

"Knock yourself out, kid," Terry said. "Maybe when we're done you can help us find our car."

Terry and I put on rubber gloves and shoe protectors and went in. I have limited ladies room experience, but it was obvious that this one had class. For starters, the toilets were discreetly out of sight. There was a row of four rosewood doors that I imagine were there to conceal the unsightly plumbing fixtures from female guests who only used the facility to brush their hair, fix their makeup, or do a line of coke.

To the right of the entrance was a marble countertop with three sinks. Above it, stretched across the entire wall, was a mirror. Below it, stretched across the plush green carpeting, was Eleanor Bellingham-Crump.

Even in death, she appeared to fit the profile of the clientele at The Afton Gardens. About forty-five, medium brown shoulder-length hair, a classic houndstooth jacket, matching skirt, and tasteful leather shoes. The only thing that set her apart from the other patrons was the pair of scissors protruding from her ribs.

Kneeling beside the body, snapping pictures, was Jessica Keating. "Hey guys, I was hoping you'd catch this case," she said. "How's your weekend going so far?"

"Unfortunately we caught the case just as we were about to sit down to eat," I said, squatting down next to her. "So we're both a little cranky."

"I had a leg of lamb in the oven," she said. "I guess all three of us got screwed out of Sunday lunch."

"Four of us," Terry said, dropping down to one knee. "She looks kind of dead."

"Good observation," she said. "I'll have to remember that for my report."

Terry leaned in to get a closer look at the scissors. "Hmmm, any idea what might have caused it?"

"At her age, any one of life's little disappointments could have done her in," Jessica said, "but I'm going to go with splenic hemorrhage caused by a pair of razor-sharp scissors entering her body at the left costovertebral angle."

"I love it when you talk dirty," Terry said. "Dumb it down for me."

18

"Somebody stuck the scissors under her last rib, rammed it up into her spleen and twisted the sucker real hard."

"Sounds lethal," Terry said.

"It's like putting a hamster in a blender. She bled to death in seconds."

"How come there's not a lot of blood?" I asked.

"It's all on the inside," Jessica said. "Clean, quick, effective. It's the same technique used by the Marines, the Green Berets, and the Navy SEALs."

"You think our killer has a background in the military?"

"Either that, or he has Internet access," she said. "Mike, these days if you want to know how to kill somebody, ask Google."

"I want to know who killed her," I said. "Can I Google that?"

"No, but I've got something that might help," Jessica said, standing up. She pointed to the sinks.

I had been at floor level since I walked into the room. Terry and I both stood up. There, on the marble countertop, was a leather-bound book, about twelve by ten.

"A photo album," I said.

"A scrapbook," Jessica said.

"I collect crime scene souvenirs," I said. "Can I go through it?"

"Not yet," she said. "We're still tagging and bagging it, but I looked at a few of the pages. It's all about Mrs. Bellingham-Crump."

I stood over it and looked down. The cover was black, with three words embossed in gold at the center.

JUSTICE FOR BRANDON.

"Who's Brandon?" I asked.

Jessica gingerly opened the book. As soon as I saw the newspaper clipping on the first page I remembered who Brandon was.

Brandon Cooper. Ten years old. About nine months ago, he was crossing in front of a school bus when a car mowed him down. He was killed instantly. The driver claimed she never saw the flashing yellow lights, or the red STOP sign extending from the left side of the bright orange bus. Or the four-foot boy.

The cops agreed that she couldn't see. She was blind drunk.

A jury would have put her away for a long time, but she never went to trial. No charges were filed. Eleanor Bellingham-Crump was protected by her husband's diplomatic immunity.

But it didn't keep someone from murdering her.

# CHAPTER 6

**IT DIDN'T TAKE** long to figure out that the only thing Terry and I could do in the ladies room was get in the way of the CSI team. So we left Jessica to commune with the dead, while we interrogated the living.

Our trusty guide dog Officer DeJean led us to the dining room. It had none of the old-world gravity of the wood and leather lobby. It was all chrome, glass, and sunlight—quite cheerful, although the three women seated at a window table looked anything but.

Terry and I introduced ourselves. Olivia Kind was the same age as the victim. Glynnis Campbell and Billie Trent were in their thirties. All three were smartly dressed, expensively bejeweled, and unquestionably shit-faced.

I turned to DeJean. "I thought you said they were on their first round of drinks."

He panicked. "They were." He turned to them. "Ladies, didn't I tell you, no more alcohol till the detectives interviewed you?"

"We must not have heard you," Olivia said.

"Or it was the fifty bucks we gave the bartender," Glynnis giggled. She was the prettiest of the three by far. Even in LA, where hot babes are a commodity, Glynnis would stand out.

"For fuck's sake, we were traumatized," Billie said. "We're having lunch with our friend, and she gets herself shanked in the crapper. Damn straight we're going to drink."

Billie was not pretty. Or damn straight. She was butch. Close-cropped black hair, and a black pantsuit. "I'm sorry for your loss," I said, "but alcohol makes you a less-than-reliable witness."

"We didn't witness shit," Billie said. "Eleanor went to the can. Ten minutes later Olivia goes in looking for her, and she comes out screaming 'Eleanor was stabbed.' I ran in, Glynnis called 911, end of story."

"Let's see if we can get a little more beginning of story," Terry said. "What's your relationship with the victim?"

"Casual acquaintance," Billie said.

"A minute ago you said she was your friend. Pick one."

"This is LA, Detective—it's all the same thing."

Terry turned to Olivia. "And how about you?"

"Definitely one of her dearest friends," she said. "I'm also her decorator. My husband and I were in church with Eleanor and her husband, Edward. Then the men went off to play golf and talk business at the club, and she and I came here with Glynnis and Billie."

"What kind of business?"

"Surely you've heard of my husband, William Kind. He's a distributor."

"Of what?"

She looked at him like he had pointed at the moon and asked, what's that big round yellow thing. "Movies," she said. "What else do people in Hollywood distribute?"

"And what business does a movie distributor have with a British diplomat?"

"Edward Bellingham-Crump is the British consul-general here in LA," she said. "Let's just say he can open doors that might otherwise be closed to me and my husband."

"What kind of doors?" I asked.

"Foreign distribution rights. Plus, Hollywood people adore the

Brits, so Eleanor and Edward were the perfect couple to invite to a dinner party. He's very charming, very droll, and she was . . ." Olivia groped for a compliment.

"Memorable," Billie said. "I remember the time she fell face-down in her vichyssoise."

"Oh, Billie," Glynnis said. "That's terrible. The poor woman just died."

Terry turned to Glynnis. "How about you? What's your relationship with the victim?"

"Friend," she said. "Also her personal fashion consultant."

"And is your husband in business with Mr. Belling-ham-Crump?" I said.

"Why don't you ask me," Billie said, "seeing as I'm her husband." She let out an inebriated laugh. "Do you guys really expect to find the killer? You can't even spot a pair of lesbians."

"You completely threw me off with your girlish charm," Terry said.

"Hey, pal, you want to see girlish charm?" Billie said. "Sit down and watch me kick your ass in arm wrestling."

"I doubt it," Terry said. "It's hard to arm wrestle when you're in handcuffs. And if you're still hot to kick my ass, we can do it at the station."

Billie sat fuming. She opened her mouth and let out a loud burp. Glynnis winced, but said nothing.

I stepped in. "Olivia," I said, "you discovered the body."

"Yes. I'll never forget it for as long—"

"And you saw the book," I said.

Olivia gasped. It was a little on the theatrical side. I wondered if she was putting it on.

"I saw it, but I didn't touch it," she said. "I watch *CSI*. I know better than to get my personal fingerprints on it."

"What book?" Glynnis asked.

"It was in the bathroom," Olivia said.

"It said *Justice for Brandon* on the cover," I said.

Glynnis opened her mouth, and then thought better of it.

"You recognize the name?" I said.

She shrugged. "I'm not sure. Wasn't that the name of the little boy who ran out in front of her car?"

Terry exploded. "Ran out?" he said. "She was driving drunk."

Glynnis gnawed at her pretty little lower lip. Billie sat in tortured silence, bubbling over with hate for the cop who had gotten tough with her girlfriend.

Olivia tried to help us see things in a better light. "But that was all behind her," she said. "Eleanor didn't drink and drive anymore. They revoked her license."

"And which one of you sober ladies was the designated driver to take her home after lunch?" Terry asked.

Nobody answered.

We interviewed them for another ten minutes. None of the three saw anything suspicious. And as far as I could tell, none of them really gave a shit about the late Mrs. Bellingham-Crump. Their relationship with her was based on the fact that she brought money, influence, and the cachet of British society to the table. They were sauced, but I doubted if they'd be any more helpful sober.

We gave them each our cards and told DeJean to take their car keys and drive them home.

"Pisses me off," Terry said. "A woman gets drunk, kills a kid, and those harpies cheer her up by getting her drunk again. And by the way, I could arm wrestle that butch bitch to the ground left-handed."

We checked in with Detective Chris High. Chris is a Brit who left Manchester for LA because we have more sun, more surf, and more homicides. He runs the Hollywood Apprehension Team. When a detective gets a warrant, the HAT Squad makes the arrest. Today they were helping us out by canvassing the hotel staff, the guests, and the parking lot attendants.

"Nobody saw bloody anything," he said. "Two of the bloody

security cameras in the lobby don't work, and the third one just shows people coming and going. We'll go through it, but I don't expect to see anyone wearing a sign that says Killer. And of course, there's no video surveillance in the ladies loo."

"We're going to break the news to the victim's husband," I said. "He's the British consul-general. Do we call him your lordship or something like that?"

High laughed. "He's not the bloody ambassador. He's just some wanker with a cushy job. But knowing his type, I can tell you he's going to throw you lads off your game."

"How so?"

"When you tell him his Mrs. is dead, you'll be watching for his reaction," High said.

"Homicide 101," I said. "If he had a hand in it, he's been rehearsing his reaction. Terry and I are pretty good at telling the difference between genuine grief and an I-can't-believe-she's-really-dead soap opera performance."

"That's the thing," High said. "This man may not react. He's a Brit and a lifelong diplomat. He's learned to control his emotions. Stiff upper lip and all that. So just because the poor bloke doesn't start bawling when you tell him his wife is dead doesn't bloody mean he killed her."

"Good advice," Terry said. "But it also doesn't bloody mean he didn't."

# CHAPTER 7

**THE BELLAGIO COUNTRY** Club was just what we expected: a vast expanse of plush green fairways and rich white people.

The woman at the front desk looked at our badges, nodded, and quietly informed us that she would get the manager.

Half a minute later, the manager, a good-looking young man wearing a blue blazer, white golf shirt, and Nantucket reds stepped out of the office.

"Graham Jaenicke," he said. "How may I be of service?"

Jaenicke is polite for a living, so he acted as if he were delighted to have two LAPD homicide detectives drop by the club on a Sunday afternoon. I let him know how he could be of service.

"I'll be right back," he said.

"Very congenial fellow," Terry said. "And I loved the duds. He was a vision in red, white, and blue. I didn't know whether to shake his hand or salute."

Jaenicke returned with the news. "Mr. Bellingham-Crump's foursome should be at the fourteenth hole," he said. "We have a strict no cell phones policy, so I'll send a golf cart out to bring him back."

Ten minutes later Bellingham-Crump arrived. He was in his late forties, six feet tall, with graying hair, a trim athletic body, and a firm handshake. He wore green golf slacks and a white shirt with the club logo on it.

In addition to their strict no cell phone policy, the club also had a no-shabbily-dressed-cops-interrogating-our-members-in-public policy.

Nantucket Red shepherded us into his office. "Why don't you conduct your business in here, Detectives?" he said. "You'll be far more comfortable."

"And far less embarrassing," Terry muttered to me as we entered the office and closed the door.

Cops don't make country club calls unless they've got something really rotten to tell you. Bellingham-Crump stood stone-faced, waiting for us to lay it on him.

"Sir," I said, "I have some bad news about your wife."

His eyebrows arched. It wasn't exactly anger, but he definitely seemed peeved. "She doesn't have access to a car," he said. "What trouble can Eleanor possibly have gotten herself into this time?"

"She's been murdered," I said. "Stabbed to death at The Afton Gardens Hotel. I'm very sorry for your loss."

Not all stereotypes are true, but in this case Chris High had gotten it right. Edward Bellingham-Crump barely blinked. "Are you sure it's her?" he asked.

"Yes, sir."

He removed his glasses, pinched the bridge of his nose, and slowly massaged the area below his brow. We stood quietly as he let it sink in. After a minute he wiped his eyes and put his glasses back on. "Do you know who did it?" he asked.

"Not yet, sir," I said. "We're hoping you can help us with that."

We gave him the details, leaving out the part about the scrapbook.

"I work for the British government," he said. "Do you think killing my wife could have been politically motivated?"

"Was your wife political?" I asked.

He shook his head. "No. Any attack against my government would more likely be aimed at me. Although Eleanor did have

27

. . ." He stopped. More likely out of embarrassment than some code of international diplomacy.

"Sir, please say whatever comes to mind. It can only help us."

"Yes, of course. My wife had some personal problems. She was recently the victim of some very bad press."

I wanted to remind him that mowing down a fourth grader in your Jag tends to get the media's knickers in a twist, but I decided to be more—I don't know—diplomatic.

"Yes, we heard," I said. "Have you been in touch with Brandon Cooper's family since the accident?"

"I made a condolence call the day it happened, but they refused to meet with me. Naturally, I paid the funeral expenses."

"Did they sue you?" Terry asked.

"No," he said. "I think the Coopers were advised by their attorneys that it would be fruitless to sue someone with diplomatic immunity. They agreed to accept a personal settlement from me in exchange for dropping all future litigation."

"How much did you give them?" Terry asked.

"I'd rather not disclose the amount. Suffice to say it was not enough to compensate for the loss of their child."

Terry, the father of three, didn't respond. He just drilled a silent stare into Bellingham-Crump.

"Detectives, my wife was not a monster," Bellingham-Crump said, "and I assure you that Her Majesty's government dealt with the incident most sternly. They also generously paid for Eleanor to go to a top-notch rehabilitation facility here in California."

"They may want a refund," Terry said. "She ordered a double vodka tonic at lunch."

"She abstained from alcohol during the week," Bellingham-Crump said. "She wasn't particularly enamored of Olivia Kind or the other two women, but she knew they wouldn't divulge her secret. None of those cackling hens are poster girls for the Temperance Union. I knew, of course, but I turned a blind eye."

"What time did you last see her?" I asked.

I made it sound like it was just a casual fact-check, but Belling-ham-Crump is a pro who knows when a question is dead serious. He needed a tight alibi. He didn't waste a word providing one.

"Eleanor and I went to Mass at ten. I said good-bye to her at the church at eleven-thirty. She drove to The Afton Gardens with Mrs. Kind. I drove to the club with her husband, Bill, and changed. I had a twelve forty-three tee time. I can provide any number of witnesses."

"Were there any threats on your wife's life after Brandon Cooper's death?" I asked.

"For obvious reasons, Detective Lomax, our home address is kept confidential, but after the accident, a number of letters were sent to me at the Consulate. The usual outcry—people demanding justice and telling us to go home."

"Did you consider going back to England?"

"Did *I* consider it? I thought it best to leave LA. My government agreed. But Eleanor was against it. She felt that she had already ravaged one family, and she begged me not to let the accident destroy my career. In reality, it already had. Having a wife who drinks too much is a major liability when you're angling for an ambassadorship. But Eleanor rang up her father. He's an earl, and I'm certain he pulled some strings, because when the dust settled, I was told I could stay, but the issue would be revisited in six months."

"These letters that you got," Terry said. "Did you show them to your wife?"

"To what end?" he said. "They were vile, ugly rants, filled with obscenities. One person sent a box of dog feces." He paused, then lowered his voice. "Eleanor already hated herself. Why would I want to expose her to any further hatred?"

"It could help us find your wife's killer if you exposed them to us," I said.

"I'm sorry," he said. "I disposed of it. All of it."

*Getting rid of evidence. How convenient.* "Why didn't you just file it away for future reference?" I said.

"Shall I have filed the box of dog shit as well?" he said. "As far as I'm concerned, Detective, it was all dog shit."

"Were any of the letters signed?"

He shook his head. "I doubt if any of the senders were traceable."

"We'll never know," Terry said.

"Tell us what you remember," I said. "Any little detail could help."

He closed his eyes. "Most were typed. Many of them poorly worded. One was in pencil in a child's composition notebook. All rather rudimentary, except for one card—it was handcrafted. On the outside was a picture of a child's classroom. On the blackboard in red letters it said, *Human Blood Is Heavy.* Inside, it said something like *The Person Who Sheds That Blood Can Not Run Away.* I hope that helps," he said.

"It would have helped if you hadn't gotten rid of it," Terry said.

I could see Edward's veneer crack just a little. This man was not used to being reprimanded—at least not by a couple of street cops.

"Detective Biggs," he said, "hate mail is something I've dealt with my entire career—every diplomat does. There are people out there who resent the special privileges and immunities we enjoy. What they don't appreciate is that American diplomats around the world are afforded the same courtesy. It's the essence of international relationships that a host country is expected to tolerate the actions of another nation's emissary living in your midst."

"With all due respect," Terry said, "I think most Americans wouldn't give a rat's ass if you ignored a thousand parking tickets, but run down one of our kids, and our accommodating attitude goes sour in a big hurry."

"I make no excuses for my wife's actions, and I can assure you there were consequences, but answer this: is the international law that protects me and my family any different from the unwritten law that protects your rich, your famous, and their miscreant offspring? I find it fascinating, sir, that Americans are more forgiving toward a coked-up film star than they are of an otherwise decent family woman, who had an admittedly tragic lapse of judgment. This interview is over. I would like to see my wife and make arrangements to bring her home to England—something I should have done months ago."

"She's at the morgue," I said. "You can identify her, but I'm afraid this is a criminal investigation, and the body won't be released for several days."

"Gentlemen," he said, raising his voice, "if I choose, I can assure you that I have enough leverage to have her in London before the Queen has her first cup of tea tomorrow morning." He took a deep breath and modulated his voice from angry husband to professional diplomat. "That said, I don't want to hinder your investigation, so for now I'll acquiesce to your rules."

"Thank you, sir," I said. "Again, our condolences. I'm sorry for your loss. We'll do everything in our power to find your wife's killer."

I extended my hand. He softened and shook it, less firmly this time.

Terry, too, reached out his hand. Bellingham-Crump graciously accepted the gesture. Terry looked like an understanding mortician, about to say, "I'm so sorry for your loss."

But instead he said, "Was your wife having an affair?"

It was a totally unexpected kick in the balls, and the cracks in Bellingham-Crump's diplomatic armor were on the verge of becoming steaming fissures. He probably would have liked to beat Terry's head in with a nine iron. But he maintained his composure.

He smiled faintly. "Ah, American diplomacy," he said. "It

flourishes in every corner. To my knowledge, Detective, Eleanor was not, nor has she ever been involved with another man. But if you find out otherwise, please be so generous as to let me know."

And with that, Edward Bellingham-Crump took his leave.

# CHAPTER 8

**CINDY AND TED** Cooper lived on Homewood Road, a friendly, tree-lined street, in Brentwood.

As soon as Terry and I got out of the car we caught the sounds of kids splashing in backyard pools, and the smells of Sunday barbecues. It felt so welcoming, so safe, that it was hard to imagine the horror that had taken place on this very spot a few months before.

The house was simple, two stories with an attached garage. We had to dodge the spray from the automatic lawn sprinklers as we went up the paved walk. Before we could ring the bell, a man opened the door. He was in his late thirties, well tanned, with sandy hair and serious brown eyes.

"I'm Ted Cooper," he said. "My wife and I were expecting you."

We showed him our badges, which he barely looked at. Then he escorted us into the living room and introduced us to his wife, Cindy.

"You're here about Mrs. Bellingham-Crump, aren't you?" she said.

"What about her?" I asked.

The husband jumped in. "Give us a break, will you, Detective. A diplomat's wife is murdered at a bar. How long do you think it takes to hit the Internet? We've already gotten five phone calls

33

telling us the news. And since nobody wanted her dead more than we did, we figured LAPD would show up."

"We're deeply sorry for the loss of your son," I said, "but I hope you understand that you're connected to the murder victim—"

He interrupted. "Connected? I guess that's a polite way to describe our relationship with the drunken bitch who ran down our son."

He grabbed a picture frame from the mantel and shoved it toward my face. "This is Brandon. This is how we're connected to Eleanor Bellingham-Crump. Our only son was your murder victim's last victim."

I took the picture from him. It was a young boy with sandy hair and brown eyes, the ten-year-old version of Ted Cooper. The boy was wearing a Little League uniform, and the camera had caught him with both arms thrust in the air, savoring a sweet moment of victory. I passed it to Terry, who looked at it for half a minute, then set it gently back on the mantel.

"Our condolences on your loss," Terry said. "My partner and I are obligated to ask you a few questions, but we can come back another time."

"Let's just get it over with," he said. "Have a seat."

We all sat down.

"Are Cindy and I suspects?" he asked.

"No, sir, but I have to ask where you were today at noon."

"We were on the Santa Monica pier collecting signatures and donations for our Justice for Brandon Fund."

"What kind of justice are you looking for?" I asked.

"Not Texas justice, if that's what you're getting at. Right after Brandon was killed, the Brits offered us a cash settlement of fifty thousand dollars. Can you believe that? Fifty thousand, for the life of a beautiful, talented, young boy. We contacted a law firm to see if we could sue for more. They were very nice, but they told us we were pissing up a rope. So we took the money and started a campaign to change the law that gives drunks like Mrs. Bellingham-Crump diplomatic immunity when they mow down innocent children."

"Which law firm did you retain?" I asked.

"Karen Winters," Cooper said. "She's not exactly a law firm. It's just her and a paralegal, but at least we didn't have to shell out a big retainer fee. Karen believed in our cause and she's helped us set up a not-for-profit corporation. She hasn't taken a penny, and she and her assistant have put in hours and hours."

"Karen is totally behind us," Cindy Cooper added. "A lot of people are. They believe in Justice for Brandon."

"Do you think any of your supporters might prefer revenge over justice?" I asked.

"I'll bet a lot of them would," Cooper said.

"Anyone in particular that you might be able to single out?"

He gave me a smile that was loaded with contempt. "We have a petition with five thousand names, an e-mail database of thousands more, and there are two dozen fourth graders at Brentwood Elementary who are still grieving for my son. I'll give you the list. Take your pick."

# CHAPTER 9

**BY THE TIME** we got back to Big Jim's place, it was dark and drizzling.

"It's about time," Big Jim said. "I've got three women here who are practically starving to death."

"Well, that sure trumps us," Terry said. "All we had was one woman who bled to death."

"Hey, just because your murder victim had a bad day, doesn't mean she gets to ruin it for everyone else," Jim said.

"You're right, Dad," I said. "And I promise that nobody else will get to ruin our evening except you."

Jim smiled. "Thank you, son. I'll do my best."

Dinner was obscene.

"That is a lot of meat," Marilyn said when Jim brought the platter of burgers to the table. "Where'd you get the recipe? *The Joy of Coronary Disease?*"

We dug in. As hungry as we were, there was still enough left over to feed a homeless shelter.

After dinner Angel brought out coffee and a plate of cookies, and then we all turned our attention to the guy who was waiting to be the center of attention.

"I think we're ready, Dad," I said. "What's your big surprise?"

"My what? Oh yes, my surprise. I almost forgot." He beamed. "Ladies and gentlemen, Big Jim Lomax is happy to announce that he is going into the movie business."

"Dad, you've been in the movie business for forty years."

"As a trucker," he said. "But now I'm going to be a screenwriter. I sold an idea to a movie producer."

"That's fantastic," Diana said. "Who bought it?"

"Norman Untermeyer."

"I never heard of him," Marilyn said.

"I have," I said.

"Cool," Diana said. "What has he done?"

"He pulled my wisdom teeth," I said. "Norman Untermeyer is a dentist."

"Well, he's branching out," Jim said. "You can't get rich pulling teeth. He's got some money, and he's planning to make a movie. My movie."

"How much did he give you?" I asked.

"No actual cash," Big Jim said. "But as of now all my cleanings are free. Once I write the script, we'll talk real money."

"At the risk of being obvious," I said, "what do you know about writing a script?"

"That's the whole point," Jim said. "I don't have to know how to write a script. I'm the concept guy. I have the plot, the story, the characters. All I need is someone who's good at . . . you know, word shit."

"Oh, I get it," I said. "All you need is someone to do all the work."

"No. I just need somebody to help me write some dialogue. Ninety percent of a movie is the big idea, and I've already got that."

"So what's it about?" Terry asked.

"Okay," Jim said. "It's about a couple of ex-cops who become—are you ready for this—they become long-haul truckers."

I laughed out loud. "You're writing a movie about Teamsters?"

"No, not Teamsters, Mike. They don't join the Teamsters

union. They just travel across the country, delivering shit by truck."

"Like what?"

"Like it doesn't matter *what* they deliver. That's just the setup. The real story is that they're driving this big-ass semi all around the country and because they're ex-cops they can't stop solving crimes wherever they go."

"It sounds like it could be fun," Diana said. "Ex-cops who become truckers and solve lots of crimes. I like it."

"Ah, the voice of reason," Jim said. "Thank you, Diana."

"What's the movie called?"

Jim smiled. "*Semi Justice.*"

I almost spit out my coffee. "Semi *Justice?* Isn't that like Half *Justice?*"

"Don't be stupid," Jim said. "A semi is a truck. It basically means Trucker Justice. Jeez, Mike, it's not that complicated. Terry, what do you think?"

"I like it," he said. "Ex-cops riding around in a big rig, solving crimes wherever they go—it's kind of like The Lone Ranger and Tonto in an eighteen-wheeler."

"Exactly," Jim said pounding his palm on the table. "And do you think the guy who came up with The Lone Ranger and Tonto sold it right away? He probably had to pitch the idea to guys like Mike, who'd be saying 'a masked man and an Indian, riding around, solving crimes and leaving silver bullets—who would want to watch that?' It takes vision to see how a good idea can pay out. I got vision. Dr. Untermeyer has got vision. And so do you, Terry. You want to help me write it? I know the trucking business inside and out. You know cop things, and you're funny. We team up; we can't miss. What do you say?"

"I never wrote a movie script," Terry said, "but once you've got the story, how hard can it be? Hell, I'll give it a shot."

"How much money do you think you guys can make?" Marilyn asked.

"Millions," Jim said. "With sequels and video games and action figures and all the rest of that movie merchandise, the sky's the limit. And even though it's my idea, we split it fifty-fifty."

"Okay," Marilyn said. "But only on one condition. Until we see some actual money, the girls and I get free dental work."

"I don't know," Jim said. "Do the girls need braces?"

"No, that's all done and paid for," Marilyn said. "I'm just talking about cleanings and normal stuff."

"Deal," Jim said. "With Terry's cop credentials, Norman would be crazy not to do it. I'll call him first thing in the morning."

He reached across the table and shook Marilyn's hand. Then he shook Terry's. "You got a damn good agent there, Detective," Jim said.

"And she can cook," Terry said. "This could be fun. I'm psyched."

"I think it's exciting," Diana said.

"We all think it's exciting," Angel said.

"Except Mike," Jim said. "I think Mike thinks that the whole thing is dumb."

"No, not at all," I said. "I just think it's Semi Dumb."

# CHAPTER 10

TERRY AND I showed up at the crime lab at seven o'clock Monday morning. Jessica Keating must have been there for hours, because the *Justice for Brandon* scrapbook had been disassembled, photographed, and Jess had spread big blowups of the pages everywhere.

"There are way too many clues here for me," Terry said. "This looks like a scene from *The Da Vinci Code on Steroids*."

"It's a lot less confusing when all we have to go on is a tire track and a pubic hair," I said. "I don't even know where to start."

"Dr. Keating, at your service," Jess said. "Let's start from the beginning. How much do you know about scrapbooking?"

"A little less than I know about brain surgery," Terry said. "I'm vaguely aware that some people do it, and I know I'm not one of them."

"That's what I figured," she said. "I, on the other hand, am a third-generation Midwestern scrapper. I even have a merit badge in scrapbooking."

"I thought LAPD only gave merit badges in crime solving and cookie sales," Terry said.

Jess kept going. "For a lot of people scrapbooking is more than a hobby. It's an obsession. They can labor over a single page for days . . . even weeks."

"Just to cut and paste a couple of pictures?" Terry said.

"That's what you do for a photo album. Scrapbooking is an art. It's all about telling a story or preserving a memory through creative design. Look at how this is crafted," she said. "The early pages have photomontages of Brandon Cooper's life—birthday parties, Little League, family outings—they paint the picture of a happy, healthy child."

"Stop right there," I said. "Where did the killer get all these personal pictures of Brandon?"

"His mother posted them online," Jess said. "She belongs to a social networking site that's kind of like Facebook for proud parents. It gives them a public place to share their kids' achievements. The killer just pulled shots of Brandon off the Web site. It makes the front section of the scrapbook all the more poignant. Now, here's where it starts to get ugly."

She pointed to the blowups from the middle section. "Notice how the color palette goes from warm to harsh. Even the font changes to one that is angrier. That's not the work of an amateur. That's rather elegant design."

"Write that down, Mike," Terry said. "We're looking for someone elegant."

I studied one of the pages. The background was a collage of newspaper clippings about Brandon's death. Overlaying that was a mosaic of pictures that illustrated the horror of the event—bottles of booze, skid marks, a school bus, police cars, emergency medical units, a chalk outline in the road, and in case all that was too subtle for you, a Photoshopped Jaguar emblem that dripped blood.

Jess continued to walk us through the book. "These next few pages track the public's outrage when it was announced that Mrs. Bellingham-Crump would not be charged. And finally the scrapbooker begins to make overt threats. This one is particularly inventive."

The page had the feel of a Rockwell painting. It was a school nurse's office, with a prominent sign that said *Make Sure Your Child Gets His Immunity Shots*. But some of the words had been changed, so it now read, *Make Sure Your Diplomat's Wife Gets Her Immunity Shots*. Next to it was a picture of Eleanor Bellingham-Crump with a skull and crossbones superimposed over her face.

"You really know a lot about this crap," Terry said. "So you think whoever made this one is pretty good at it."

"Better than good," Jessica said. "The M's and P's are beautiful."

"What about the other twenty-four letters?" Terry asked.

"M's and P's," Jessica repeated. "Memorabilia and photographs. A lot of people include the usual predictable souvenirs—matchbooks, airline tickets, concert stubs—but the real artists are much more original. This is very creative and extremely well crafted. Whoever did this has been scrapbooking for years. She's probably got a cropping case the size of a Honda."

"Sounds like Martha Stewart on a rampage," Terry said. "I knew they should never have let her out of the slammer."

"We appreciate the education on the fine art of scrapbooking," I said. "But what about that forensics thing LAPD pays you to do?"

"Unfortunately, forensics is where I come up short," she said. "There are no prints, and the scrapbook itself is the kind you can easily buy online or in any scrapbooking store in America."

"There's more than one scrapbooking store?" Terry said.

"Oh, honey, you have no idea. Scrapbooking is a multi-billion-dollar industry. In the Midwest it's practically a way of life. My grandma scrapbooked, my mom scrapbooks, and defying all California stereotypes, I still scrapbook, although these days mine are mostly digital."

"Grandma, Mom, and you," I said. "Any of the men in your family do this?"

"Grandpa had a collection of license plates and beer bottles, my dad has electric trains, and my husband belongs to a fantasy football league. It's pretty much a chick thing."

"So you think our killer is a woman?"

"I have no physical evidence to support it," she said. "And while most scrapbooks are done by women, most violent premeditated murders are not."

"So we don't have much," I said.

"There's one thing I can give you," she said. "Our scrapper has cats. Even with the page protectors, I found traces of cat hair from two separate cats on at least half a dozen pages."

"Unfortunately, cat hair isn't like DNA or fingerprints," I said. "We don't have a database that can lead us to a suspect."

"Maybe we could round up all the suspicious-looking cats and question them," Terry said.

"This scrapbook took a lot of work," I said. "But it also took a lot of passion. Somebody put their heart and soul into this. Somebody who really wanted justice for Brandon."

"Ted and Cindy Cooper come to mind," Terry said.

"That's what I'm thinking," I said. "They could have put together the scrapbook, then hired someone to do the killing on a Sunday morning, when they'd have plenty of witnesses to vouch for their whereabouts. We should subpoena their bank records."

"Ted Cooper seemed too smart to leave a paper trail on their personal account," Terry said. "He's more likely to dip into the Justice for Brandon Fund. Funneling money out of a not-for-profit is harder to spot."

"Especially if the lawyer who is handling the finances is just as dedicated to the cause as he is," I said. "Let's go pay a visit to Ms. Winters."

"But first let's stop at one of those cool scrapbook stores," Terry said.

I looked at him. "What for?"

He clutched both hands to his heart. "This case has become so fascinating, I suddenly have an urge to preserve all these precious memories."

# CHAPTER 11

KAREN WINTERS LEGAL Services was in a strip mall on South Figueroa, tucked between a dry cleaner and a pet supply store.

"It may be a storefront law firm," Terry said, "but you can tell she caters to an upscale clientele. No neon."

I opened the door and an electronic chime announced our arrival. The man at the front desk stood up and welcomed us like we were the prize patrol from Publisher's Clearing House. "Good morning, gentlemen. How can I help you?"

He was trim, about medium height, with Matt Damon boyish good looks that made it hard to tell which side of thirty-five he was on. He was wearing the traditional uniform of the storefront lawyer: shirt with the sleeves rolled up, tie loosened at the neck, and jeans. He was so eager to help I hated to break the news to him.

"Detectives Mike Lomax and Terry Biggs," I said. "LAPD Homicide."

He shrugged, but kept on smiling. "Which one of our illustrious clients brings you here?"

"We'd rather discuss that with Ms. Winters," I said. "Is she in?"

"She's on the phone. I'm Cody Wade, her paralegal, but I also make a mean cup of coffee. If we ever strike it rich, the first thing we're buying is a cappuccino machine like the big law firms. Can I get you gentlemen anything?"

"No, thanks," I said. "How long do you think she'll be on the phone?"

"Minutes. I'll slip her a note and let her know you're waiting." He headed toward a glassed-in office in the rear.

"Friendliest damn lawyer I ever met," Terry said.

"He's just a paralegal," I said. "They don't go sour till they pass the Bar."

"Look at this," Terry said.

There was a table against the wall filled with Justice for Brandon paraphernalia—signs, pamphlets, pins, donation envelopes, and a clipboard with a petition attached.

Cody bounced back into the room. "Karen will be out in a few minutes. Are you sure I can't get you some coffee, water, anything?"

"No, we're good, thanks," Terry said. "I see you're one of the collection points for Justice for Brandon."

"Global headquarters actually," Cody said. "We're big supporters of Mr. and Mrs. Cooper. It's a good cause."

"I've been meaning to donate," Terry said, "but I'm on a cop's salary, so I can't afford much."

"Hey, no . . . we don't ask for much," Cody said. "We have a few big donors and a lot of little ones."

"I guess you're right," Terry said. "A buck here, a buck there, it all adds up."

"It does, and every donor is a voice added to our cause. The louder we get, the better we'll be heard."

Terry reached into his pocket and took out a five-dollar bill. "Here," he said. "Keep up the good work."

Cody grabbed a pin from the basket on the table, and handed it to Terry. "Thank you, thank you. Would you like to sign our petition?"

"Not really," Terry said.

"Fair enough. Can I have your name and address for our database?"

"I'd rather just be anonymous," Terry said, "but I bet you get a lot of people who say that."

"On the contrary," Cody said. "Most people are proud of the affiliation."

"So," Terry said, slipping the pin in his pocket, "where do all these Justice for Brandon donations go?"

"The goal is to raise enough money to lobby Congress for a Brandon's Law—one that will prevent anyone guilty of a capital crime from hiding behind diplomatic immunity."

"Well, that woman who ran down little Brandon won't be hiding behind diplomatic immunity anymore," Terry said. "So I guess part of the mission is accomplished."

"Oh, no, no, no," Cody said. "That was totally messed up. Whoever killed her definitely didn't help our cause."

"But now that she's dead," Terry said, "do you agree that Brandon got justice?"

"I think you've got the wrong impression of what we do," Cody said. "Justice and revenge are not the same thing. You know what Gandhi said: an eye for an eye would make the whole world blind."

"So you don't think Brandon's parents will be happy that somebody killed the woman who ran down their son."

"I know the Coopers," Cody said. "That woman's murder won't change their mission. They're trying to fix the system. Let me check on Karen for you."

He headed back to the boss's office.

"That was some real nifty police work, Detective Biggs," I said. "Did you think he was going to come right out and say, thanks for the donation? It's really going to help us offset our hit man expenses."

"It was fun trying," Terry said. "And all it cost was five bucks."

A few minutes later Karen Winters came out of her office. She was fifty, with short blond hair, no-nonsense makeup, simple black slacks, and a gray sweater—more Macy's than Saks.

"We're investigating the murder of Eleanor Belling-ham-Crump," I said.

She frowned. "Yes, the Coopers told me you questioned them."

"We don't mean to open up wounds," I said, "but somebody murdered the woman who killed their son. We had to talk to them."

"They have a solid alibi for the time of the murder. Why are you here?"

"We have a few questions about the Justice for Brandon Fund."

"Like what?"

"Like where does the money go?"

"Oh, you know, the usual. Filing fees, research, mailings to Congress, and of course, the occasional contract killing." She pointed a finger at Terry. "How dare you walk in here and ask my paralegal if he thinks our clients could be guilty of homicide. That's a cross between entrapment and sheer stupidity. You want to see our books? Get a subpoena. But I suggest you save your energy. The Brandon Fund is all being spent to help change the law."

"I've got to ask the tough questions, Counselor," Terry said. "It's the first thing they teach us in cop school."

"And I don't have to answer them. That's the first thing they teach us in law school."

"Ms. Winters, it's clear that Mrs. Bellingham-Crump was responsible for Brandon's death," I said. "Can you at least answer this—why did you advise the Coopers not to sue?"

"Sadly, I advise a lot of my clients not to sue. I know the system, and it's stacked against the little guy. That's why a lot of law firms don't take on deserving cases. It's not about who's right or wrong. It's about who can afford to fight to the finish. I don't want to watch my clients go bankrupt trying to fight City Hall, or in the case of the Coopers, Her Majesty's government."

"Do you think the Coopers regret not suing?" I asked.

"Now you're beating around the same bush I told you was off limits," she said. "The Coopers were not involved in the murder of Eleanor Bellingham-Crump. I have two strict policies here at my little law firm. Always leave the toilet seat down in the coed bathroom and don't murder anybody, even if they took the life of your only child."

Terry nodded in agreement. "An eye for an eye would make the whole world blind. Gandhi."

"I'm impressed, Detective," she said.

"That's the second thing they teach us in cop school."

# CHAPTER 12

**"THE MAN IS** a triple threat," I said once Terry and I were back in the car. "He solves crimes, he writes screenplays, he quotes Gandhi."

"Did I say Gandhi? I meant Hulk Hogan."

"It doesn't matter," I said. "That woman would have thought you were an idiot no matter what you said."

"It was all part of my master plan to give her a false sense of superiority, so she'd let her guard down."

I flashed my badge at him. "Hi, I'm Detective Biggs from Homicide. So, Mr. Paralegal, here's five bucks. Do you think your clients are ruthless murderers?"

"Hey, I took a shot," Terry said. " She was still wrong to call it entrapment."

"Yeah, but she might have hit the nail on the head when she called it sheer stupidity."

"Even so," Terry said, "I still think we should subpoena the Justice for Brandon records. I wouldn't put it past Ted Cooper to use some of the money to get some blood along with the justice."

"The Coopers are crusaders, not avengers. Besides, if they used the Justice for Brandon money, Winters would know about it."

"Right," Terry said. "And she'd probably hide behind attorney-client privilege. Maybe you noticed—she likes throwing the

49

rules in cops' faces."

My cell phone pinged. I flipped it open. It was a text message from Diana. I tapped out an answer and sent it.

"Care to share?" Terry said.

"Diana asked me to try to come home early. She has a surprise for me."

"That's never good. When Marilyn says she's got a surprise, she's either bought something we don't need, or she's got a new hair style that she knows I'm gonna hate."

This time, my cell phone rang.

"Uh-oh—now she's calling," Terry said. "Whatever you texted back, your girlfriend's not happy about it."

It wasn't my girlfriend. It was my boss.

"I need you and your partner at the station," he said.

"Sounds like you have a problem," I said.

"I never have problems. I only have opportunities, and I've got a doozy for you and Biggs," Kilcullen said. "Remember Garet Church, the SAC from the FBI?"

"Sure. Terry and I worked the Familyland case with him."

"He's on his way over. He wants to talk to you. Get your asses back here. Now."

He hung up.

"The boss wants us back in the office. Garet Church is coming over."

"I'll bet this has something to do with the diplomat's wife," Terry said. "Damn! You know how I feel about the FBI. The only thing they're good for is preventing the unauthorized reproduction, distribution, and exhibition of DVDs and videotapes."

"Come on, Garet Church is a pretty straight shooter."

"He's a Federalé. They're all a little bent."

"At least he's not as crazy as Kilcullen," I said.

"You mean he didn't get pissed at his bowling ball, take it to the firing range, and blast it to smithereens? If you're gonna set the bar that low, then, sure—nobody's as crazy as Kilcullen."

Church was waiting for us in Kilcullen's office. He gave us each a quick handshake and about five seconds of long-time-no-see foreplay.

"I'll cut right to the chase," he said. "You guys just caught the murder of Eleanor Bellingham-Crump."

"Emphasis on *just caught*," I said. "We don't have much to go on yet."

"Well, I've got something that will either help or screw you up," Church said.

Terry threw me a look. He was betting on screw it up.

"Lay it on us," I said.

"We're pretty sure that Bellingham-Crump was the victim of a serial killer," Church said. "As far as we can tell, she was number three in a series."

# CHAPTER 13

**"THE FIRST MURDER** took place in LA a few weeks ago," Church said. "The guy was stabbed with a pair of scissors, and the killer left behind a scrapbook."

"There are too many homicides in LA for us to hear about them all," I said, "but you'd think something like that would make the eleven o'clock news. How did it slip through the cracks?"

"Two detectives from the Wilshire station worked the case," Church said. "The victim was a real scumbag, so they didn't work too long or too hard. Then the killer took his show on the road—Portland, Oregon. He murdered a priest."

"That would get a lot more attention," Terry said.

"Oh, it did. Especially this priest. Six months before the murder he was relocated by the archdiocese for misconduct."

Terry's face tightened. "Let me guess. He wasn't rigging bingo games."

"No. It was kids."

"Son of a bitch," Terry said.

"It gets even more interesting. Would you like to know where this pedo-priest was transferred from?" Church didn't wait for an answer. "Los Angeles. Eventually the Portland cops picked up that they had the same MO and the same scrapbook signature as the first LA murder, and they called us in."

"So then the killer comes back to LA, wastes Eleanor

Bellingham-Crump, and leaves another scrapbook," Terry said. "Who called you in for that?"

"One of our agents caught it this morning on NLETS," Church said. "I'm sure you would have picked it up soon enough."

"If we had the manpower," Terry said. "It must be nice to have a bunch of federal agents with nothing else to do but surf the network looking for cases they can poach from us poor struggling locals."

Church smiled. "Chill out, Biggs. This isn't a turf war. In fact, I came here to ask your lieutenant if LAPD would be willing to work on this with the Bureau."

"And I agreed," Kilcullen said.

"Not to play hard to get," Terry said, "but why? My partner and I just got started on this case. You guys have been at it for a couple of weeks. Why do you even want to team up with LAPD?"

"Because I've got the best profilers and database analysts your tax dollars can buy," Church said. "But I need guys with street savvy, and you two are the smartest homicide cops in this city. If that's what you were fishing for, savor it, because it's the last time I'm gonna blow smoke up your ass till you catch the murderer."

"Funny thing," Terry said. "Mike and I were just talking about the Familyland case, and how terrific it was to work with Special Agent In Charge Church. We were saying how we can't wait to work with you again."

"You're full of shit, but even so, working with me personally is not going to happen. I'll be in D.C. for the next four weeks polishing up my anti-terrorist skills. But it's still my task force, my rules. Are you in or out?"

"Are you kidding?" Terry said. "Mike and I are having a blast trying to solve this one murder—and now you're giving us a shot at having three times as much fun. We are definitely in."

"Good," Church said. "I'm teaming you up with Special Agent

Simone Trotter. You guys have any problem working with a woman?"

"Hell no," Terry said. "At the end of a tough day chasing bad guys we don't care if our boss goes home and slips into a sexy little cocktail dress. It'll almost be like working for J. Edgar Hoover himself."

# CHAPTER 14

**TERRY AND I** drove to the FBI offices at 11000 Wilshire to meet with Agent Trotter. Church had given us a brief background on her.

"Simone is French-Canadian, born in Quebec. She went to Ithaca College, and became a US citizen so she could join the Bureau. She's smart; came up through Linguistics; speaks seven languages."

"Good to know," Terry said. "Even if she can't solve these murders she can probably help my youngest daughter, Emily, with her French homework."

Church shook his head. "I know you have fun sticking it to me, Biggs, but I bet you'll like working with Simone. She doesn't fit the classic Quantico mold that you guys love to hate."

Thousands of Hollywood movies have helped shape the stereotypical image of an FBI agent—tall, blond, and stoic. Simone Trotter was none of the above. She was small, dark-haired, with a mouth that never stopped. She was in her early thirties, younger than us, but she immediately took control of the meeting. She kicked it off by giving us a background on our own case.

"Let me save you guys some time and tell you what I already know about Eleanor Bellingham-Crump," she said. "She comes from money and title. Daddy is an earl. Twenty years ago, she took a job as a press secretary at the British embassy in Capetown, which is where she met her husband, Edward. He had a working-class background, but he's bright, and with a little help from his new father-in-law, he managed to get some plum assignments. He had a promising career, but he moved more often than most diplomats, mainly because Eleanor was a member of the liquid-lunch crowd."

"We heard she was no slouch at breakfast or dinner either," Terry said.

Trotter went on. "The day she ran down the Cooper boy, she got plastered at a restaurant in Brentwood. The manager offered to drive her home, but she insisted that she only lived a few blocks away—actually it's one point six miles. When she came up behind the school bus it was stopped, lights flashing. Witnesses say she never slowed down. She tried to drive around it and hit Brandon Cooper just as he was crossing in front of the bus. The kid died on impact. She refused a sobriety test, and ultimately she played her husband's diplomatic get-out-of-jail-free card. She did a twenty-eight-day stretch at a rehab, but several local bartenders can testify to the fact that she is definitely not a star graduate. Did I leave anything out?"

"You know more about our case than we do," Terry said. "If you can tell us who killed her, we can all go home early."

She laughed. Not a big hearty har-har-har, but it was enough to pass the ultimate litmus test—she responded to dumb cop humor. Church was right. We were going to like working with Simone Trotter.

"You guys have been on this case since yesterday," she said. "What have you got so far?"

We told her. It didn't take long. Then it was her turn to tell us about the other two victims.

"The first one was a twenty-two-year-old badass named Tavo Maldonado," she said, spreading out some crime scene photos on her desk. "He was the night manager of an adult pleasure palace and he raised dogs."

"I'm guessing not for the Westminster Kennel Club dog show," Terry said.

"Dog fights," she said. "He owned half a dozen pit bulls that he would keep juiced on steroids, so they were always primed and ready to kill. He lived with his girlfriend, Marlena Rios, in her aunt's house in West LA. The dogs were fenced up in the yard, but the neighbors knew enough to steer clear, because sometimes Tavo would forget to lock the gate and the dogs would get out. About a year ago the guy next door got attacked by one of the dogs, but he shot and killed it before it could do much damage."

"So he had bad blood with Tavo," I said. "Did you question him?"

"Yeah. He's got a solid alibi. He's doing ten to fifteen for armed robbery."

"Poor bastard," Terry said. "He'd be a free man today if he'd have let the dog chew his arm off."

Simone laughed again. "Unfortunately, not everyone in West LA carries a gun." She threw a picture on the desk. It was in vivid color, most of it red.

"This is the late Eddie Chang. He was a delivery guy for a Chinese restaurant. One night he shows up at Tavo's house. He hadn't been there before and made the mistake of going toward the side door. The dogs start barking, Chang panics, picks up a rock and throws it at them."

"Poor guy," Terry said. "He obviously didn't read the fortune cookie that says *never throw a rock at a bunch of pissed-off pit bulls.*"

"Exactly," Simone said. "One of the dogs busted through the fence, and the whole pack of them piled on and ripped him apart. By the time 911 arrived, Chang had bled out."

"And an hour later, I'll bet the dogs were hungry for another Chinese deliveryman," Terry said.

Simone flashed me a pretty smile. "Does he ever stop?" she

asked.

"I've known him ten years," I said. "And so far, he hasn't shown any signs of letting up. Try to ignore him. When did Tavo get murdered?"

"Two weeks ago. It was a Saturday night. Technically, it was after midnight, which would mean all three killings were on a Sunday. He worked at Lovey's Leather and Lace, an upscale sex shop. It was about one in the morning, and Tavo steps out into the alley behind the store to smoke a joint. Someone shoved a pair of scissors in him."

"Did he put up a fight?" Terry said.

"Nothing. He was totally blindsided. Died on the spot."

"Massive splenic hemorrhage?" I asked.

"Yeah, there's a whole lot of that going around lately," she said. "The third victim was Father Francis Fleming. He was originally from LA, but the archdiocese transferred him to Portland about six months ago."

"They should have castrated him instead of setting him up with a whole new set of young boys," Terry said. "I'm betting somebody stuck a pair of scissors right through his cassock."

"Pretty much," Simone said. "That was a week ago Sunday, up in Portland. The killer left behind a scrapbook for both Fleming and Tavo. That's how we linked them, and that's how we picked up on your case."

"Bellingham-Crump's scrapbook is still in our lab," I said. "When can we get a look at the other two?"

"First thing in the morning," she said. "The priest's scrapbook just arrived here from Portland. We did a side-by-side with the Tavo scrapbook. They both use the same paper, same ink, same rubber stamps, and the same cat hair is on each book."

"The Bellingham-Crump scrapbook has cat hair all over it," I said.

"Sounds like it's the same pissed-off, crazy, scrapbooking cat lady all three times," Terry said.

"Don't jump to the conclusion that it's a woman," Trotter said.

"Yeah, I know," Terry said. "Women don't serial kill and men don't scrapbook, but if I had to put five bucks on one or the other, I'd say our killer is a woman."

"Why's that, Detective?"

"Tavo Maldonado doesn't look like he would let a guy sneak up and shank him in a dark alley without putting up a fight," Terry said. "But if he's smoking weed in the back of his sex shop, and a woman came along, she'd have a much better chance of getting close."

I watched Trotter as she processed Terry's logic. "Makes sense," she said. "You sound like a man who knows a few things about women."

Terry laughed. "Agent Trotter," he said. "I've been married four times, which means that I really don't know shit about women."

"In that case, Detective Biggs," Trotter said, "I guess you're lucky that none of them had a pair of scissors."

# CHAPTER 15

**WE WENT BACK** to the office so we could fill Kilcullen in on our meeting with Agent Trotter. But first we stopped at Wendy Burns's desk and asked her to join us.

Wendy is our direct boss. She's a Detective III and the most even-tempered, patient, unflappable cop I've ever worked with. She decides which homicide teams get which cases. But her most important job is being the voice of reason whenever Lt. Kilcullen gets unreasonable, which is usually.

"Do you need me to stand between you and the bullets?" she asked as we walked toward Kilcullen's office.

"No," Terry said. "We just got this case, so we haven't had time to screw it up yet, but Kilcullen is going to get all gooned up anyway."

"Any particular reason, or just general principles?" Wendy asked.

"He's gonna go off on a tear about how we're working with the Feds, and how we have to solve it single-handedly, and show them how smart LAPD is."

"So solve it single-handedly, and show them how smart LAPD is," she said.

"If you keep him out of our airspace, we might have half a chance," Terry said.

We spent about fifteen minutes filling them both in on the three murders.

"It sounds more like a vigilante than a serial killer," Kilcullen said. "Charles Bronson lives on."

"There's a good possibility that in this case Charles Bronson is a woman," Terry said.

"Is that the FBI's theory?" Kilcullen asked.

"No," I said. "It's Terry's, and it makes a lot of sense. This is a front-page case, boss. I know you're big on teamwork and cooperation and all that crap, but there's nothing more we'd like to do than to solve it single-handedly, and show those hotshot Federal agents how smart LAPD is."

Wendy stifled a laugh.

Kilcullen didn't notice. He was too busy being impressed with the fact that I had been sitting at his feet long enough that I was beginning to sound just like him.

"I like the way you're thinking," he said.

I held up my hands, deflecting the compliment and waving it back in his direction. A silent gesture that said, "you, *sensei*, are a shining power of example. A beacon. And I am honored to bask in your glow."

He ate it up with a spoon. "Well, thank you. You know you guys have my total support."

I looked at my watch. Five-thirty. Diana wanted me home early. "We've got a lot of work to do," I said. "We'll keep you posted."

"Go get 'em, boys," Kilcullen said. "Burn that midnight oil."

As soon as we were out the door Terry patted me on the back. "Nicely done," he said. "You realize, of course, that we don't actually have that much to do till we get a good look at those other scrapbooks tomorrow morning."

"In that case, I'm going home. Diana has a surprise waiting for me."

"If you're lucky," he said, "it might include a little of that midnight oil."

Two minutes later I was in the car calling Diana. "What's the surprise?" I asked.

"If I told you, it wouldn't be a surprise."

"Are we going someplace?"

"No. I'm making dinner at home."

"Is it something special? If you tell me what we're having I can stop off on the way home and get some wine."

"Fine," she said. "Get something nice that goes with franks and beans." She hung up.

# CHAPTER 16

**OUR NEW HOUSE** is on Hill Street in Santa Monica. It had been run-down when we bought it, but when there's a spectacular ocean a few blocks away from your front door, you grab the fixer-upper, and then hire someone to fix 'er up.

Unfortunately, Diana and I hired the wrong someone. Hal Hooper, the contractor from hell. He promised everything and delivered nothing. The house was so uninhabitable that we were forced to move in with Terry and his family.

And then one day, we got lucky. Hal Hooper fell off a roof and couldn't finish the job. Even better, it wasn't our roof, which meant we could dump him without having to worry about a lawsuit.

We quickly replaced him with my friend Kemp Loekle, a master craftsman who is happy to charge cop-friendly prices if he likes the cop he's working for. After living there for only six months it no longer feels like a new house. It feels like home.

Diana's car was in the driveway. I backed in next to it. I've been backing into driveways ever since I joined LAPD. It's a pain in the ass, but on those dark, rainy nights when I have to jump into the car and race to a crime scene, I invariably congratulate myself on being a smart buttoned-up cop.

The little voice inside my head informed me that Diana's surprise could mean that when I opened the door a path of rose petals would lead me to the bedroom, where she would be waiting in something sheer and wenchy from Victoria's Secret.

*Victoria's Secret doesn't go with franks and beans*, I reminded the voice.

The voice came right back at me with its usual brand of logic. *The franks and beans are all part of the ruse. I'm betting it's oysters and champagne.*

I studied myself in the rearview mirror. The wear and tear of the day was showing, but at least I didn't smell too bad. I ran my fingers through my hair.

*You look fine. And after one glass of champagne, it won't matter.*

I opened the front door and went in. No rose petals.

Diana's voice beckoned. "In here." Sadly, it was not coming from the bedroom. I headed toward the kitchen and caught an unmistakable smell.

*Franks and beans.*

Diana was at the stove. She was wearing jeans and one of my old plaid shirts tied at the waist. Sexy, because she looks sexy in anything, but definitely not the surprise I was hoping for.

*That's not Victoria's Secret*, the little voice told me. *It's more like L. L. Bean.*

Diana took the paper bag I was carrying and pulled out the twenty-dollar bottle of Chardonnay I had brought home.

"This looks yummy," she said.

"It's better than yummy," I said. "I had this notion that you were cooking up some kind of incredible gourmet dinner. I thought that was going to be the surprise."

"I'm the surprise," a voice said.

I turned to see a lump curled up in the kitchen window seat. The lump sat up. It was a kid. Asian. With dark straight hair, dark eyes, and an expressive angelic face.

I walked over to the window. "I'm Mike," I said. "You're the nicest surprise I've had all day."

The kid grinned, revealing a lot of empty dental real estate. One of her front teeth was just starting to poke through. The other space was still vacant. "I'm Sophie," she said. "I'm staying for dinner."

"I hope we're having franks and beans," I said. "They're my favorite."

Her reaction was something that can best be described as pure glee. In my line of work I don't get to see a lot of glee, pure or otherwise. "No they're not," she said. "They're *my* favorite. When you came in you said you had a notion that Diana was cooking up a gourmet dinner."

"And you know what gourmet means?" I asked.

"Duh," she said, posing with both hands in the air for effect.

"And you're telling me that franks and beans are not gourmet."

"No," she said, extending the two letters into about five syllables.

"And all this time, Diana has been telling me they are like fine French cuisine. I think she calls them *boof and hairy coats*."

She giggled out of control, then regained her composure, and put on her sternest schoolmarm face. "I take French," she said. "I think you mean *boeuf et haricots*."

"Duh," I said, mimicking her style. "That's what I just said. Boof and hairy coats."

"He's funny," she said to Diana.

"You don't know the half of it, kiddo," Diana said.

"So, Sophie," I said. "How old are you?"

"Guess."

"Let's see. I didn't know what *gourmet* meant till I was forty years old, but you look a little younger than that, so I'm going to guess thirty-seven."

She shook her head. "Subtract thirty."

"So you're nineteen," I said.

Another head shake. "Now subtract twelve."

"I'm not as good at math as I am at French, so help me out,"

I said.

"I'm seven."

"With an asterisk," Diana said. "She's in second grade and she's ready for sixth grade, but her mom wants her to live like a normal kid."

"Whatever," Sophie said, tossing it off as if being a pint-sized genius were just another burden of childhood.

"You met Sophie's mom," Diana said. "Carly Tan. She's one of the nurses on my floor. She had to work late tonight."

"Bogus," Sophie said. "She had to go to traffic school. She was speeding and that's part of the punishment."

Diana's mouth opened. "You know about that?"

Sophie puffed herself up. "Detective Tan, ma'am. She sees all, knows all."

Dinner was nothing short of magical. At some point I got around to asking Sophie the traditional lame what-do-you-want-to-be-when-you-grow-up question.

"An author," she said.

"That's great," I said. "What have you written so far?"

"You mean fiction or nonfiction?"

At this point her vocabulary no longer surprised me. "Fiction," I said.

"I wrote a story about an enchanted swimming pool."

She took me through the plot and the main characters.

"How about nonfiction."

She shrugged. "Thanksgiving dinner, but it wasn't that exciting. Do you have any good stories about being a policeman? I would write about that."

And so it went. By the time Carly Tan came to pick up her daughter at nine-thirty, I was totally mesmerized.

"Thank you, thank you, thank you," Carly said. "I hope she hasn't been too much trouble. She loves to talk."

"I noticed," I said. "And if you try to stop her from talking I'll have the boys downtown send you back to traffic school."

Carly's finger went to her lips. "Mike . . ."

"The jig's up, Mom," I said. "The kid knows all about the speeding rap."

"And we didn't tell her," Diana said.

"That little scamp," Carly said. "How did she —"

I put on my tough cop face and looked Carly square in the eye. "Detective Tan, ma'am," I said. "She sees all, knows all."

I gave Sophie a high five. More of a low five actually, because I had to kneel down to get there.

She wrapped her arms around my neck, kissed me on the cheek, and whispered in my ear. "Thank you for the boof and hairy coats," she said.

I stood up, feeling a warm glow all over. Diana opened the front door, and the two of us watched Sophie skip down our front walk, looking back only once to make sure her mother was close behind.

"Do I bring home nice surprises or what?" Diana said.

"She's fantastic," I said. "I miss her already."

And then the little voice inside my head spoke.

*Now you know how Brandon Cooper's parents must feel.*

The warmth that had spread over me turned to an icy chill, and in that moment I knew, understood, and completely accepted why someone would want to rid the world of Eleanor Bellingham-Crump.

*It doesn't matter, Detective Lomax. You still have to catch the guy who did it.*

# CHAPTER 17

**"THIS IS ALL** yours," Agent Trotter said the next morning as she walked Terry and me into an office on the seventeenth floor of the Federal Building. From the outside, the building is steel and glass, and since there aren't many skyscrapers in Westwood, most of the offices have decent views. Not ours. The room was about fifteen by twelve, windowless, with a whiteboard, cork walls, file cabinets, and an expansive government-issue conference table.

She handed us each a key. "This is the best place to store your files. I'm the only other person with access."

The three scrapbooks were on the table.

We started with Gustavo Maldonado. It wasn't hard to understand why Tavo got iced. Or why the cops didn't waste a lot of time trying to catch whoever did it. Tavo was a scumbag. He bred dogs to kill one another in a bloody public spectacle. And if that weren't foul enough, he didn't seem to give a shit if the dogs got out and killed the neighbors.

Having taken the Jessica Keating crash course on scrapbooking, I was able to see the similarities between this one and the one for Eleanor Bellingham-Crump. Tavo's scrapbook was organized so that the early pages focused on his penchant for dogfighting. There were handmade dogfight flyers, counterpointed by newspaper ads that protested animal abuse.

"This section looks like it was pasted together by the board of directors of PETA," Terry said.

I turned to a double page spread that was filled with pictures of Lovey's Leather and Lace, the adult pleasure palace where Tavo was working the night he was murdered.

"I was expecting a sleazy porn shop," I said. "But this is a pretty classy porn shop."

"The store is owned by Lovey LaRue," Simone said. "It's actually rather high end."

"Right," Terry said. "It's like Victoria's Secret, only from the looks of some of the kinky stuff she sells, Lovey has a much more interesting secret."

"One that seems to attract customers from Beverly Hills and Bel-Air."

"If this store caters to such an upscale clientele, how did a sleaze like Tavo Maldonado get a job there?" I said.

"Good question," Simone said. "Why don't you go ask Lovey?"

"Need anything while we're at the store?" Terry said.

"Honey, I'm divorced and not looking to make the same mistake twice, so let's just say that I'm stocked up on all the paraphernalia a single girl needs," Simone said. "But if you pass a RadioShack, I could use some double A batteries."

Terry laughed. Simone Trotter was definitely his kind of cop.

I turned the page. The focus of the book moved from Tavo, the victim, to Eddie Chang, Tavo's victim. There were newspaper clippings about the vicious attack, including one from the *Chinese Daily News*.

"My Chinese is limited to hold the MSG, please," Terry said. "Do you have a translation?"

"Sorry," Simone said. "LAPD had all the Chinese translated when they first got the case, but the transcript is probably buried somewhere. I didn't need it. I can read it. It describes the dog attack on Eddie, and condemns dogfighting, and basically calls for justice."

"Justice for Brandon, and now Justice for Eddie," I said. "I think we have a theme emerging."

The next few pages were happily festooned with menus, napkins, a guest check written in Chinese, a paper umbrella, and other mementos from The Empress Garden, the restaurant where Eddie worked.

"Handcrafted with love," Terry said. "Let's look at the next one."

The cover of Father Fleming's scrapbook was wrapped in dark purple velvet. "This is the most elaborate of the three scrapbooks," Simone said, "and if you ask me, the most creepy."

"That's because pedophile priests outrank everybody else on the creepy scale," Terry said.

"I take it you're Catholic," Simone said.

"Born and lapsed," Terry said. "And you?"

"Catholic and practicing."

"Does that mean you actually go to church?" Terry asked.

"Don't sound so surprised," she said. "A lot of Catholics still do the whole nine yards—mass, communion, confession—"

"I'm sure Father Fleming was one of them," Terry said.

We went back to the scrapbook. The first four pages were filled with pieces of the scripture cut out of a Bible. It looked so normal, you might have mistaken it for a tribute to Father Fleming. But on closer inspection, the verses were all about sins of the flesh, homosexuality, and transgressions against children.

There were newspaper articles about Catholic sex abuse cases, complete with documents that had been evidence in a trial brought against a California priest in 2005. One was a note, handwritten by a bishop, which clearly indicated that he was aware of the recurring offenses.

*Father J. has slipped again, this time with a 13-year-old boy. The parents are not going legal, but Father J. needs to take a vacation, or a medical leave of absence until we can find a long-*

*term solution.*

A second document indicated that the bishop had transferred Father J. to a parish in Phoenix.

"There's your long-term solution," Terry said. "Musical pedophiles. As long as they keep moving, it's harder to lock them up."

"Do we know if the documents in the scrapbook are real, or are they forgeries the killer put together to make his point?" I asked.

Terry shook his head. "I'd bet they're real. It's easy enough to go online and find all kinds of court case evidence. That's why God gave us the Freedom of Information Act and Google."

"Fleming was killed in Portland," I said after we'd gone through the book a second time. "For now, let's focus on the two LA murders."

"That would be much better for my stomach lining," Terry said. "Father Fleming is kicking up a lot of old shit that I thought I had buried."

I didn't ask him to unbury it any further.

We each took a scrapbook. Terry started with Bellingham-Crump; I took the Tavo book. It was a slow process, mainly because we had no idea what we were looking for.

After an hour, we both needed a break. "Let's get some coffee, then swap scrapbooks and see if that helps," Terry said.

FBI coffee is no better than LAPD coffee, and I was staring into the murky brown beverage when it hit me.

"The receipt from the Chinese restaurant," I said.

"What about it?"

"That receipt belonged to the killer. He put it in the book."

"Right, but there are no prints," Terry said.

"But it's a receipt that Tavo's killer got from the Chinese restaurant."

"So the killer had dinner at The Empress Garden, loved the food, loved the service, and instead of leaving a fifteen-percent tip, he went out and murdered the guy who killed their deliveryman," Terry said. "We know that the killer ate there at some point, because the book is filled with menus, napkins, and other shit from the restaurant. How does this help?"

"We show someone at the restaurant the receipt, and see if they remember anything about the person who ordered it."

"Mike, that's the equivalent of asking a toll collector if he remembers who gave him that five-dollar bill."

"I realize it's a total long shot," I said. "But there's a major upside if we take the time to do it."

Terry shrugged. "And what's that?"

"Lunch."

# CHAPTER 18

**ON THE WAY** to The Empress Garden I told Terry about Diana's surprise.

"That was fast," he said. "Your father just asked you guys to have a baby, and the next day Diana brings home a full-grown kid."

"First of all, that was just happenstance," I said. "Even Big Jim with his black belt in meddling couldn't have orchestrated that. Second of all, we only had the kid for a couple of hours. It's like a rent-a-car. If you give it back at the end of the day, you don't have to make monthly payments on it."

"How'd it feel to have a kid around the house?"

"Sophie is terrific, but I would hate to have to eat franks and beans on a regular basis."

"Fear not," Terry said, as we pulled into the parking lot at The Empress Garden. "Lunch today is going to be amazing. Are you feeling adventurous?"

"No, but I'm guessing you are."

"You know me—Captain Adventure."

"What do you have in mind, Captain?"

"Don't order anything off the menu."

"You've eaten here before?"

"No," Terry said. "But this place is two miles from Tavo's house. There are probably dozens of Chinese restaurants between here and there. If he ordered from this one, logic would dictate that it must be fantastic."

"If your logic is based on the assumption that a guy who works in a porn shop and raises killer dogs is a connoisseur of Eastern cuisine, then yes, I'm sure it'll be incredible."

The Empress Garden was relatively full, mostly white-collar types on their lunch break, but there were several tables of Asian men. The hostess, a pretty young woman wearing jeans and a UCLA T-shirt, sat us at a table and was about to give us menus when Terry held up his hand.

"Surprise us," he said. "We'll have whatever looks good in the kitchen."

She smiled. "Cool," she said. "My grandmother loves it when the customers let her do her own thing. You won't be sorry." She walked to the kitchen and was barking instructions in Chinese before the door closed.

"I would have settled for the number one combo plate," I said. "Do you really think we're going to get a better lunch by doing it this way?"

"Yes. Just don't let her know you're a cop until after we eat."

Terry has some strange quirks, and this one is a contender for the strangest. He's convinced that there's someone working in the kitchen of every restaurant who hates cops. And if they know the food is for us, they'll spit in it. Or worse.

"You flash your badge, and you know what they'll send out?" Terry said. "Snot and Sour Soup. Egg Poo Yung. Pork Dumpings. Flied lice with real lice and real flies."

He ran through half a dozen more appetite suppressants and only let up when a waiter put the first course on the table.

Terry dove in. "This is excellent," he said. "I wonder what it is."

I took a forkful. "Tastes like it might be Moo Goo Gai Phlegm."

We had three more dishes and finally had to ask them to stop. The waiter brought hot towels, a fresh pot of tea, and fortune cookies.

A few minutes later a tiny woman wandered over to our table. Her face was gaunt and skeletal, her classic Asian features connected by deep wrinkles and dark liver spots. Her gray stringy hair was held in place by a dark blue headband that had twin dragons on it. She looked to be somewhere north of eighty years old. She was wearing a stained chef's coat that was covered by an even more stained apron.

Terry and I stood. "You must be the empress of Empress Garden," he said.

She smiled broadly and I could see the ochre-tinged teeth of a lifelong smoker. "Sonia Woo," she said. "You like my cooking?"

"Very much," Terry said. "Especially the duck. What did you do to it?"

"First, I take duck and do this." She pointed a finger and drew it bladelike across her neck. "Fffffffft," she said. "Everything else is big secret."

"Well, it was excellent," Terry said, and did a quick head bow.

The old woman returned the bow. "Good. You come back tomorrow. Bring lots of friends."

"We'll be back soon. But first we have a question," Terry said, taking out his badge. "I'm Detective Biggs, and this is Detective Lomax from LAPD. We're investigating a—"

That's as far as he got before Sonia scurried off.

"I rest my case," Terry said. "You see what happens when they know you're a cop?"

The young hostess returned, with Sonia hanging behind her. We introduced ourselves again.

"I'm Judy Woo," she said. "My grandmother is very upset. What seems to be the problem?"

"We didn't mean to scare her," Terry said. "My partner and I are investigating a crime and we wonder if you can help us out."

Sonia's eyes darted to Judy, and the young hostess put her arm around the old lady's shoulder. "If I can," she said. "What's the crime?"

Terry didn't answer. Instead he took out a photocopy of the guest check that had been in Tavo's scrapbook. "Do you recognize this?"

"It says The Empress Garden right on top," Judy said. "It's ours."

"Do you happen to know who bought this meal?"

"We get a lot of customers," she said, looking at him like he was an idiot.

"Take a close look," he said, handing her the check.

Judy rolled her eyes and took it from him. "Unless you have a credit card receipt, there no way for us to tell one guest check from—"

Whatever she saw stopped her cold. She turned to her grandmother and started talking in rapid-fire Chinese.

Sonia grabbed the check, held it inches away from her rheumy eyes, and squinted at it. A few seconds later Granny went batshit. She pointed a finger at Terry and started shaking it at him yelling, "no deliver, no deliver."

Terry looked at Judy. "What's going on?"

"No deliver," Sonia yelled. "That lady, she a bitch. Bad, bad lady."

"What lady are we talking about?" Terry said.

"The one who ordered the dinner on this guest check," Judy said.

"You know who it is?" I said.

"My grandmother knows. Ask her."

But at this point, Sonia Woo was beyond asking. She pumped a gnarly fist in the air, and ran back to the kitchen screaming, "no deliver, no deliver."

Judy ran after her.

Terry gave me a baffled laugh. "What the hell was that all about?"

I shrugged. "I have no idea," I said, "but this definitely looks like a job for Captain Adventure."

# CHAPTER 19

IT TOOK TEN minutes to calm Grandma down. Judy finally brought her out of the kitchen and the four of us sat down at a table in the rear.

By now the lunch crowd had thinned out. Our waiter quietly set down some fresh tea and more cookies.

"Judy," I said, "what got your grandmother so excited when she saw that guest check?"

"You know that my cousin, Eddie Chang, was killed about six months ago," Judy said.

"We didn't know he was your cousin," I said, "but yes, we knew he was killed by Tavo Maldonado's dogs."

"Tavo a bassard," Sonia said, and went off on another tirade. Judy gently patted her grandmother's spindly arm, and the old lady quieted down.

"A few months after Eddie was killed, a woman came to the restaurant," Judy said. "She ordered the food that was on that guest check. She said it was her son's birthday, so she put a birthday card in the bag and asked us to deliver it to him. She paid in cash plus an extra twenty-dollar tip for the deliveryman."

"The delivery address isn't on the guest check," I said.

"The guest checks are paper, and if they get wet they fall apart. We always write the address out in big numbers on an index card and staple it to the bag. Makes it easier for the delivery guy to see."

"Where was it delivered?" I asked.

"To the store where Tavo Maldonado worked."

"Lovey's Leather and Lace," I said.

Judy nodded. "The deliveryman was my brother Bobby. When he got to the store, he recognized Maldonado."

"He knew who he was." I said it, rather than asked it.

"Detective, after Eddie was killed, Tavo Maldonado's picture was in the *Chinese Daily News* many times. We all know who he was."

"What did your brother do once he recognized Tavo?"

"He freaked. He ran to his car and brought the food back here."

"What about the birthday card that he was supposed to deliver?"

"He brought that back, too. And we have the carbon of the guest check you gave me. I saved them in case that woman ever came back."

"Don't expect her," I said, "but it would help if you gave them to us."

"No problem." Judy got up and headed to the front of the store.

That was Sonia's cue to unload on us. "Tavo a bassard," she said. "His dog kill Eddie. Now Eddie wife, Dandan, all alone."

We let her rant until Judy came back and handed me a small plastic bag. "They've been handled a lot, but I figured we might as well not get any more fingerprints on them," she said, handing me the bag. Inside were a square white envelope and a yellow guest check.

"Thanks," I said. "Can you describe the woman who ordered the food that was supposed to be delivered to Tavo?"

"I wasn't here that day. My grandmother took the order. That's her handwriting on the check."

I turned to Sonia. "The woman who said she was Tavo's mother—do you remember what she looked like?"

"Yes. White woman."

"What else?"

"Nothing else. She all white. White skin, white hair, white

dress, white shoe."

"Was she old? Young?"

Sonia waved both hands in the air. "I say white hair. White hair old. She all white, like death."

"What about her eyes? Brown? Blue?"

"Round. She have round eyes like you."

"Judy," I said, "do you think Sonia could sit down with a police artist and help us get a sketch of this woman?"

"We can try, but you know how a lot of you guys can't tell one Chinese waiter from another? Grandma has a hard time telling white people apart."

"We're white cops," I said, "and we have a hard time telling white people apart."

Sonia let loose a croupy laugh. "You funny white cop," she said. "You come back. Bring family. I make you special Chinese banquet."

"We'll be back if you promise to help us find this woman."

"She ghost lady, but you find her, you bring her here to Sonia Woo."

"Oh really," I said. "And what would you do if I brought her here?"

Sonia gave me a big yellow-toothed grin. "Same like duck," she said, drawing a bony finger across her neck. "Ffffffft."

# CHAPTER 19

"**SONIA WOO IS** a great cook, but a lousy eyewitness," I said when we got back to the car. "White woman, white hair, white skin? Not much help."

"I don't know," Terry said. "In LA that eliminates a huge chunk of the population. All we have to do is question all the geriatric female albinos in the county. And just to be on the safe side, the mimes who work in drag."

I took Tavo's so-called birthday card out of the bag. Someone in the restaurant had already opened the envelope. The outside of the card had a photo of a snarling pit bull. Inside was a picture of a fortune cookie, with the fortune unfurled beneath it: *Injustice is relatively easy to bear. What stings is justice.*

"It's a shame Tavo never got to see this," Terry said. "I'll bet he'd have enjoyed the lighthearted artfulness and the subtle undertones of irony."

"This woman in white," I said. "She had to know that the scrapbook would lead us back to The Empress Garden. So she dresses like . . . a nurse? Is that a clue or did she just do it to throw us off?"

"I think she wore white so Sonia would remember her," Terry said. "In China, white is the color of death. A little factoid I picked up watching the Beijing Olympics."

We had agreed with Simone that any evidence we came up

with could go to the LAPD Crime Lab, and they'd share their findings with the Feds. So even though the card looked like it had been handled by half the Chinese army, we delivered it to Jessica Keating. Then we headed for Lovey's Leather and Lace.

It was on the cusp between the ultra chic Beverly Hills and the rough and tumble West Hollywood. We pulled into the parking lot behind the store.

"This is where Tavo was killed," Terry said. "Totally secluded, one streetlight, no surveillance cameras. The killer knew what she was doing."

Considering it was Tuesday at 3 P.M. the lot was pretty full. A Mercedes, a pickup truck, a Saab convertible, a plain vanilla Buick with a Hertz sticker on the window, and six others. Lovey seemed to attract a rather diverse clientele.

The veil of shame and secrecy that had once been the hallmark of the sex trade had been lifted. Lovey's front window proudly featured cock rings, dildos, floggers, and other paraphernalia of the sexual revolution.

Inside, customers strolled comfortably down spacious aisles marked BONDAGE & DISCIPLINE, ANAL TOYS, and CLIT KITS.

I tried to match the shoppers with the cars in the parking lot. A thirty-something woman who looked like she did most of her shopping on Rodeo Drive had to be the owner of the Mercedes. A couple in the Marital Therapy aisle had *tourists from Iowa* written all over them. I pegged them for the rent-a-car. I couldn't find a guy with a tool belt to go with the pickup truck, so I assigned it to a woman with spiked hair who was checking out strap-ons.

We heard Lovey LaRue before we saw her. She jangled. She strode toward us in a billowing dress of dark purple velvet trimmed in black lace. She had enough costume jewelry around her neck to anchor a battleship, and dozens of bracelets on each wrist. All that hardware made a racket.

Lovey was tall and statuesque, with bottle red hair, three coats of makeup, and the pungent aroma of perfume that's sold by the jug, not by the ounce.

"Welcome to my little shop, gentlemen," she said in a voice rubbed raw with whiskey. "I'm Lovey LaRue, and you boys are definitely not gay."

She caught me by surprise, and the best I could do was "no ma'am."

"And since two straight dudes would no sooner show up here than go to a Cher concert, I'm guessing you're LAPD."

"We're looking for Marlena Rios," I said.

"And I'm looking for some ID."

Normally, we wave our badges in front of somebody's face and they accept it. Lovey took our IDs and studied them.

"James Michael Lomax, Jr." she said, looking at mine. "Do I call you Jim?"

"You call my father Jim," I told her. "You call me Mike."

"And Terrance Martin Biggs. Do I call you Terry or Marty?"

"You call me Detective Biggs," Terry said. "We're looking into Tavo Maldonado's murder. Do you know where we can find Marlena Rios?"

"She didn't do it," Lovey said, handing back our IDs.

"Well, that saves us a shitload of time," Terry said, "Now we can just cross her off our list of suspects, and go out for donuts."

"Marlena moved back to Mexico," Lovey said. "Permanently."

"Funny, but to me, that sounds suspicious," Terry said.

"Somebody came to the store and stabbed her boyfriend. She figured it was payback for his dog killing that Chinaman. She was afraid she was next."

"What can you tell us about Tavo?" I asked.

"I liked him."

"He was a lowlife," Terry said. "Not exactly a natural fit for a store that caters to the Beverly Hills crowd."

"You're wrong," she said. "He was a magnet. Women loved

to ask him questions about what would satisfy a man. He was smart, sensitive, and the bad-boy exterior got a lot of them even hornier than when they walked in."

"Did he ever go home with one of the customers?"

"No, it's against our corporate policy," she said. Then she coughed up a raspy laugh. "Get real, Detective. For all I know he was knocking off a piece of ass every night. In case you hadn't noticed, sex is what I sell."

"What about the dogfighting?"

"So he was into dogfighting," she said. "Let me tell you, honey, everyone is into something that frosts somebody's ass."

"He didn't just frost somebody's ass," I said. "His dogs ripped out somebody's throat. After the delivery guy was killed, did Tavo get any threats?"

"Not that he told me."

"Was there an older woman, white hair, asking about him?" I said.

"Younger women, especially the Latinas. No one like you described."

"Tell us about the night he was murdered."

"We're open late Saturday. Guys get lucky at a bar, come in here with a girl who's willing to try anything, and they'll drop a bundle on toys and other stuff that will give them bragging rights in the office Monday morning. Just before closing, Tavo went out back for a smoke. Somebody jumped him, stabbed him, and left behind some kind of a scrapbook. Can you believe it? A scrapbook," she said leaning against a rack of dog leashes, whips, and riding crops. "That's really twisted."

"You have surveillance videos for that night?" I asked.

"Not for the parking lot. Just for inside the store. LAPD already took them. I'm surprised to see you guys come fishing around. I didn't think the cops gave a shit about finding the killer."

"Well, we do, and if you can think of anything that might help, give us a call," I said, handing her a card.

"I don't know anything else about the case," she said. She reached into the pocket of her dress, pulled out two business cards of her own, and handed one to each of us. "But if you ever need any goodies to help perk up your sex life, you give me a call."

"Thank you, ma'am," Terry said, pushing the card back at her. "But God already gave me all the goodies my wife needs."

Lovey shook her head. "Honey, I got news for you. God did not give you everything you need to keep a woman happy in the sack."

"Y'know, you're probably right," Terry said. "He gave me almost everything I need. LAPD threw in the handcuffs."

# CHAPTER 21

**IF YOU ASK** someone to guess how many police artists work for LAPD, the odds are they won't get it right. The answer is one.

Over the years, the sketch artist has gradually been replaced by software programs like Smith & Wesson's Identi-Kit. But when the witness is as potentially unreliable as Sonia Woo, having a computer draw a picture doesn't always work. You need a skilled interviewer who can draw the jumbled details out of the witness's head.

That's where Nancy Segerberg comes in.

Nancy is a soft-spoken grandmother who's as good a listener as she is an artist. People remember the obvious things about a suspect, like dreadlocks or horn-rimmed glasses, but those are useless details, because a few minutes later that same suspect could be bald and wearing contact lenses.

Nancy asks slow, deliberate questions that help people zero in on facial features that can't easily be changed, like the shape of a jaw, the size of the nose, or how far apart the eyes are set. Then she translates it into a sketch.

By the time Terry and I got back to the station, Nancy had spent over an hour with Sonia Woo. I stuck my head in the door where the two of them were working together with Sonia's granddaughter, Judy, looking on.

"How you guys doing?" I asked.

Nancy shook her head and frowned.

"Language barrier?" I said.

"Not at all," Nancy said. "Mrs. Woo has a very definite picture in her mind, and with Judy's help she was able to give me a crystal clear description. I don't think you'll have any problem finding the woman she described."

"Really?" I said.

"Yes. The suspect and her three cronies are on Lifetime Television about six hours a day, seven days a week."

Nancy handed me the sketch pad. The picture was a perfect drawing of Betty White, the actress from *The Golden Girls*, a sitcom that was in constant reruns.

"Mike, it looks like Mrs. Woo gave me a description of her favorite television character," Nancy said.

"I was afraid something like this could happen," Judy said. "She watches the program every chance she gets. She's even got a small TV in the kitchen at the restaurant, so she's seen those episodes of *The Golden Girls* dozens of times."

"Four crazy lady," Sonia said. "Make me laugh. Woman who come to restaurant and send food to Tavo, she look like this." She pointed at the picture of Betty White. "And her name White. I tell you, she all white."

"So should we put out an APB," Terry said, "or should we just call Ms. White's agent?"

"I'm really sorry," Judy said.

"Oh, please, don't apologize," Nancy said. "It's hard enough for people to describe a person of their own race. It's even harder across racial lines. I'm afraid that to your grandmother one old white-haired Caucasian woman pretty much looks like another."

"The other possibility," Terry said, "is that your grandmother is right, and Betty White is our killer."

"I'm the one who should be apologizing," Nancy said, packing up her pads and pencils. "About a half hour into our session, I could see where she was headed, but whoever came into the restaurant that night just reminded her of that actress, and I couldn't get her to shake the image."

"It's okay," I said. "At least you helped us narrow it down to a type."

"Right," Terry said. "And when we catch the killer, we already know who can play her in the movie."

I escorted Sonia and Judy to their car, then went back to my desk to check messages. By the time I got there Terry was sitting at his computer, staring at the screen.

"I got an e-mail from your dad," he said.

"What does he want?"

Terry shrugged. "Just the usual Hollywood writer bullshit. You know, like who should play him in the movie, who should play me?"

"You're a character?"

"Yeah, the two truckers are called Big Tim and Jerry. He wants Brian Dennehy to play him. I'm thinking Leo DiCaprio could be me."

"You're casting a movie that hasn't even been written yet?" I said. "If the only thing you've done is change Big Jim and Terry to Big Tim and Jerry, I don't think Brian and Leo are going to be interested. Hell, I don't even think Betty White would be interested."

"For your information, we've already started writing the script. Big Jim just pitched me an opening sequence for the film. You want to hear it?"

"More than life itself," I said. I sat back in my chair. "Lay it on me, Jerry."

# CHAPTER 22

**TERRY STOOD UP.** "Okay, as the movie opens, it's twilight."

I laughed.

"What's so funny?"

"I never heard a cop use the word *twilight* before," I said. "I guess it's a screenwriter thing."

"Anyway, it's twilight. The sky is purple, and we open on a long shot of this big semi rolling down this dusty stretch of highway out on the plains. We'll shoot it in Iowa or Nebraska or one of those places where they have plenty of wide open spaces."

"And plenty of twilight," I added.

"After we get the establishing shot, we cut inside the truck, and there's our two heroes, Big Tim and Jerry—Brian Dennehy and Leo DiCaprio, and you hear Dennehy's voice-over on the sound track. He says, '*My partner and I used to be detectives with LAPD. After we retired, we opened a trucking business.*'"

"Leo DiCaprio is retired?" I asked. "Isn't he kind of young to retire?"

"Come on, Mike. They're cops. Lots of cops retire young."

"And what about Brian Dennehy?" I said. "Isn't he old enough to play Leo's grandfather?"

"So some cops retire old," Terry said. "Let me finish. Then Dennehy says, '*After we retired, we opened a trucking business. But deep down inside, we're still cops at heart. So now we're crime-fighting truckers. You might say we went from the halls of justice to the hauls of justice.' "*

"I don't get it," I said. "What does he mean they went from the halls of justice to the halls of justice? It's the same thing."

"Jeez, Mike, the second hauls is spelled different. Hauls. Like long-haul trucking."

"How the hell are people supposed to know that?" I said. "It's a sound track. Is Brian going to spell it for them? How about he says this? '*You might say we went from the H-A-L-L-S of justice to the H-A-U-L-S of justice.*' A Teamster who can spell? How authentic is that? Hauls, halls? That's almost as bad as *Semi Justice*. As far as I'm concerned, that still means half-assed justice."

"Damn it, Mike, when you see two ex-cops riding in a big semi, Semi Justice can only mean one thing—trucker justice. Can't you even see that?"

"Hey, I'm not knocking it," I said. "A movie about half-assed justice might be good. A lot of people paid good money to see *Dumb and Dumber*."

"You've been gooned up about this movie from the get-go," Terry said. "I think maybe you're a little jealous of the bond I have with your father."

"I don't care what Big Jim does in his spare time," I said. "I'm just pissed that he's sucking you into doing all the work."

"I think you're jealous that he'd rather work with me."

"Who would rather work with you?"

Terry and I turned around. It was our boss.

"Are you serious, Biggs?" Kilcullen said. "Somebody would rather work with you?"

"Hard to believe, isn't it?" Terry said.

"Who's his second choice? Inspector Clouseau?" Kilcullen said, laughing at his own joke. "I guess I should take comfort in the fact that you're actually working. Have you guys made any headway?"

"We were just about to call Simone," I said.

"Don't bother," he said. "I just spoke to her. The FBI ran the cat hair from the Crump scrapbook against the first two. It's a perfect match."

"So that means we've got three victims, two cats, and one killer," I said.

"Yeah, and zero progress," Kilcullen said.

"We've made some progress," Terry said.

"Like what?"

"Like we found a great Chinese restaurant, and we're hot on the tail of Betty White," Terry said. "Come on, Lieutenant, give us a little time. The FBI couldn't solve it either, and they're two weeks ahead of us."

"Tell me what you've got so far," he said.

We filled him in on the birthday card for Tavo and the white-haired woman.

"So we're looking for a little old lady with a twisted sense of humor and a taste for Chinese food," Kilcullen said. "Do you realize that all three victims were killed on the same day of the week? The priest and the diplomat's wife were both on a Sunday, and Maldonado was killed late Saturday night, but it was after midnight, so technically, that's three Sundays. Does that tell you anything?"

"Yeah," Terry said. "The guy doesn't like to kill anyone on a school night."

"Or he's busy during the week," Kilcullen said. "Or maybe he works nights. But in my book three Sundays in a row is a pattern, and in case you hadn't noticed, Sunday is coming around again real soon. I don't care if the FBI couldn't crack it. It's your case now. Don't let the bodies pile up."

"Hold on," Terry said. He picked up a pen and a notepad and started writing. "Don't . . . let . . . bodies . . . pile . . . up. Great direction, boss."

"You're pretty funny, Biggs," Kilcullen said. "A guy with your kind of talent should think about writing a movie."

That stopped Terry cold.

Kilcullen grinned. "Do you think I'm clueless, Biggs?"

"I'm writing it on my own time," Terry said.

"I figured that," Kilcullen said. "What I can't figure out is why. Is somebody paying you?"

"No," Terry said, shaking his head. "But the job comes with a great dental plan."

# CHAPTER 23

**WHEN I WOKE** up the next morning there was a text message on my cell phone: *meet me @ 11000 asap*. It was time stamped 4:49 A.M.

"The man is whacko, but he sure is dedicated," I said, flipping the phone shut.

"Terry?" Diana said, pouring us each some coffee.

"Yeah. He must have been working the case in his head in the middle of the night and he texted me."

"That's not whacko," she said. "Whacko would have been if he called you in the middle of the night."

"He wants me to meet him at FBI headquarters."

"You guys are going to solve this, right?" she said. "Don't let the FBI beat you out."

"Hey, it's not us against them," I said. "We're a team."

"A team?" she said, rolling her eyes. "Now look who's whacko."

I drove to 11000 Wilshire. Terry was in our office with the FBI files spread out on the table. "I'm an idiot," he said.

"When did you finally come to that conclusion?" I said.

"About four a.m., and then I couldn't get back to sleep."

"I've known you were an idiot for years, and I sleep like a baby," I said.

"This killer is methodical, right?" Terry said.

I nodded.

"She, he — whatever — our killer likes patterns," he said. "Same murder weapon, same method of killing, different scrapbook layouts, but everything she does fits a pattern."

"What's your point?"

"Where's the card for Father Fleming?"

"What card?"

"The killer sent Tavo that bogus birthday card with the warning about the sting of justice."

"Tavo never got it," I said.

"Right, but the killer sent it," Terry said. "She also sent one to Eleanor Bellingham-Crump, with that quote about washing away human blood."

"Hubbie threw it out, so Eleanor never got the card either," I said.

"Doesn't matter. What matters is that the killer sent it both times. And since she's practically ritualistic, I'm betting she sent a warning card to Father Fleming."

"Even if she did, the first two cards didn't get delivered," I said. "So there's a good chance that the one for Fleming didn't get to him either."

"Or maybe it did, but we haven't found it."

"The Portland cops and the FBI tossed his room and his office. Nothing turned up," I said. "But let's just say he did get a card. He probably destroyed it."

"Maybe not," Terry said. "That's what woke me up this morning. This priest had a history of transgressions. The church transferred him to another parish, but I'll bet they kept a sharp Catholic eye on him. And I guarantee you they told him that if anyone accused him of anything, he'd have to let them know."

"He's not going to rat himself out."

"Mike, ratting yourself out is what confession is all about. Besides, if he got a card from the killer, it would have been threatening justice for his *past* sins — stuff the church already knew about. So I'll bet he showed it to another priest, probably his boss, the monsignor."

"Didn't Portland PD interview the monsignor and all the other priests?"

Terry held up a police file. "Monsignor Callahan was interviewed by Detectives Fukushima and Weinstein. I'm going to go out on a limb and guess that a Buddhist and a Jew don't know how a priest thinks."

"But you do."

"Sadly, yes." He looked at his watch. "It's seven-fifteen. He'll be awake. Let's call him."

Terry picked up a phone and started dialing a number that was written on the file. He pointed at an extension and gestured for me to listen in.

A church secretary took the call, and a minute later a man with a deep resonant voice came on. "This is Monsignor Callahan."

"Good morning, Father," Terry said. "This is Terrance Biggs in Los Angeles. My family and I are parishioners at St. Victor's, and we were all immensely fond of Father Francis Fleming. Our hearts grieve for his loss, and we pray that the person who brutally murdered him will be caught."

"Thank you, Terrance. We all grieve him, and we, too, pray that the police apprehend the killer and bring him to justice."

"As Providence would have it, that's part of my job," Terry said. "I'm a homicide detective with the Los Angeles Police Department, and my partner and I have joined Portland PD and the FBI to look for his killer."

"I see," Callahan said in a noncommittal monotone.

"We may have a breakthrough in the case, and I wanted to ask you some questions about Father Francis."

"Son, I've told the Portland police and the FBI everything I know."

"Father, I was an altar boy. I had two aunts, God rest their souls, who were nuns, so I understand the priestly vows. Did you tell the police *everything* you know, or did you leave any details out because you had to stand behind the obligation of the confessional?"

"Son, you know that if I did leave anything out I wouldn't be able to tell you any more than I could tell the Portland police," he said. "But in this case I was able to answer everything they asked."

"Did they ask you about any hate mail Father Fleming received?"

"Oh yes," he said. "Father Francis was the target for a lot of anger. He received multiple pieces of hate mail. He destroyed them all, but it was hardly a secret, so I was able to give the police the details on as many as I could remember."

Terry covered the mouthpiece of the phone with his hand and turned to me. "He gave them *details*? Portland PD didn't give us details. They wrote one short sentence in the report. *Victim received threatening letters from a variety of anonymous sources*."

He went back to the Monsignor. "Father, I'm missing some of those details. Can I ask you about one in particular? It might have come from someone connected to the murder."

"Of course," the priest said.

"This one might have caught your eye because it would have been on quality paper, artfully done, and very well crafted."

"I don't find any message of hate well crafted," the monsignor said. "But I think I know the one you're referring to. It didn't come in the mail. A woman delivered it."

Terry's thumb shot up in the air. "Can you describe it?"

"She cut up pages from the Holy Bible and then highlighted some of the passages."

"Do you remember the specific words that were highlighted?"

"No, not the exact passages," Callahan said. "All I can tell you is that it was a misguided attempt to take the Holy Scripture and use it as justification for harassment."

"Did you see the woman who delivered it?" Terry asked.

"No, but Francis told me that she came to his confessional seeking the Sacrament of Penance. She said 'forgive me Father, for I have sinned,' and passed an envelope through to his compartment. It was that card you spoke of. By the time he opened it and stepped outside of the confessional, she had walked down the aisle and was leaving the church."

"Did he see what she looked like?"

"Only from behind. She was an older woman. White hair."

"Where is the card now," Terry asked.

"It was burned."

"I see," Terry said. "Father, bless you for your help. If you think of anything else, here's my phone number."

He gave the monsignor his number, and hung up.

"*It* was burned," Terry said. "Not *I* burned it, or *Fleming* burned it, just it was burned. As if God Himself showed up in Portland, Oregon, and consumed it with fire."

"But at least we know you were right," I said. "Fleming got a warning card."

"And Betty White delivered it," Terry said.

"You lied through your teeth to the monsignor," I said. "You realize, of course, that you're going straight to hell."

Terry smiled. "I know. And as soon as I get there, I'm tracking down that pedophile priest."

# CHAPTER 24

**WE DECIDED TO** spend the morning sifting through the evidence one more time. Around eight o'clock, Jessica Keating called with the inevitable news. The hodgepodge of fingerprints on Tavo's birthday card was useless.

"But I may have something for you," she said. "The scrapbooks our killer is using are made by a company called Memories Forever. I checked with them, and as I suspected, this is one of their most popular models. It's sold in thousands of scrapbooking stores and online, so tracing the buyer would be impossible. But a few months ago, they retooled their machinery, and all the plastic page protectors they've manufactured since January are slightly different from the one they've been making for years."

"How different?" I asked.

"Infinitesimal. It has to do with the way the pages are crimped. You need a microscope to tell the difference. Lucky for you guys I just happen to have one. Memories Forever is sending me samples of the old and new pages. It's a long shot, but if our killer bought the new protectors, we might have something to go on. I'll have an answer for you this afternoon."

Two hours later, Karen Winters called.

"I believe we were just contacted by the person who killed Mrs. Bellingham-Crump," she said.

"In person? Phone? E-mail?" I asked, signaling Terry to get

ready to move out.

"No," Winters said. "An envelope was delivered this morning by our regular mail carrier."

"What was in it?"

"A page from a photo album," she said.

Twenty minutes later we were in Karen Winters's private office, along with her paralegal, Cody Wade.

"It was addressed to the Justice for Brandon Fund," she said, pointing to the twelve-by-ten page on her desk. "Cody opened it and immediately brought it to me."

Cody nodded. "Once we realized what it was, we stopped handling it," he said. "But it's got our fingerprints all over it."

Terry and I came around to the other side of the desk to get a better look. The page was tucked neatly into a plastic protector. In the center was a picture of something I had seen before. Only I had seen it up close and personal. It was Eleanor Bellingham-Crump lying dead on the ladies room floor at The Afton Gardens Hotel.

"Unless that's a police photo," Winters said, "it was shot by the killer."

"First he stabs her, then he shoots her," Terry said. "This dude is nasty."

The rest of the page was adorned with the killer's signature handiwork—a cocktail napkin, swizzle sticks, and other souvenirs from the hotel where the murder took place. It was clear what this was—the final chapter in Eleanor Bellingham-Crump's scrapbook.

A note was clipped to the top. It read: *Please accept this contribution to the Justice for Brandon Fund.*

Karen shook her head. "That's a page out of one very twisted photo album," she said.

"Not that it makes it any less twisted," Cody said, "but it's more like a scrapbook."

Terry and I both turned to him, ready to ask the same question.

He passed the baton to me. "Scrapbook, photo album," I said. "What's the difference?"

"You stick a photo in a sleeve, and basically it's archived and you've got a photo album," Cody explained. "Scrapbooking is more creative. There are more elements than just pictures. Scrapbooks tell a bigger story. They can be very creative pieces of art."

"You seem to know a little bit about scrapbooking," I said.

"Oh, God, I know a lot about scrapbooking," he said. "My mother ran a battered women's shelter. I grew up in that environment. Scrapbooking was one of Mom's favorite activities for the women who lived in the shelter."

"Why would a battered woman want to put together a memory book?" I asked.

"It's like therapy. It helps them get their feelings out," Cody said.

"Do you do scrapbooks?" I asked.

He laughed. "No, man, I'm much more of a beer and video game guy. That's my therapy."

"You say this was delivered by the post office," I said.

"Yeah," Cody said. "It's postmarked LA."

I turned to Karen. "Do the Coopers know about this?" I asked.

"No. As soon as we realized what we were dealing with, we called you guys. I'm not even sure I'll tell the Coopers. It would only upset them. I don't think they'd be happy to hear that their son's death inspired vigilante justice."

"The killer may have left some fingerprints on this page," I said. "You and Cody definitely did. Can we take your prints so we can eliminate you?"

She laughed out loud.

"Should I take that as a no?" I said.

"I'm going to take a guess and say that whoever did this is not stupid enough to get his prints all over it," Karen said. "And I'm not interested in having my prints or my paralegal's in your case file."

Cody gave me a halfhearted shrug that said, *I don't give a shit if you take my prints, but whatever my boss says, goes.*

I knew I could track their prints down at any one of a number of state agencies, but I also knew that Karen Winters was right. The killer was too smart to leave fingerprints on the page.

An hour later we were in the crime lab with Jessica, comparing the newest page to the rest of Eleanor Bellingham-Crump's scrapbook.

"It's a match," she said. "No question. Same paper, same plastic, even a trace of cat hair."

My cell rang. It was Simone Trotter.

"Terry and I were just about to try to catch up to you," I said.

"Well, this would be the perfect time," she said. "Guess what Portland just called in."

"I'm gonna take a wild guess and say a scrapbook page with a picture of a dead priest on it," I said.

"Wow, Garet Church said you guys were good, but . . ."

"We're good, but we're not psychic," I said. "We got a similar page for Bellingham-Crump. It was mailed to the Justice for Brandon Fund."

"The page they have in Portland was mailed to Monsignor Callahan. He got it this morning and called the locals, who called us," she said. "Apparently the monsignor knows Detective Biggs quite well. He was pleased to hear that the Bureau brought in a devout Catholic cop, who was a devoted parishioner at St. Victor's and one of Father Fleming's most loving admirers. Funny, but that doesn't sound like the same Detective Biggs I talked to yesterday morning."

"Terry has had a lot of spiritual growth in the past twenty-four hours," I said. "He's practically born again."

"The Bureau has a policy against flat-out lying to witnesses to get answers out of them," she said.

"It's a great policy," I said. "I think it's something LAPD should look into. In the meantime, I'll try to get Terry to play by your rules."

"Fine. Now, if the killer sent a final page for the Fleming scrapbook and a final page for Mrs. Bellingham-Crump, wouldn't you think there's a final scrapbook page for Tavo Maldonado?"

"I'm guessing there is," I said, "and it's waiting for us at the Chinese restaurant."

"Get it from them," she said.

"Yes, ma'am," I said. "But this one's gonna have to be a pickup, not delivery."

# CHAPTER 25

**JUDY WOO WAS** not at the restaurant, which meant we had to deal directly with Sonia. She looked surprised to see us. And not particularly happy. "You catch white lady?" she said.

"Not yet," I said.

"You come for more good cooking?" She said it without an ounce of enthusiasm, knowing the answer in advance.

"Not today," I said.

"Everybody work here all legal," she said. "Everybody have green card. No trouble, just good food, low price. You come back, talk to Judy. She tell you, everybody all legal."

"Sonia, we're not from Immigration," I said. "We're investigating a murder."

"Everybody know who kill Eddie. Tavo dogs. Tavo fault."

"I know. We're trying to find who killed Tavo."

"Who give a shit?" she said, then yelled out in Chinese, and got instant responses from all those in the place who understood her. She smiled at me. "Nobody here give a shit. Can't help."

"Did you get a picture of Tavo Maldonado," I said.

"Tavo a fat bassard. Why I need picture of a fat bassard?"

"We think someone might have sent one to you. Did you get the mail yet today?"

She shrugged, then called out in Chinese to the man sitting behind the cash register. He reached under the counter, pulled out a handful of envelopes, got off his stool, and walked them over to Sonia.

She riffled through them. "Bill, bill, bill, crap, bill," she said. "No picture. Who would send Sonia picture of Tavo?"

"The person who killed him."

"White lady?" she said. "Tavo dead. Why she send me picture?"

"Killers do strange things," I said. I handed her my card. "If anything shows up in the mail, will you call us right away?"

She took the card without looking at it. "Judy call you. Everybody work here all legal. Everybody have green card." She folded her arms across her chest and stood in the classic defense pose.

"I know," I said. "Everybody's legal."

She didn't offer us a table. It didn't matter. It was definitely not the right time to test Terry's theory about the kitchen help spitting in our food.

We left the restaurant and walked back to the car. "Well, that was a waste of time," I said. "So tell me, Detective DiCaprio, what would you and Brian Dennehy do now?"

"We'd probably pull off the Interstate into one of those truck stops that has cheap gas, greasy food, bathrooms with real showers, and a totally cheesy gift shop."

"That sounds smart," I said. "Or at least semi-smart. Do you think the old lady was telling the truth?"

"Probably. It's hard enough to lie in your native language; it's even harder to lie in broken English. Anyway, why would she lie?"

"Because now that she's had time to think it over, she probably doesn't want us to catch the white lady who killed the bassard who killed Eddie Chang."

"You're right," Terry said. "Which means, if she did get a picture of Tavo sprawled out dead in an alley, she's never going to give it to us. She'll probably frame it and hang it over her bed next to the picture of JFK, or Elvis, or Mao, then do a little dance around it."

"So that means she's probably lying to us," I said.

"Just the opposite. It means she's probably telling us the truth."

"How so?"

"The killer wants closure. He or she wants these final pages to be added to their respective scrapbooks," Terry said. "But the only way for that to happen is to send each page to someone who would definitely call the cops."

"Like Karen Winters," I said. "Or Monsignor Callahan."

"But not Sonia Woo," Terry said. "The killer would figure she's never going to give it to us."

"Ergo, no closure," I said.

"So he sent it to somebody else. Somebody who cared about Tavo and would be more likely to call us."

"Lovey LaRue," I said.

"Bingo. She'll probably be calling us any minute."

"Why wait?" I asked. "How do you feel about driving back to the porn shop?"

"Are you kidding?" Terry said. "This long-haul trucker's got a semi already."

# CHAPTER 26

**"WELL, LOOK WHO'S** back for seconds," a husky voice called out as we walked through the front door. "Hello, Detective Lomax, Detective Biggs."

"Hello, Lovey," I said.

"Yesterday was business," she said. "I'm guessing today is pleasure."

"Just the orgasmic pleasure one gets from solving a homicide," I said. "We have a few more questions."

If an exhale can sound uncooperative, hers did. She nodded for me to continue.

"Did you get any mail today?" I asked.

"Just my AARPS newsletter," she said. She waited for me to ask what the initials stood for, but I didn't bite. So she answered it herself. The American Association of Retired Porn Stars.

She laughed. Terry and I didn't.

"Just kidding," she said. "I never did porn. I was a class act all the way."

I swept my hand across the wide array of sex toys. "And it shows," I said.

"I used to dance," Lovey said. "I worked in Vegas—The Sands, back in the day when the Rat Pack still owned the strip. Those were the days. If my knees didn't buckle and my tits didn't sag, I'd still be dancing."

"You're dancing now," I said. "Let me repeat the question. Did you get any mail today?"

"The usual crap. What are you looking for?"

"Pictures of the late Gustavo Maldonado laying dead in the alley," I said.

"Don't you guys have enough of those already?" she said.

"We don't have one on fancy paper with pretty decorations," I said. "But I bet you do."

"Bad bet," she said. "House wins."

"How about if I play one more hand," I said. "This time with a search warrant. And you're really not going to like what it says on it."

"I know what a search warrant looks like. I've seen them before."

I smiled. "But this one won't say Lovey LaRue. It will have your real name on it."

"That is my real name," she said.

"It's your real alias. Has been for decades," I said. "But we dug your real name out of our database, and I can see why you stopped using it. We'd be glad to spare you the embarrassment, but once we file a warrant, it's in the public domain. And when we do catch Tavo's killer, that name you've tried to keep secret all these years will be on page one of all the papers."

"You prick," she said. "Wait here." She headed for the back of the shop.

"That's the biggest load of horseshit you ever served up," Terry said. "Search warrants are in the public domain? Her real name will be on page one of all the papers?"

"She bought it," I said.

"What is her real name, anyway?"

"Damned if I know," I said. "But I was betting she would hate the thought of anyone finding out."

"Good bet," Terry said. "House folds."

Lovey came back with an envelope identical to the one we had seen in Karen Winters's office. With total disregard for all things forensic, she yanked the contents out and put it on the counter.

It was the final page for Tavo Maldonado's scrapbook. On the right side was a picture of Tavo lying face up on the asphalt with a pair of scissors in his spleen. On the left was a square of white paper. At the top it said, *Coverage Of Gustavo Maldonado's Murder By The Los Angeles Media.* The rest of it was blank, except for two words at the very bottom. *Good Riddance.*

"Do you have any idea who the hell would send this to me?" Lovey asked.

"Now you're asking," I said. "Why didn't you call us when you got it?"

"I don't reach out to LAPD every time some religious nut threatens me or my business," she said.

"You think this is a threat to you?" I asked.

"They sure as shit aren't threatening Tavo. He's dead. I think the message is clear. He's first, you're next."

"So if you thought you were next, why didn't you call a cop?"

"Yeah, like LAPD is going to protect some old broad who runs a sex boutique," she said. "I don't call cops. I call 1-800-CHICANO. You see that Mexican guy who's browsing through the bondage toys? And that woman over there by the lubricants? They're my instore security."

"Just those two?" I said.

"The two of them, me, and Mrs. Glock," she said, reaching under the counter and pulling out a Glock 9mm handgun.

"Easy on the trigger, Lovey," I said.

She tucked it back under the counter. "And yes, I have a CCW permit," she said. "But since you've already done your homework on me, you know I've had a license to carry a concealed weapon for the past ten years. That's probably where you got my real name."

"You have the right to protect yourself," I said, "but I don't think this page you got in the mail is from some religious nut who doesn't like the business you're in."

"Then why did I get it?"

"You're just the messenger," I said, picking up the scrapbook page and sliding it back into the envelope. "All you were supposed to do is deliver it to us. Thank you for being so cooperative."

"Alright, maybe I was a little slow about it, but I delivered," she said. "You're not going to start giving out my real name, are you?"

"No, ma'am," I said. "We'll just let that be our little secret."

"You'll be in good company," she said. "There's only one other person who knew my real name. Frank. Frank Sinatra. I loved that man."

"You knew Sinatra?" I said.

"Honey, we had an on-again, off-again affair for fifteen years," she said. "He would dump me, but then he would always come back. He couldn't stay away. He said I gave the best head this side of Hoboken."

She flipped her fire-engine red hair and winked a mascara-caked eye at me; the septuagenarian Vegas showgirl, waiting for a predictable male response.

The best I could do was, "Yes ma'am. We'll just let that be our other little secret."

# CHAPTER 27

"**I'VE GOT GOOD** news," Jessica Keating said when we got to the lab with the latest scrapbook page. She took it and put it under a microscope.

"If you're looking for fingerprints, don't hold your breath," I said. "That piece of evidence has seen more than its fair share of fingers."

"I don't care about prints. I'm looking at crimps. I got samples of the new and the old page protectors from Memories Forever. The reason they changed their manufacturing process was to make the pages last longer. The new ones have something called the satin stitch crimp."

She adjusted the scope and stared into it for about thirty more seconds. "Bingo," she said.

"Bingo?" Terry said. "I thought you lab guys are supposed to yell out 'eureka.'"

"I've checked all three scrapbooks," she said. "And guess what? Our killer only used the satin stitch crimped pages— including this one. Do you know what that means?"

"Our killer's memories will last longer than other people's crap crimp memories?" Terry said.

"The new design wasn't available in stores until after the first murder," Jessica said. "The killer could only have bought them direct from the company's Web site. They're e-mailing me the names and addresses of every buyer. I had them break it down by state. I should have it in a few minutes."

"Shoot the list over to Muller, and have him start by running down everyone in the LA area who bought those scrapbook pages," I said. "We're going to the office for a group grope."

Kilcullen insists on holding joint task force meetings whenever we work with another department. By the time we got back to the station, Simone, Kilcullen, and Wendy Burns were waiting for us in the break room. Agent John Breiling from the FBI's Portland office was sitting in by speakerphone.

The first thing we did was agree on a pronoun. Some of us were calling the killer *he*, others were saying *she*, and Kilcullen was saying *he/she*.

"Just because some witnesses ID'd our suspect as a woman doesn't prove anything," Simone said. "It could easily have been a guy in drag."

We settled on *she*.

We rehashed the case for twenty minutes, and finally Kilcullen focused on the three newest pages. "Why did she send out those extra pages?" he asked.

"She's looking for closure," Simone said.

"Closure?" Kilcullen said. "What the hell is jamming a pair of scissors into somebody's spleen? If that isn't closure, what is?"

"She wanted to put the finishing touch on each scrapbook," Simone said. "The scrapbooks are critical to her, and they weren't complete without a picture of the dead victim."

"Complete?" Kilcullen said. "Does she think we're going to take the last page and add it to the back of the book?"

"That's what she'd like," Simone said. "According to the profile we did, she's incredibly thorough—probably a firstborn or an only child—and she probably expects us to do what she would do if she could. Remove the back cover of each scrapbook, insert the last page, and finish the job for her."

"Excuse me." It was Breiling, the Portland agent on the

speakerphone.

"Go ahead, John," Simone said.

"If she's hoping we'll tuck the last page into each scrapbook, why didn't she send them directly to us? Why mail the final pages to three different people, who might or might not turn them over to us? Isn't that putting closure at risk?"

The room went quiet.

After ten seconds Breiling broke the silence. "Are you guys still there?"

"It's a good question, John," Simone said. "We need a minute to come up with a halfway decent answer."

"I have a theory," Wendy said. "Maybe she isn't looking for closure."

"Meaning what?" Kilcullen said.

"If she sent the pages directly to us, we'd keep it under wraps, just like we're doing with the scrapbooks," Wendy said. "Maybe she doesn't like that we're not telling the public about the scrapbooks. What if she wants everyone to know that she's an avenger who is hell-bent on serving up justice, even if the system won't?"

"It's not real justice," Kilcullen said.

I wrote on my notepad and passed it to Terry. It's *semi-justice*.

"She thinks it's justice," Simone said. "Her victims each thought they were getting away with manslaughter, or pederasty, or vehicular homicide. She wants the world to know that they didn't get away with shit."

"Then why didn't she just send the final pages to the press?" Breiling asked from the squawk box. "She sent it to a lawyer, a priest, and that old lady in the sex shop. They turned the pages over to us. So who are they going to tell?"

"They'll tell *somebody*," I said. "The lawyer says she won't tell the Coopers, but I don't believe her."

"What about the priest?" Breiling said. "Isn't he bound by the church to keep it quiet?"

111

"Bullshit," Terry said. "Father Callahan will tell every pedophile he knows—and trust me, he knows a few. He's gonna warn them that there's a crusader out there. Keep your dicks in your frocks, boys. And once the word gets out, it will snowball."

"He's right," Wendy said. "People will be talking about The Scrapbook Vigilante."

"Not sexy enough," Terry said. "How about The Crepe Crusader?"

"How about the Sunday, Bloody Sunday Killer," Kilcullen said. "Three Sundays, three murders. Who retires when they're batting a thousand? He—or shit, she—is good at what she does, and she's rubbing our noses in it. You don't call the seven-ten split, and then not roll the ball. Mark my words, there's going to be another murder in four days."

"Did Forensics come up with anything on the three new scrapbook pages?" Wendy asked.

"They match up with the originals," Simone said. "Same paper, same rubber stamps, same cat hair."

The meeting dragged on for another half hour. It would have been a total bust except for Muller.

Detective Robert Muller is to LAPD what Bill Gates is to Microsoft. There's no better Comp Tech in the department.

"Hey dudes," he said. He's past thirty, but he never outgrew his love of teen-speak. "I've got something."

He put a computer printout on the table.

"This is every Los Angelino who went online and bought scrapbooks with the new satin stitch crimp page protectors from Memories Forever."

"Long list," I said.

"Right," he said. "So, let's narrow it down. Multiple murders, multiple scrapbooks, so here's the list of people who bought more than one."

He produced a second, much shorter printout.

"And here's the list of white-haired, older women who ordered twenty scrapbooks."

The third printout had one name on it. Lori Gibson.

"How do you know she has white hair?" Kilcullen asked.

Muller grinned and produced a printout of Lori Gibson's California driver's license.

She looked a little bit like Betty White.

# CHAPTER 28

**LORI GIBSON LIVED** in a working class neighborhood in South LA. The house was small and white. The lawn was dry and brown. There were three vehicles in the driveway: a ten-year-old Honda Civic, an even older Jeep Cherokee, and a recent vintage Harley-Davidson Fat Boy.

A low wrought-iron fence separated the house from East 27th Street. The gate was open. We went up the walk and rang the bell.

A man in his early sixties opened the front door. He used his left hand, because his right arm was in a sling.

"LAPD," I said, flashing my badge.

He couldn't hear me. He was deaf. He made that perfectly clear by signing with his good left hand. He leaned in and looked at my ID.

"Lori Gibson," I said, mouthing the words slowly.

He nodded and beckoned us in. The house smelled of home cooking, the kind you really feel good about coming home to. I inhaled, knowing that was as much dinner as I was going to get for at least two hours.

The woman whose picture was on the driver's license was in the living room, along with the guy who obviously owned the Harley in the driveway.

He stood up. "Hi, I'm Jim Gibson."

I identified myself again. "We'd like to ask Lori Gibson a few questions."

"She's my mom. And you already met my dad. They're both hearing impaired, but I'm a professional interpreter. Do you guys have a problem if I interpret? I'm certified. Actually, I do a lot of work in the court system."

Looks are deceiving. Gibson's arms were tattooed, his ears were pierced, and he had the heft, girth, and facial hair of a Hells Angel. His black T-shirt had a big yellow smiley face on it that said, *I am having a nice day. Don't screw it up, asshole.* It was hard to imagine him as the sign language interpreter in a staid LA courthouse.

"Go ahead," I said.

He turned to Lori, and his hands started flying. She looked surprised to see cops in her house and signed back.

The son laughed, shook his head, and told us what was so funny. "She thinks this is about the fender bender she had in the Walmart parking lot last week. I told her not to worry. What's up, anyway?"

Without giving away any of the details of the case, I asked him about the twenty scrapbooks Lori had bought from Memories Forever.

They had an animated conversation. The father watched, and at one point he chimed in, his left hand moving quickly, and his almost useless right hand dangling from the sling.

Jim turned to me and Terry. "My mom asked me if you guys know anything about scrapbooking," he said.

I looked at Lori and shook my head.

"You can talk directly to them," he said. "They can both read lips."

"We don't know much about scrapbooking," Terry said. "It's one of the things they forgot to teach us at Police Academy."

Gibson didn't have to interpret. The three of them laughed.

"My mom is a scrapbook consultant," he said. "She's been doing this long enough so that people who are new to scrapbooking look to her for help. She has a Web site, and sometimes she'll go to the local scrapbook store and supervise at a kids' party. She's also a reseller. She has an online account with Memories Forever, and she buys things to sell to other scrapbookers."

"Tell us about these twenty scrapbooks."

"My mom got an e-mail through her site," he said. "This woman wanted to buy twenty identical scrapbooks, plus a lot of page protectors, and my mom wrote back to say that with that big an order the woman would be better off opening her own account with the company. This way she wouldn't have to pay my mom's fee for being the middle man."

Lori shook her head and I could actually understand by her hand motions that she was waving off the woman, trying to prevent her from wasting money.

"But the woman said she'd rather do it this way," Gibson said, "because she didn't trust online credit card transactions, and she'd rather pay cash. So my mom ordered the stuff, and the woman came to the house and picked it up."

"Do you remember her name?" I asked.

Lori signed.

"She thinks it was Ann," Gibson said. "She can go look it up in her computer."

"Please," I said.

Lori held up a finger and left the room. The father signed something and Jim responded.

"What happened to your father's arm?" Terry said.

"He fell off a step stool."

"Having your arm in a sling must really cut down on your conversation," Terry said to the father.

The guy laughed, shook his head, and signed.

"He says my mom does all the talking all the time anyway," Gibson said.

Lori returned with a piece of paper and handed it to me. The name on it said Ann A. Venger.

"Shit," I said. "Sorry for the language."

"Hey, if I don't sign it she won't know if you said shit or shoot," he said. "What's the problem with the name my mom gave you?"

"It's phony," I said, and handed the paper to Terry. "Lori, can you describe what she looked like?"

The answer came back as expected. Average build, late fifties, white hair. I produced the sketch that had been done from Sonia Woo's description. "Do you recognize this woman?" I asked.

Lori took the picture and gave me a puzzled grin. She showed it to her husband and her son.

"Mom says that's one of the old ladies from the TV show, *The Golden Girls*," he said. "I think she's right."

We talked for a few more minutes. Lori vaguely remembered that the car the scrapbook buyer came in was old and gray. Or old and light blue. And her e-mail was a disposable Yahoo address. It was clear that the killer had used Lori as a go-between, so she could buy scrapbooking supplies without leaving a trail. We thanked the family and left.

"Ann A. Venger," Terry said, once we got outside. "An avenger. Very F. N. Funny."

# CHAPTER 29

**IT WAS AFTER** 9 P.M. when Diana and I sat down to dinner. We went to Vito's, an old-school Italian restaurant about a mile from our house. It has excellent food and even more excellent homemade desserts.

"Screw the calories," I said. "Tonight I'm diving headfirst into a bowl of passion fruit and honey zabaglione. Today is one of those days when I totally earned it."

We ordered, and I spent the next ten minutes telling Diana about Terry's conversation with the monsignor, the scrapbook page that showed up at the lawyer's office, and our return visits to the Chinese restaurant, and Lovey's Leather and Lace.

"You're right," she said. "You definitely deserve dessert. Sounds like you had a jam-packed day."

"And you've only heard the first half of it," I said. "But why don't we talk about you for a while."

"I had a wonderful day." She smiled, and I could see her eyes start to moisten.

Diana is a nurse in the Pediatric Oncology Unit at Valley General Hospital. Her patients are all kids with terminal illnesses, so when she says she had a wonderful day, that's code. It means nobody died on her shift, which in a cancer ward is the gold standard for wonderful.

"I had lunch with Carly Tan," she said. "You made quite a first impression on that little girl of hers."

"I have that effect on women."

"If I remember correctly, I bailed out of our first dinner date before we even had dessert."

"That first date didn't count," I said. "My father invited me to dinner and then ambushed me by trotting you out."

"Hmmm, isn't that what I did with Sophie?" she said, grinning at me. "Anyway, Sophie adores you. She can't stop talking about you."

"Tell me everything you heard," I said, "and don't leave out a single compliment."

"Sophie went to school yesterday and told all the other kids about this cool cop she met. Then last night she showed Carly the beginning of a short story she's writing."

"About a cool cop?"

"About you and Sophie. You're a team of private detectives."

"Private?" I said. "What about the department?"

"That's just what Carly asked Sophie, and the kid had the perfect answer. She said LAPD can't hire a seven-year-old girl to be a cop, but if you're private detectives you can open your own agency and no one can stop you."

We ate dinner and eventually I got around to telling her about the rest of my day. She was fascinated when I told her about Lori Gibson.

"It was the first time Terry and I ever interviewed a witness using sign language," I said.

"Can you sign?" she asked.

"No. Can you?"

She held up her right hand, put her pinky and index finger straight up and her thumb at a ninety-degree angle.

"I need an interpreter," I said.

"It's the universal sign for I love you. Here's the I, the L, and the Y," she said. "Babies can learn sign language at a much younger age than they can learn to speak, so a lot of my hearing

119

patients know how to sign, and this is always the first one they want to teach me."

"Well, thanks for teaching me," I said. "That doubles my sign language vocabulary."

"What else do you know?"

"I'm not sure I should be signing it in public," I said.

"Don't worry, nobody will hear you. Let me see what you know."

I made a fist with my left hand, inserted the index finger of my right hand, and slid it in and out.

"That's gross," she said, "Where did you learn that?"

"Fifth grade," I said. "It's the universal sign for forget about dessert. Let's go home, get naked, and see what comes up."

Which is exactly what we did.

It was a hell of a lot better than Vito's zabaglione.

# CHAPTER 30

**THE NEXT MORNING** Terry and I sat down with Muller and told him that Lori Gibson was just a third party vendor.

"We have to track down the woman who bought the scrapbooks from her," I said. "Two witnesses have stated that she's in her fifties or sixties. If she's that old, and she's systematically killing people, she's probably in our database. She can't have gone all those years without having some kind of a record."

"That's not entirely true," Terry said. "Some of them don't really go batshit till they hit menopause. One day they're sweet as the baby Jesus, and the next day their hormones go haywire, and they'll turn on you like a hammerhead shark with a toothache."

"Is that really what happens in menopause?" Muller said. He's in his early thirties. Like most guys his age, he knows more about video games than female life cycles.

"Ignore him," I said. "He's exaggerating."

"Am I?" Terry said. "Muller, how old is your wife?"

"Annetta? Thirty-three."

"You've got ten, twelve good years ahead of you," Terry said. "Then her biological clock will strike midnight, and she'll go from Cinderella to Lizzie Borden. Her thermostat will spike, and she'll radiate enough heat to roast a Butterball turkey in six minutes. She'll produce so much testosterone they'll make her a card-carrying member of World Wrestling Entertainment. And everyone will piss her off—flight attendants, telemarketers, and most of all, you. Then one day she'll mysteriously snap out of it and either decide to open a small bookstore, or run for some amusing public office, like Governor of New Jersey."

Everybody knows Terry wants to go into standup comedy after he retires from LAPD. It finally dawned on Muller that Terry was just trying out some new material.

"Oh, crap," Muller said. "Is this one of your stupid routines?"

"It might have been if you'd have laughed," Terry said.

"Excuse me, Detectives." It was Kelly Jo Brownfield, one of the recent crop of uniforms assigned to our station.

"What's up, Kelly Jo?" I said.

"There's a really cute guy out at the front desk. He's here to see you and Detective Biggs."

"Name?"

"His name? Oh, damn. He told me, but I got distracted. Cory, Colby . . ."

"Does he look a little like Matt Damon?" I asked.

"Yeah. That's what distracted me."

"Is his name Cody Wade?"

"Yes," she said. "God, you're a good detective. What should I do?"

"Take him home and handcuff him to your bedpost till we're ready for him," Terry said.

"I wish," she said.

"Bring him into Interview One," I said. "We'll be right there."

"Take your time," she said. She ran her hands through her hair and headed back to the front desk.

"Cody Wade is a paralegal who works for the law firm that represents the Justice for Brandon Fund," I told Muller. "I can't imagine what he wants, but while we're talking to him, why don't you start looking for age-appropriate white women who have some kind of a record of violence."

"If you believe Biggs," Muller said, "that'll be all of them."

"But this woman isn't the type to get arrested for whacking her old man on the head with a frying pan in a domestic brawl," Terry said. "She's smart. More than smart—she's a fucking mastermind."

"The FBI profiler said she's thorough," I added.

"Did we really need a profiler from the federal government to point that out? Thorough? How about obsessively, compulsively meticulous," Terry said. "And cunning. When she bought those scrapbooks from Lori Gibson, she could have made up any one of a million aliases. But she knew we could track down the sale, so she picked Ann A. Venger. She's taunting us. She wants us to know that she's one step ahead of us."

"Reminds me of the Zodiac Killer," Muller said. "He kept tweaking the cops by sending letters to the newspapers."

"Bad analogy," Terry said. "Zodiac murdered thirty or forty people and he never got caught. This broad is going down."

"I have a thought," I said to Muller. "It might help you narrow down your search. These killings have a kind of surgical precision to them. It takes a little bit of knowledge and a lot of skill to stab someone in just the right spot, then twist it so the victim bleeds out instantly."

"Good idea," Muller said. "I'll cross-check, looking for women who work in the medical—"

"Detectives!"

It was Kelly Jo.

"He left. Matt Damon—Cody Wade—he took off. When I got back to the front desk, he was gone."

Terry and I both jumped from our chairs and ran through the squad room to the front desk. Two uniformed cops were behind the counter. There was only one place Wade could have gone. Out the front door.

Terry and I ran down the front steps. The section of Wilcox in front of the station is a no-parking zone, but there are meters across the street in front of the bail bondsman's office. There was a red Honda Civic at one meter. Cody was in the front seat, smoking a cigarette.

Terry and I crossed the street and went to opposite sides of the car. I tapped on the driver's side window.

"Are you here to see us?" I asked.

"No," he said. "I mean I was. But I changed my mind."

"Why?"

"Because I think I might have made a mistake," he said. "I was going to tell you guys, and then I decided that would be an even bigger mistake."

"Now that you logged in at our front desk, it would be an even bigger mistake not to tell us," I said. "But as a paralegal I'm sure you already know it."

It was an out-and-out lie. He was free to drive off into the sunset. But Cody didn't want to add ignorance of the law to his growing list of mistakes, so he nodded in total agreement.

"Come on inside, and let's talk," I said.

He got out of the car, and the three of us headed back to the station. I had the feeling Officer Brownfield would be thrilled to see us walk through the front door.

# CHAPTER 31

**WE SAT CODY** down in an interview room. Bare walls. Small table. Uncomfortable chairs. It's the kind of place people want to get out of in a hurry—which, of course, is the whole idea.

"So what brings you here," I said, as if Cody and I were nextdoor neighbors who just happened to bump into each other at The Home Depot.

He shook his head. "I don't know. I'm not sure that I should say."

Given time, I could easily have broken him down. But according to Kilcullen we were three days from the next murder. I didn't have time.

I moved behind Cody and let Terry step up in front of him. He stood there for thirty seconds, towering over the young paralegal. And then he struck.

"Give me five dollars," Terry screamed.

Cody froze. "What?"

"Give me five dollars," Terry repeated. "Get off your ass and hand over five bucks."

Cody fished in his pants pocket till he produced a five-dollar bill. "What's this about?" he said.

"What's it about? I gave you five bucks for the Justice for Brandon Fund, and you're doing everything you can to obstruct justice."

"I'm not obstructing justice for Brandon," he said. "This is about something else."

"Oh?" Terry said, going from a shout to a whisper. "Is it about Eleanor Bellingham-Crump? Because then you'd be obstructing an active homicide investigation, so you'd be digging yourself a much deeper hole."

"It's about that scrapbook page—the one I got in the mail yesterday," Cody said.

"What about it?"

He deliberated, choosing his words carefully. "Would it have been wrong for me to share that information with a third party?"

"It's part of an ongoing investigation," Terry said. "I can't stop you from telling anybody about it, but I hope that third party wasn't CNN."

"Nothing like that," Cody said. "I told a close family member about it."

"Your wife?"

"I'm not married."

"Listen to me," Terry said. "You work for a law firm. Somewhere along the way you must have learned that discretion is the better part of valor—especially in a homicide case. But you weren't discreet. Are you feeling guilty? Because if you're here for us to absolve you of your guilt or your stupidity, consider yourself absolved. Just understand that the more information you leak, the harder our job is."

"I know," Cody said. "But I may be able to make your job easier."

"Getting to the point often makes my job easier," Terry said. "Now, let's give it a whirl. Who did you tell about the scrapbook page?"

"My mom," he said.

"Your mother?"

"Yes. My mom. Gladys Wade."

Terry exhaled hard and massaged his forehead with his

fingertips. What had sounded like a promising lead was turning stupid on us. "I had a real unhappy childhood," Terry said, "so my partner handles all questions dealing with moms. Go ahead, Detective Lomax."

I was now the official designated driver on the train to nowhere. "Okay," I said. "You obviously think you've got something that can help, so walk us through it."

"I went to visit my mom yesterday," he said. "I go every Wednesday. I left work early and got there at two o'clock. That's our regular visiting time—two on Wednesday. Usually we just talk about this and that, have a snack; it's all very low key. But yesterday I had this scrapbook page on my mind. And like I told you, my mother ran a battered women's shelter. She used to teach scrapbooking to the women who lived there. She always believed it was real good therapy for them. So I told her about the page we got at the office."

He looked at us as if his mother's love of scrapbooking justified his behavior. Surely once we knew about Mom and her scrapbook philosophy our cold hard stares would melt into warm smiles, and we would give him our blessings to leak the details of our homicide investigation to anyone he thought might get a kick out of it.

It didn't take long for him to figure out that wasn't going to happen.

"I knew I shouldn't be talking out of school like that," he said, "but it's not always easy to find such interesting stuff to talk to my mother about."

"What exactly did you tell her," I said.

"I told her about the picture of Mrs. Bellingham-Crump dead in the bathroom, and about the mementos from the hotel, and the note, and how somebody had put a lot of time into crafting this creepy-ass death tribute."

"And what did she say?"

"That's the thing," Cody said. "She didn't say anything. I

thought maybe I spooked her, but she didn't look upset. She was totally calm. Cold, almost, like, dumbstruck. And then finally, she said, 'did you get any others?'"

"Others?" I said.

"That's what she said. I said, no. A picture of one dead body is plenty for me, thank you. So she said, 'what about LAPD? Did they get any others?' So I told her if the cops got more scrapbook pages about Mrs. Bellingham-Crump, they're not going to tell me. And she said, 'I don't mean her; I mean did the police say anything about any other murders?'"

"Why would your mother ask such a bizarre question," I said.

"She said 'because if this is the first murder, there's going to be more coming.' That's why I came here," Cody said. "My mom thinks there's going to be more murders and more scrapbooks, and now I'm afraid to open the mail. I don't want any more pictures of dead bodies. It's like murder porn. I had to pop an Ambien last night, just to catch a few hours sleep."

"Your mother thinks there might be more scrapbooks?" I asked.

"Yeah," Cody said. "And she said, if there are, she probably knows who made them."

"Well, we didn't mean to gang up on you, but I'm glad you came here," I said. "We'd like to ask your mother a few questions."

"I guess that's possible," he said "I only go there once a week, but I'm sure you could make arrangements to see her whenever you want."

"Okay," I said. "And who would I make these arrangements with?"

"Her name is Lauren Swan," he said. "I have her phone number in my BlackBerry."

"Lauren Swan," I said. "I know that name. . . ."

"Well, I guess since you're a cop, you would know it," Cody said. "She's the assistant warden at the state prison in Corona."

I wasn't ready for that.

"Cody," I said slowly, "does your mom work at the prison?"

He smiled. "Oh no, sir," he said. "I thought you knew. Mom's an inmate."

# CHAPTER 32

**I CALLED SIMONE** Trotter and told her Cody's story.

"It sounds like his mother is a prison snitch," she said. "Usually, they're not worth the time you take to talk to them."

"She's not a snitch," I said. "At least not yet. At this point, she hasn't offered to tell us anything. But she knows there was more than one murder and more than one scrapbook. I want to know how she knows. Terry is calling Corona and setting up an interview."

"Ninety-nine times out of a hundred it's a con job, but let me know when, and I'll meet you there," she said. "What's the mother in jail for?"

"Conduct unbecoming a mom," I said. "Specifically, involuntary manslaughter. Terry and I are going to get the gory details from the son."

"What's his story?"

"He seemed like your basic, idealistic legal do-gooder the first few times we talked to him. Today he looks like he's ready to wet his pants, because Mommy told him he might be getting more pictures of dead women."

"Did you tell him that he's not the only one on the killer's mailing list?"

"I didn't want to burden him with the truth," I said. "He showed up, took off, had to be dragged back in, and now he's coming to grips with the fact that he's damned if he talks to us and damned if he doesn't."

"You really know how to find reliable witnesses," she said.

"Hey, compared to the three drunken women at the hotel, the Chinese grandma who fingered Betty White, and the gun-toting porn shop lady, this kid is more reliable than the six o'clock news. I'll see you later."

Kelly Jo was standing outside the interview room to make sure Cody didn't have another change of heart.

"How's he doing?" I said.

"No problem," she said. "I talked to him for a while. He's kind of a wimp."

"But you'd still sleep with him," I said.

"In a heartbeat."

Terry and I went into the interview room. Cody was still sitting at the table. This time we sat down with him.

"Tell us how your mom wound up in jail," I said.

"She was railroaded," he said.

"Aren't they all?" Terry said. "Especially the ones that shoot a guy between the eyes."

"She explained that in court," he said.

"Humor us, and explain it again," I said.

"My mom runs a battered women's shelter," he said. "It's not a job; it's a calling. My father used to beat the shit out of her regularly. One day, this guy shows up at the shelter. We don't know how he found it—the address is unlisted to protect the women. He goes to my mother's office and he says he wants to talk to his ex-wife, and Mom says no, absolutely not. He starts screaming at her, and then he got violent."

"Define violent," I said.

"He picked up a ceramic bowl that was on my mother's desk, and he threw it against the wall."

"Did he have a weapon?"

"It turns out that he didn't. But my mother didn't know that at the time. For all she knew, he could have had a gun or a knife."

"Or an arsenal of ceramic bowls," Terry said.

"He was a two hundred-and-fifty-pound wife beater," Cody said. "He didn't need a weapon."

"So then what happened?" I said.

"Mom just snapped. She had seen it before. First the bowl gets smashed, then your head. A bunch of shrinks testified that my mother was suffering from PTSD. She had been beaten; her residents had been beaten, so she took a stand. Instinct. Fight or flight."

"It was more like gun or run," Terry said. "She shot him."

"She had a gun in her desk drawer. It was something she confiscated from one of the women years ago."

"So it was unregistered," I said.

"She never thought she'd ever use it. She just wanted to threaten the guy. She was aiming over his head. . . ."

"But she missed. That's the problem with guns," I said. "If you fire one, you can't say that the bullet was intentional, but where it ended up was an accident. It's cut and dried. He's dead, and she killed him."

Cody shrugged. "We thought a jury might be sympathetic, but the DA was a hard-ass, and said if she got convicted he'd push for fifteen years. At the time it was a tough political climate. Lots of anti-gun sentiment. Karen recommended that my mother cut a deal rather than take a chance. So she pled out for seven years, up for parole at three and a half. The good news is she comes up for parole in a few weeks."

"Well, we'd like to talk to her and see what she's selling," I said.

"She's not selling anything," he said. "She didn't tell me to call you. I just told you—she's up for parole in a few weeks. Why would she want to be connected to another murder?"

"It would help her case with the parole board if she helped us," I said.

"She doesn't need your help," he said. "She's a model prisoner. Karen and I both feel she has a great shot at parole."

"Well then, I'll wish her the best of luck in person," I said. "We're going to pay her a visit."

"Not without a lawyer you won't," he said. "I'll call Karen."

"The sooner the better," I said.

He took his cell phone out of his pocket, then he paused.

"Is she right?" he said. "Is there another murder besides Mrs. Bellingham-Crump?"

"Good question," I said. "Let's go ask your mom."

# CHAPTER 33

**TERRY AND I** went back to Muller's office.

"You know that important project you're working on for us?" I said.

"Let me guess," Muller said. "You got something more important."

"Gladys Wade, an inmate at Corona—what do we know about her?"

"If she's a guest of the California Department of Corrections and Rehabilitation, we probably know everything, including the results of her latest pap smear," he said, tapping on the keyboard.

In seconds, the computer corroborated Cody's story, although the state's version didn't include phrases like "she was railroaded."

"Ms. Wade seems to think there's more than one scrapbook murder," I said, "which is not exactly a factoid she would have picked up watching *Jeopardy*. Get a list of people who visited her in Corona over the past twelve months."

The list was short. Cody showed up religiously every Wednesday. Plus, there were a handful of other visitors, all female, each with the same address on Nichols Canyon Road.

"I cross-checked," Muller said. "That's the address of the battered women's shelter."

"I thought that was supposed to be unlisted," I said.

"Not to a computer cop on a mission," Muller said. "I can also hack into their phone records if you don't have time to get a subpoena. But the best I can tell you is who she talked to, not what was said."

"We'd be better off if you just went back to the original most important project, and searched the database for women whose hobbies are scrapbooking and mass murder," Terry said. "We're going to Corona to talk to Gladys now."

"Good timing," Muller said. "She's coming up for parole, so she'll probably sing like Mary Poppins, hoping to score some brownie points."

"Don't bet on it," Terry said. "Her lawyer will be there."

The California Institution for Women on Chino-Corona Road was built back in the 1950s when the state had a more progressive attitude toward rehabilitation. So it has more of a campus atmosphere than some of the maximum-security men's facilities, where the murderers are closely monitored to keep them from murdering each other.

Terry, Simone, and I were escorted into an interview room. Karen Winters was waiting with her client.

Gladys Wade was much more attractive than her mug shot. Her eyes and hair were both a soft brown, and despite her sixty years, she had a youthful Sally Field air about her. She looked amiable, but nervous.

"I explained to Gladys that Cody told you some of the things she told him in a privileged conversation," Karen said.

"But I'm not mad at him," Gladys said. "I'm sure he did what he thought was right."

Karen's eyes disagreed, but her mouth stayed shut.

"Cody told you about the murder of Eleanor Bellingham-Crump," I said.

"I saw it on the TV first," Gladys said.

"But your son told you about the scrapbook page he received in connection with her death," I said.

Gladys nodded.

"And you suggested that there might be other murders, and other scrapbook pages," I said.

Karen stepped in. "It was only a suggestion," she said. "Not a confession. That scrapbook page is the sign of a ritualistic, thoroughly organized killer, and that often indicates serial murderers."

"A good profiler might come to that conclusion over the course of an investigation," Simone said, "but we're wondering how your client saw one scrapbook page and immediately thought there might be others."

"She's naturally intuitive," Karen said.

"Aren't we all?" I said. "And then she said if there are more scrapbooks, she knows who made them. That's a serious case of natural intuition."

"I didn't say I know who made them," Gladys said. "I said I probably know."

"So then you probably know who killed Mrs. Bellingham-Crump," I said.

"I know who wanted to kill her," Gladys said.

"Gladys," Karen said. "We've had this discussion. You don't *know* for sure who killed her. You don't have to tell these people anything."

"Mrs. Wade," I said. "You're up for parole in a few weeks. Cooperating with us will help you look like a model citizen — especially if you help prevent someone else from getting stabbed to death. Your lawyer is advising you not to talk, because that's what lawyers always tell clients, but you'd be doing everyone a favor if you'd listen to your conscience and not your counsel."

"I work in the prison library a few days a week," Gladys said. "One of the inmates was collecting newspaper stories like the one about the diplomat's wife."

"To read or to cut and paste?"

Gladys shrugged. "I don't know. But I've taught a lot of the girls how to scrapbook, and she was my best student."

"What's her name?" I said.

"Not so fast, Detective Lomax," Karen said. "If you turn Mrs. Wade into a prison rat, she becomes a walking target. If she helps you catch a killer, what's in it for her?"

I knew we'd finally get to it. The negotiations had begun.

"What does your client want?" I asked.

"Same thing all these ladies in jumpsuits want. Out."

"She's up for parole," I said.

"That's a crapshoot, and you know it," Karen said. "Those sanctimonious bastards on the parole board don't make decisions based on facts. It depends how they feel that day. If they got laid the night before, Gladys walks. If they wake up with hemorrhoids that morning, she gets another year of free room and board from the state. You want information? I want guarantees."

Simone stood up. "And I want a dollar for every jailhouse monkey who tried to trade worthless information for a Get Out Of Jail Free card. Either put some of your cards on the table or we take our chips and go home."

"Fair enough," Karen said. "Gladys, tell them what we discussed."

Gladys folded her hands on her lap and took a deep breath. "Like I said, this inmate wasn't just collecting newspaper stories about Mrs. Crump. She had a file on people who did bad things to other people and got away with it. She said 'I'm gonna teach them all a lesson.'"

"Them all? Did she say who else besides Mrs. Bellingham-Crump?"

"I remember some," Gladys said. "A landlord in East LA, a Hollywood stuntman, a priest—"

"Tell me about the priest," I said. "What did he do?"

"You don't have to be a detective to figure that one out," Gladys said. "He did bad things to young boys. The church moved him to Portland."

I exchanged a look with Terry and Simone. None of the specifics of Father Fleming's murder had been leaked.

Gladys Wade definitely had something to sell.

# CHAPTER 34

**WE OFFERED GLADYS** a deal. If she helped us find the killer, the FBI and LAPD would both go to bat for her with the parole board.

"Go to bat?" Karen said. "What does that mean? Why can't you just get her out?"

"You know as well as we do, Counselor, that the board has total jurisdiction," I said. "But they usually listen when cops testify."

"Even if they do wake up with hemorrhoids," Terry said. "We're like the Preparation H of the criminal justice system."

"Fine," Karen said, "but we want it in writing from somebody on high."

"Paperwork takes time," Simone said. "For now, you've got our word."

"If I lend you twenty bucks, I'll take your word that you're going to pay me back," Karen said. "But I'm dealing with my client's freedom. If I don't have it in writing, I don't have shit."

Simone snapped back. "If someone else gets murdered while you're playing hard-ass, I will personally go to the parole board and tell them your client's refusal to cooperate led to another homicide."

"Gladys doesn't want anyone else to die," Karen said. "She's willing to tell you what she knows about potential victims. But the only real bargaining chip she's got is the name of the woman collecting the newspaper stories. You don't get that till you give us the deal in writing. Take it or leave it."

We took it.

The landlord in East LA was a slumlord named Johnny Walmark. Some of his tenants' kids ate paint chips off the walls in his rattrap apartments. One died of lead poisoning; a second had brain damage. But Walmark had signed leases stating that the tenants understood the paint was old and contained lead.

"Technically, he's operating inside the law," Karen said. "But do you think his tenants had any idea what they were signing?"

"So the guy skirts around criminal court," Simone said, "but the tenants could probably win a judgment against him in a civil suit."

"Except they're too poor to sue," Karen said.

"Tell us what you know about the stuntman," I said.

"His name is Jock," Gladys said.

"Like Jacques Cousteau?"

"No, like jock strap. He's a movie stuntman, and I know somebody got killed, but that's all I can remember. I'm sorry."

"What else?" I said.

"A woman who owns a nail salon. She was giving her customers Botox shots for half the price you'd pay at a doctor's office. But it wasn't real Botox. It was just a chemical concoction that made people feel numb. Even worse, it turned out to be toxic. One woman went blind, and a bunch of others had permanent facial damage."

"Do you remember her name?" I said.

"No. Just that she was Korean."

"Great," Terry said. "That eliminates both of the Lithuanian nail salons in LA."

She gave us three more scrapbook subjects. She didn't remember all the details, but she was able to give us a name, an occupation, a location, or the reason they were being targeted. In each case it was more than enough for us to track down the potential victim.

"That's six names," I said. "Any more?"

"Yes," she said. "I mean, I know there were more, but I can't remember any of them."

"Do you remember anything about a Chinese food delivery guy?" I asked.

She shook her head.

"How about pit bulls? Dogfights? A store called Leather and Lace? Do any of those ring a bell?"

"No, no, and no," she said. "I never wrote anything down. And I only work in the library three days a week. She could have done research when I wasn't there. I'm sorry."

"I don't think you should be apologizing," Karen said. "You were extremely cooperative. Don't you agree, Agent Trotter?"

"Cooperative, yes," Simone said. "Extremely cooperative would be to give up the name of the woman we want to question. By the way, was she released, or is she still in here and working with people on the outside?"

"Nice try," Karen said, "but you've gotten all you're going to get."

"My boss is in Washington D.C.," Simone said. "I'll have a letter signed, sealed, and notarized first thing in the morning."

"And we'll have one from LAPD," I added.

Gladys smiled. "Thank you," she said. "I'll be here."

She was wrong, but I wasn't going to be the one to tell her.

# CHAPTER 35

**"IT LOOKS LIKE** our scrapbooker has her next six Sundays planned," Simone said as soon as the door to the interview room was shut behind us.

"I'd make a piss-poor serial killer," Terry said. "I can barely plan one murder."

First order of business was to stop at Lauren Swan's office and arrange to have the Sheriff's Department move Gladys Wade to downtown LA. There was no sense making another three-hour round trip to Corona to deliver a letter, when the Sheriff's jail is only ten minutes from our office.

Simone, Terry, and I walked to our cars, each with a cell phone pressed to our ears. I called Anna DeRoy at the DA's office and explained the situation. "Do you think the DA would give Mrs. Wade a letter guaranteeing that LAPD will testify on her behalf at her parole hearing if she helps us crack the case?"

"Are you kidding?" DeRoy said. "Do you know how much pressure is coming out of the State Department to solve this case? If Gladys Wade helps you catch whoever stabbed that British diplomat's wife, the DA will personally unlock her cell door, the Chief of Police will drive her home, and your good buddy Deputy Mayor Mel Berger will give her a parade down Hollywood Boulevard."

"Thanks," I said. "That sounds like a yes."

Terry called Muller and gave him what we had on the newest scrapbook candidates. Simone called Don Hogle at the Bureau and gave him the same assignment. The two of them had worked together before, and we decided that we needed all the geek power we could get.

"As soon as our techs get a positive ID on a target, I'm sending out a team to warn them," Simone said as we arrived at our cars.

"Terry and I will take the stuntman," I said.

She shrugged. "Fine by me. Any reason why you zeroed in on him?"

"Old times' sake," I said. "My mom worked in Hollywood. She used to get punched in the face and thrown out of windows all the time."

"Wow," Simone said. "Your mom was a stuntwoman?"

"Either that or a screenwriter," Terry said. "Show business can be such a cruel taskmaster."

As soon as Terry and I were in our car, I called Big Jim.

"Dad," I said. "Do you know a stuntman named Jock?"

"Yeah, Jock Noonan."

"Tell me about him."

"Since when did you get into the movie business?" Jim asked.

"I'm not *in* the business. I just need your help."

"I don't care if you won't work with me," Jim said, "but whatever you do, don't get into bed with Jock Noonan. The guy is a total scumbag. Your mother did one feature with him. She would never work with him again."

"How come?"

"Because he treats his stuntpeople like they're G.I. Joe action figures—totally expendable. If one gets broken, screw it; he just gets another. His attitude is, hey, everybody gets banged up when they do stunts. Don't be a pussy. You cash the checks; do the stunts. He has the worst accident record in the industry, because he keeps pushing the envelope against all safety practices."

"Stupid question," I said. "Why does he keep getting hired?"

"That *is* a stupid question, Mike. Why do you think? His stunts are over the top, and a shit movie that's loaded with spectacular stunts can mean millions more at the box office around the world. 'No guts, no glory' Jock always tells the producers, and a lot of them buy into his macho bullshit."

"Thanks," I said. "That's a big help."

"Are you investigating his latest disaster?" Jim said. "I can't believe that one didn't land that asshole in jail."

"What latest disaster?"

"The speedboat accident," Jim said. "I assume that's what you're calling about."

"It is," I lied, "but there are so many versions, I figured, where do I go when I want the real scoop on Hollywood? A teamster."

"Damn right," he said. "Here's what I heard from a guy who was there when it happened. They were shooting a spy picture somewhere in Malaysia, or one of those places where the labor laws are sketchy, and the safety regs are flexible, depending on how much you pay the local government. There were two stunt guys in a speedboat being chased by a helicopter. The guy in the chopper is throwing grenades at the boat, and there are depth charges in the water that are rigged to explode in sequence, just missing the boat each time. It's a pretty standard stunt, but Jock Noonan decided he wanted to give the producer more bang for his buck."

"What did he do?"

"He doubled up on the explosives," Jim said. "As the boat was racing across the water, the first charge was so strong that the shock wave lifted it up and dropped it down smack on top of the next charge. Boom. The boat was blown to bits, and the two stunt guys were dead in the water."

"You're right," I said. "He should be in jail. That's negligent homicide."

"Not in Malaysia," Jim said. "The production company settled with the families of the two stuntmen, but according to the lawyers, Jock was untouchable. And the bastard didn't even show any remorse. His attitude was, 'hey, that's the business. It's not my fault when shit happens.'"

"Dad, thanks," I said. "You've been a big help."

"I always am," he said. "You're just not always smart enough to call. Is Terry with you?"

"Yeah. Why?"

"We're doing this trucker movie together," Jim said. "I want to talk to him."

"Sorry," I said. "Terry and I are busy doing this cop stuff together."

"It'll take two minutes," Jim said.

"Dad, Terry doesn't have two minutes—especially two Big Jim minutes. He really can't come to the phone."

"Come on, Mike," he said. "I'm busting a gut here. I have this great idea for the movie that I want to bounce off of him."

"Bounce it off your dentist. Ciao, baby," I said and hung up.

# CHAPTER 36

**"HIS NAME IS** Jock Noonan," I said to Terry, "and if there was ever any doubt that somebody would love to stick a pair of scissors in his belly, there isn't now."

"Typical Hollywood asshole?" Terry said.

"Worse. He's an arrogant bastard who got two of his stuntmen killed on a shoot, never showed an ounce of regret, and didn't even wind up with a slap on the wrist."

"And we're supposed to warn him that somebody wants to kill him?" Terry said. "Man, I know our job is to protect and serve, but sometimes I wish we could just let nature thin out the herd."

I called Muller and got Noonan's address.

"It figures," I said, hanging up. "Guess where this guy lives."

"You said *arrogant bastard, stuntman*, and *it figures*," Terry said, "so I'll go with the stereotype and say he lives within a two-mile radius of Muscle Beach."

"Damn, you'd make a fine detective," I said.

There are two Muscle Beaches: the original in Santa Monica, and the one we were headed for in Venice. LA beach communities generally attract a diverse assortment of weirdos, but Venice is freakier than most.

Even on a Thursday, Ocean Front Walk was populated with street musicians, jugglers, magicians, fortune-tellers, and of course, mimes. The local citizenry always look like they're dressed for Halloween, but the favorite spot for gawkers is the boardwalk, where the most popular fashion statement is lots of skin—with and without the body art.

There's a weight-lifting pen where the young Arnold Schwarzenegger used to be a regular. As we drove past, we could see the deeply tanned, well-oiled bodybuilders, whose lives seemed to move to the rhythm of the clanking barbells.

Jock Noonan had a small house on Zephyr Court, a few blocks from the beach. Terry parked, and we decided to take a quick look around the perimeter of the house before we announced ourselves.

The plates on the Chevy pickup in the driveway matched the number Muller had given me, and since nobody in LA goes anywhere on foot, that could only mean one thing. Noonan was home. The backyard was small and grassless, covered in heavy-duty black rubber interlocking gym floor tiles. Sitting on it was a dumbbell rack, an adjustable weight bench, and a barbell set that Terry and I probably couldn't lift together.

Behind the house was a recycling bin filled with tequila bottles and beer cans. "Whatever else you might say about him," Terry said, "at least he cares about the environment."

We went back to the front of the house, and I was about to knock on the screen door, when I heard it.

*Unnngh. Unnngh. Unnngh.*

A man was breathing hard and grunting.

"You think Jock has another set of dumbbells inside the house?" I said.

"Just one dumbbell," Terry said. "Probably with a nice set of tits."

The deep manly grunts were now being accompanied by a woman moaning, *oh yes, oh yes, oh yes.*

"He's either in there banging some chick," Terry said, "or he's working on a stunt that's definitely gonna have a happy ending."

"What's the department protocol on this one?"

"I don't know," Terry said, "but I'd hate to be the one who tells her she has the right to remain silent."

The sex got louder.

"At this point they won't even hear the doorbell," Terry said, "and we've got no probable cause to bust in."

"They sound like they're wrapping it up," I said. "Let's give them a few minutes."

"Sure, then we can run in with warm towels and a pack of Marlboros."

We stood at the screen door and listened. As the fornicating couple got louder the music inside the room seemed to crescendo with them.

"Not to be judgmental," Terry said, "but that has got to be the worst music to get laid by I ever heard."

A minute later, it was over. Terry wasted no time leaning on the doorbell.

There was no answer.

He yelled through the screen door. "Jock Noonan. LAPD. Open up."

Still no answer.

And then we heard a man's voice.

"*Thank you for letting me try the Virtual Reality Sexadrome 5000, your majesty.*"

A woman responded. "*Oh please, Professor. Call me Plutonia.*"

"Plutonia?" Terry said. "Mike, they're watching a porn movie."

"You sure?" I said.

"It's a vast improvement over those pleasure droids," Terry said.

And then from inside the house came the male voice. "*It's a vast improvement over those pleasure droids.*"

"Now that's amazing detective work," I said. I pounded on the door.

No answer from Noonan, but the woman kept talking.

"Mike, the sex is over," Terry said. "Nobody watches porn for the plot."

"Open it," I said.

Terry pushed on the screen door and inhaled. "Guess what I smell?" he said.

"Sex?"

"Death. I think we got probable cause."

We drew our guns and entered the house. "Police," I yelled.

The voices were clearer now. We headed in their direction. It was coming from downstairs. We called Noonan's name again and walked down a flight of narrow stairs.

The first thing we saw was the professor and Plutonia. They were in the center of a four-foot-wide plasma screen television. Jock Noonan was in front of the TV, sitting in a black leather recliner. His pants and shorts were around his ankles, and his right hand was dangling between his legs, next to his lifeless penis. A pair of scissors was sticking from his ribs.

"Jesus," I said. "She stabbed him while he was whacking off."

"How does someone who looks like Betty White get the drop on Iron Man Jock?" I asked.

Terry pointed at an empty tequila bottle on the floor. "I think she had a little help from Jose Cuervo. And look, she delivered a eulogy."

The killer's trademark scrapbook was on the floor behind the chair.

We called for backup and, guns still drawn, we searched the house. It was clear.

We went back downstairs. The movie was still playing. In fact, Noonan owned a Sony 400 DVD changer, which meant he could watch porn for about three weeks without ever having to leave his chair.

I took a pen and hit the stop button, interrupting a pair of natural blond alien women who were soaping each other down in the shower.

"I guess Gladys Wade was right," I said. "Jock Noonan was

definitely a candidate for a scrapbook."

Terry nodded. "And we were wrong."

"How so?"

"It's Thursday," Terry said. "We figured the killer only worked on Sundays."

# CHAPTER 37

**"THIS IS NOT** our killer's best work," Jessica said. "She really didn't put her heart and soul into this one."

I looked over at Jock Noonan, still in his death chair, pants bunched around his ankles, his final pathetic attempt at self-gratification now being captured from every angle by a crime scene photographer.

"He looks pretty dead to me," I said. "I don't know how much more heart and soul she could have given it."

"I'm talking about the scrapbook," Jess said. "It's not nearly as inspired as the others."

"Gosh," Terry said. "You would think a tequila-swilling, chicken-choking, steroid-popping Hollywood asshole would be an inspiration to any artist."

"Are you sure it's the same killer?" I asked.

"I'm not ready to testify till I take the evidence back to the lab, but look at the body," Jessica said. "Look at the position of the murder weapon. This killer is so precise, so consistent, so incredibly lethal." She paused and gave us a happy smile. "I just think her scrapbooking is getting shoddy."

"Maybe you ought to talk to her about that," Terry said. "We really should try to find her."

Simone Trotter came down the basement steps. "Well, that's a pretty sight," she said. "What have you got?"

"Jock Noonan," I said. "Hollywood stuntman. Recently retired from the biz."

"He thought he was coming," Terry said, "but it turns out he was going."

"It looks like Gladys Wade called it," I said. "Did you get the green light from Garet Church, so we can cut a deal with her?"

"Sorry," Simone said. "I've been kind of busy."

"Are you gonna let a little thing like a homicide stay you from the swift completion of your appointed rounds?" Terry said.

"One homicide, no," Simone said. "Two, yeah. We've got another body."

"Anyone Gladys knows?" Terry said.

"Our slumlord, Johnny Walmark," Simone said. "I sent a team to warn him, but they got there a few hours too late."

"A few hours wouldn't have mattered," Terry said. "The law says you always have to give a landlord a month's notice."

"We tracked down three of the other people Gladys gave us," Simone said. "They're all okay, and the Korean lady is visiting relatives in Seoul. We reached her by phone and told her to stay there."

"So it looks like Gladys has brought a new sense of credibility to the term prison snitch," I said. "LASD should have transferred her downtown by now. How long will it take us to get the paperwork so we can get her to tell us the rest of the story?"

"An hour," Simone said.

It took four. The wheels of bureaucratic progress turn slowly, no matter what's at stake. It was 8 P.M. by the time Simone, Terry, and I finally walked into an interview room in the Sheriff's jail on Bauchet Street. Gladys and Karen were waiting for us.

"I love reunions, don't you?" Terry said, as we sat down.

We handed Karen the letters of agreement, one signed by the DA, the other by Special Agent In Charge, Garet Church.

Karen put on her glasses and began reading. At one point she stopped. "Holy shit," she said. "There are five victims?"

"And counting," Terry said. "Read faster."

A minute later she handed the letters to Gladys. "These are fine. You want to read them?"

Gladys waved them off. "Just tell me what they say."

"Basically they state that if you give them information leading to the arrest of the person who murdered Eleanor Bellingham-Crump, Gustavo Maldonado, Father Francis Fleming, Johnny Walmark, and Jock Noonan, The Los Angeles Police Department, The District Attorney's office, and The Federal Bureau of Investigation will all write detailed letters to the parole board praising your cooperation, and testifying that it is their belief that you are a productive, law-abiding member of the community, and strongly urge them to grant you parole."

"So then we have a deal?" Gladys asked.

"Signed, sealed, and delivered," Karen answered.

Gladys nodded. "The killer is a woman named Hilda Beck."

# CHAPTER 38

"**HILDA WAS A** nurse," Gladys told us.

I looked at Terry. He shrugged. We suspected as much. We just hadn't turned our instincts into an arrest. Gladys was reminding us how smart we were. And how incompetent.

"She worked at The Paradise Living Center," Gladys said. "It's for people who have finished living, but haven't had the good sense to die. It's where the rich and trendy ship their geriatric relatives. If Granny has a colon full of cancer or a head full of dementia, all you need is a bag full of cash and your worries are over."

"I've heard of the place," Simone said. "They have a good reputation."

"And well deserved," Gladys said. "It's a five-star elephant burial ground. If you can afford to go out in style, it really is Paradise. Hilda was a senior floor nurse. She was very skilled, very organized, and very, very *efficient*."

"How efficient?" I said.

"Her hero was Jack Kevorkian, and Hilda was a big believer in a patient's right to die. And since a lot of them can't do it without help, she helped. They call her Mercy Nurse. I met her at Corona three years ago, and we struck up a friendship. Hilda was suspected of assisting in the suicides of an unknown number of people. I happen to know for a fact that the number was seventy-nine, but the state of California only tried her for one. She served nine years for second-degree murder."

"And now she's out and about?" Terry said.

"She was released four months ago."

"And she went right back to killing people," I said.

"I don't know that for sure," Gladys said.

"What do you know?" I said.

"When she worked at Paradise, she thought she was helping people to die with dignity. But her vision changed while she was in prison. The two of us used to talk about how many people are locked up who really shouldn't be."

"Like her," Simone said.

"And me," Gladys said. "But what bothered her the most was how many guilty people are still roaming around free."

"Like Eleanor Bellingham-Crump," I said.

"That woman killed an innocent child," Gladys said. "She should have been behind bars, but the justice system let her get away with murder. Hilda knew she couldn't change the system, so she became obsessed with the idea of going around it."

"If you knew she was planning to go out and kill people in the name of justice, why didn't you report her?" Simone asked.

"Get real, Agent Trotter," Karen said. "Do you know what prisoners talk about all day? 'I'll show them. I'll get them.' It goes with the territory. Besides, since when are cops willing to listen to prisoners? My client isn't obligated to report every inmate who threatens to kill somebody when they get out. It was only after Gladys found out about Mrs. Bellingham-Crump's scrapbook page that she put two and two together. That's when she contacted the police."

"No, she didn't," I said. "She told her son in confidence. He's the one who came to us."

"None of that matters," Karen said. "What matters is that my client gave you information that should lead you to the arrest of this serial killer."

"Which is going to happen tonight," Trotter said, pulling out her cell phone. She turned to me. "Don Hogle is still at the office. I'll have him contact CDCR and find out where this Hilda Beck lives."

"Oh, you don't have to do that," Gladys said. "I can tell you where she lives."

"You can?" Simone said. "Where?"

"My place."

# CHAPTER 39

**"YOUR PLACE?"** I said. "The battered women's shelter on
Nichols Canyon Road? Hilda Beck may be batshit, but she's not
battered."

"She doesn't live in the shelter," Gladys said. "I have a house
on East Vernon. There's a little studio in the back that Cody used
to live in. He moved into the main house when I went to Corona.
The studio has been vacant, so when Hilda got out, I told her she
could use it."

She gave us the exact address.

"And you think she's there now?" I asked.

"At this hour? Probably," she said. "But why don't you call
Cody and tell him to take a look out back."

"I'd rather not," I said. "The department frowns on cops calling
unarmed civilians and asking them to take a look out back for
mass murderers."

"At least let him open the front door for you," she said. "He
has the key."

"We can handle it," I said. "Thank you."

"Please don't break the door down. There's an extra key under
the geranium pot," she said.

Simone turned to Karen Winters. "Counselor, please remind
Mrs. Wade that we promised to help spring her from jail if we
catch this maniac. If your client wanted a no-door-breaking

clause, she should have asked for it before we signed the letter of agreement."

Karen was not amused. But she didn't say anything. She knew she had negotiated a hell of a sweet deal for Gladys Wade.

Simone, Terry, and I didn't waste time with good-byes. We sprinted toward our cars.

"I'm calling for backup," I said, flipping my phone open.

"So am I," she said. "If this turns out to be as good as it looks, I don't want LAPD taking all the credit."

"I can see the headline in tomorrow's paper," Terry said. "How many cops does it take to bag one old bag?"

We got to Gladys's house in fifteen minutes. By that time there were half a dozen squad cars waiting for us, with more on the way.

Cody Wade was waiting out front.

"Detective Lomax," he said. "Karen called me. I can't believe it. Do you really think Hilda—"

"Not now, Cody," I said. "You didn't go back there, did you?"

"No. I waited here after Karen called. I just wanted you to know that Hilda is in there. The lights are on, and her car is in the driveway."

"Is she alone?"

"She's always alone. Except for her cats."

"Thanks. Now back off," I said.

He didn't. "Karen told me that my mom wants me to make sure you don't break the door down." He held up a silver key. "This is for the bottom lock. It's a little tricky, so you might have to jiggle it. Maybe it would be easier if I went with you and I opened—"

I yanked him by the shoulders and pushed him toward two uniformed cops. "Officers, take this man and put him in a squad car before he gets himself killed."

Cody laughed. "Don't worry, Detective, Hilda would never kill me."

"No, but if you don't get the fuck out of here, I will," I said.

I grabbed the key out of his hand, and the two cops escorted him down the street.

Terry came up next to me. "The poor guy was only trying to help," he said. "When this is all over, you're really going to have to take a refresher course in Community Relations."

"We've got infrared on the house," Simone said. "We've got three clear images. Hilda is in bed, but the lights are on, so she's probably not asleep. The other two are the cats, one about sofa height, the other on the floor."

Terry drew his gun. "I'll cover the cat on the sofa," he said.

Five minutes later we were good to go. Vests on, guns ready, house surrounded. I banged on the door, and yelled out Hilda's name.

No answer. Shades of Jock Noonan.

But unlike Noonan, Hilda didn't get a second chance. I stuck the key in the door, turned it, and rushed in. Terry, Simone, and six cops were behind me.

The two cats ran like hell. Hilda Beck didn't budge.

She was stretched out on the bed. Dead. There was a scrapbook on the table next to her. Once again, shades of Jock Noonan.

The difference was there were no scissors stuck in Hilda's belly. Just a hypodermic needle lying on the floor.

# CHAPTER 40

COPS DON'T ALWAYS treat the dead with total respect. Especially when the deceased is Suspect Number One in a string of homicides.

As soon as we found the body, Simone started cursing up a storm at Hilda. I just couldn't tell in what language.

"Garet told us you speak seven languages," I said. "Which one are you giving her hell with?"

"I'm *fluent* in seven languages," Simone said. "I can curse in a dozen more, and I'll use them all before I'm done with this harpy slag. I've worked this case night and day, and this is not the way it's supposed to end. I wanted a report that says the brilliant and tenacious Agent Simone Trotter hunted down and captured a mastermind serial killer. Now all it will say is one of our field agents, who couldn't find her ass with a flashlight, stumbled onto the killer after the old bitch cow offed herself."

"We don't know for sure yet that it's a suicide," Terry said.

"Right," Simone said. "Just because we've got a dead woman in the bed, a needle on the floor, a bottle of morphine on the—"

"A label that says morphine," Terry said. "If I slapped a Heinz logo on the bottle, would you think it was ketchup?"

"And, oh look," Simone said. "That might be a suicide note. Or maybe Hilda left us a grocery list. Hey, I know the drill. I've had my share of stage suicides."

"So have we," Terry said. "My favorite was the woman who shot her husband through the head and left a typed suicide note. She only made one little mistake. After she killed him, she took the gun with her. Mike and I figured this was either cold-blooded murder or this guy killed himself with a .38 caliber finger."

"This one looks a lot more convincing," Simone said. "But who knows? Maybe that dumbass Cody Wade came in here and killed her just before we showed up. He had the key."

"Would you like to interrogate him?" Terry asked. He winked. "Alone, perhaps? Over a long weekend?"

The frustration on Simone's face morphed into a shit-eating grin. "He is pretty fucking sexy for a dumbass, isn't he?" she said.

"Hands off him, bitch," Terry said. "I saw him first."

The grin turned to a laugh. "He's all yours if you read me the note."

Terry put on a pair of rubber gloves, picked up the piece of paper, and began reading. "Milk, eggs, orange juice, morphine."

Civilians would be horrified if they had any idea how much clowning around goes on at a murder scene. Terry got the laugh he wanted, cleared his throat, and started again.

*"I ran out of time. I wanted to kill them all because they all deserve to die. God knows it and I know it, but the politicians and the judges don't know it, so I had to be the one to do God's work. There are lots more who should be killed, but I won't go back to prison, so I hope somebody finishes what I started."*

"I hope somebody finishes what I started?" Simone said. "Let's not make that public. Is that all she wrote?"

"No, there's one more thing," Terry said. "Cody Wade is queer as a three-dollar bill, so stay away from him, FBI lady."

Simone laughed again. "You never let up, do you Biggs?"

The crime scene unit hadn't arrived yet, but we decided to take a quick look inside the scrapbook that was on the table next to the bed.

"I'm betting this one is autobiographical," I said.

It was. Hilda's last scrapbook was all about the life and hard times of Hilda. It was filled with mementos of her days as a young nurse, articles about her arrest, the trial, and a bunch of souvenirs that reflected her time in jail.

"She bought twenty scrapbooks," I said. "So there's got to be more."

It didn't take long to find them. Each one was earmarked for a potential victim, including the people Gladys Wade warned us about.

"When you read about some of the scumbags she wanted to kill, you feel bad she didn't get to go through with it," Terry said.

"She wants somebody to finish what she started," Simone said. "You volunteering?"

"Why now?" I said. "She's been killing people left and right, and just when we zero in on her, she kills herself. How did she know we were on to her?"

"Somebody told her we were on the way," Terry said.

"Karen Winters," Simone said.

"She's not that stupid," I said. "She knows we can check her cell phone records."

"Cody?" Simone said.

"I think LAPD warned her," Terry said. He was standing at Hilda's dresser. The top drawer was open. He removed a handheld police scanner from the drawer and held it up.

"RadioShack," he said, "Probably cost a hundred bucks. We were rounding up every squad car in LA, and she was listening in."

Jessica Keating and her crime scene crew arrived, so we went back outside to break the news to Cody Wade.

He didn't seem upset about her death. Just puzzled about her life.

"It doesn't make sense," he said. "I knew about the euthanasia, of course. That's what she went to prison for. But why would she murder a bunch of people she didn't even know?"

"Oh, she knew a lot about them," I said. "Scrapbooks full. When did you last see her?"

"About six-thirty. I was at my computer. Her car has to go past my window, so I saw her pull into the driveway."

"Was anyone with her?" I said.

"No. Hilda is a loner. The only one I've ever seen her with is Bruce."

"Bruce who?"

"Bruce Gadansky. He's her parole office. Nice guy. Sometimes he stops in to see me and ask me a few questions. I have his card if you want it."

"Can you think of anyone who would want to kill her?" I asked.

He nodded his head slowly. "She was a tortured soul. I think the person who would most want to kill Hilda was Hilda."

"Yo! Detective Lomax! Detective Biggs!"

It was coming from behind the yellow tape, where the usual crowd of press people, paparazzi, gawkers, and stalkers were corralled.

It was Gary Miller, *LA Times*. Gary is not your stereotypical coffee-swilling, chain-smoking, flask-in-his-pocket movie reporter. He's a vitamin-popping, tree-hugging, health freak, who just happened to have a passion for crime. Terry and I like him, but we had nothing to say to the press.

"Should we ignore him?" I asked Terry.

He called again. "Yo! Mike! Terry! Over here."

"Ignoring a reporter only makes them more curious," Terry said. "Let's go over and lie to him. They like that."

We walked over and said hello.

"What are you boys doing here?" Miller said.

"I don't know about Mike, but I'm totally pissed off because I couldn't get on *Dancing with the Stars*," Terry said.

"You're working the case of the diplomat's wife," Miller said. "Is this connected?"

"We're all connected, Gary," I said. "Especially in friendly Southern California. Besides, we juggle multiple cases all the time."

"Not with all these FBI guys milling around," Gary said. "This has to be connected to the big one. Come on, give me something,"

"Gary, all we've got is a dead body," I said. "It's not even classified as a homicide yet. Not exactly newsworthy."

"We gotta go," Terry said. "We'll let you know if there's anything worth writing home about."

"Yeah, sure," Miller said.

"No, really," Terry said. "I swear on my second wife's life."

We went back inside.

"What's the verdict?" I asked Jessica.

"Given all of five minutes to look at the body, I'd say the cause of death appears to be an overdose of morphine," Jessica said. "But we won't know for sure until we get a toxicology report."

"Is it or is it not a suicide?" Simone asked.

"It looks like a duck, it walks like a duck, and it quacks like a duck," Jessica said. "So I guess I'll have to call it a duck. But I can't be positive. We all know suicides can be faked."

"But why?" Simone said. "I can understand why she'd kill herself, but where's the motive for somebody else killing her?"

"Motives are for homicide detectives," Jessica said. "I work with evidence."

"And what does the evidence tell you?" Simone said.

Jessica shrugged. "Based on the evidence, I'd say she died of an apparent suicide."

"You mean an apparent duck," Terry said.

# CHAPTER 41

**WE STAYED AT** the crime scene till 2 A.M. and were back at the station five hours later. Lt. Kilcullen was waiting for us in his office. He didn't look happy.

"Good morning," he said.

"Morning, boss," Terry said. "Your scowling face looks angrier than usual. Didn't anyone tell you that we put another killer out of business last night?"

"Do you know a reporter by the name of Gary Miller?" he asked.

"*LA Times*," I said. "I know him, you know him, half the station knows him."

"Right," Kilcullen said. "And you saw him last night."

"He was behind the tape," I said. "He knows we're the lead on Bellingham-Crump, but we blew him off."

"Yeah, he mentions that in the piece he wrote."

"I don't know what there was to write," I said. "We didn't talk to him."

"No," Kilcullen said. "But Cody Wade did."

I flashed back to last night. Terry and I had been talking to Cody when Gary Miller gave us a yell. Any smart reporter would then jump all over the guy the cops were just talking to. Any smart cop would have known to keep a key witness like Cody under wraps. Sometimes you get sloppy when you work an eighteen-hour day.

"I looked at the morning paper," I said. "There was nothing—"

"Have you heard about this new inter-web thing?" Kilcullen said. "The morning paper gets updated every two minutes. Let me read to you from the latest version of their home page."

He put on a pair of glasses and leaned into the monitor. "'LAPD tracks down secret scrapbook serial killer.' Catchy headline," he said. "'The murder of the wife of British diplomat Edward Bellingham-Crump last Sunday in a bathroom at The Afton Gardens Hotel turns out to be the tip of an extremely lethal iceberg. The stabbing of Eleanor Bellingham-Crump was one of at least five murders allegedly committed by Hilda Beck, who was recently released from prison after serving nine years for euthanizing a patient at The Paradise Living Center. Last night, Beck reportedly took her own life, a source close to the case told this reporter. He claimed that Beck was a vigilante on a mission. Her victims were people who themselves committed heinous crimes, but because of loopholes in the law, or in the case of Mrs. Bellingham-Crump, diplomatic immunity, managed to circumvent justice. So Beck appointed herself judge, juror, and executioner. She was also the official chronicler, leaving a scrapbook diary of her victims' sordid, evil pasts at the scene of each crime.'"

"Sorry, boss. What do we do about this?" I asked.

"I wanted to soft pedal the details until we got the autopsy on Beck," he said, "but now we'll have to hold some kind of a joint press conference with the Feds, and announce that we have a suspect in the Bellingham-Crump case."

"A dead suspect," I said. "But she did leave a confession, along with some more scrapbook material. All we have to do is tie up the loose ends."

"But now that your buddy Gary Miller outed us, somebody is going to have to stand up in front of a bunch of reporters and be charming and vague," Kilcullen said.

"Let me guess," I said. "When you say somebody, you mean me."

"Who else would I mean? You and Biggs let the cat out of the bag."

"There were two cats," Terry said. "We turned them over to the pound."

The press conference was at noon. Simone Trotter was there to take credit for the joint capture, but her boss didn't want her taking questions, so I stood in the line of fire. I did some blah, blah, blah about British-American relations, and our government's deep regret over the tragic death of a diplomatic visitor residing on our shores, and the diligent efforts of the joint task force to bring the killer to justice, and I closed with the promise that in a few days we'd have the forensics that would help us bring the matter to closure.

Not a single reporter in the room gave a shit. They were on a blood quest for more good stuff on the secret scrapbook serial killer.

"Why weren't we warned that there was a serial killer loose in LA?"

"Did Hilda Beck leave a suicide note?"

"Did she have a hit list of other people she wanted to kill?"

And the most popular question of all: "When can we see the scrapbooks?"

By the six o'clock news on Friday evening, a cult hero was in the making. Hilda Beck, Vigilante Scrapbooker.

The good news was, it was Friday at six o'clock. Terry and I finished the paperwork and we were getting ready to leave when Kilcullen stopped by our desk to bestow upon us his managerial blessings.

"Tough week," he said.

"Yep," I said.

"Guhjahboyz," he mumbled, which I took to mean, good job, boys.

"Thanks," I said.

"Yeah, thanks," Terry said.

"Mmmmph," he said. "Enjoy the weekend."

From Kilcullen, that's as good as it's ever gonna get.

# CHAPTER 42

**ALL I WANTED** to do on the weekend was catch up on my e-mail, my sleep, and my sex life. Not necessarily in that order.

On Saturday Diana and I had brunch at an outdoor café, walked on the beach, made love, and took a two-hour nap. At night we went to one of those neighborhood art theaters where the seats all have holes and the movies all have subtitles. Four out of five ain't bad.

At ten o'clock Sunday morning the phone rang. It was Carly Tan.

"Hey, Carly. Diana's in the shower," I said. "Can she call you back?"

"That's okay," Carly said. "This call is more for you."

"Another traffic ticket?"

"No, this is more serious," she said. "I have a kid who has a crush on you."

"Tell her I already have a girlfriend."

"She loves Diana, too."

"You want us to babysit?" I said.

"I don't need a sitter. But Sophie asked for a playdate. She wants to know if she can hang with you guys today."

"Are you kidding?" I said. "How much do we have to pay you?"

"You mean it?" Carly said. "You don't have anything planned?"

"Our plans were to chill out and do nothing," I said. "But now Sophie can bring some purpose and meaning to our dull middle-aged lives. What does she like to do?"

"You can ask her," Carly said. "I'll bring her over before you change your mind."

Sophie was as adorable as I remembered. She was wearing blue jeans, a yellow headband, and a green T-shirt that said I CAN CHANGE THE WORLD.

"So you want to change the world," I said. "Where would you like to start?"

She giggled. "First, we're going to need some sustenance," she said. "So let's start at Chuck E. Cheese."

"I don't understand," I said.

"You never heard of Chuck E. Cheese?"

"Oh sure, but what is this sustenance thing you speak of?"

Another giggle. "Food."

When somebody says Chuck E. Cheese, food is not the first thing one thinks of. True, it's a restaurant chain, but it's a dedicated-to-kids place where the fun, the games, the rides, and the other diversions are more important than the sustenance. Probably just as well, since a large unappetizing animatronic rat sings to you while you eat.

After lunch we headed for the California Science Center, where there are hundreds of hands-on ways for kids to explore the universe. Sophie tried them all.

Next we stopped at a Starbucks.

"I'm buying," I said. "What'll you two ladies have?"

"I'd love an espresso," Diana said.

"Me, too," Sophie said, and I could tell from the look in her eyes that she meant it.

"No can do, kiddo," I said. "They can't serve caffeine to seven-year-olds, and if they do, I'd have to arrest them."

"Then make it a decaf espresso," she said.

We settled on a hot chocolate and two sips of my decaf

cappuccino.

"How many bad guys have you caught," Sophie asked, adding two packets of sugar to the chocolate.

"Not enough," I said. "There are still plenty out there. Why do you ask?"

"I'm writing a story about you."

"Instead of writing about me and bad guys, why don't you write about me and you and Diana, and what we did today?"

She rolled her eyes. "We didn't do enough for a whole story."

"If you don't go into a sugar coma from that hot chocolate, we will."

"Can we go to the Westside Pavilion mall?" Sophie said.

"What's there?" I asked.

A big grin spread across her face. "Everything."

So we went to the Build-A-Bear workshop, where Diana and Sophie each stuffed their own teddy bears; a bookstore, where we bought one book for Diana and three for Sophie; then we drove to the Farmer's Market, and finally we had dinner at a Chinese restaurant.

Sophie ordered her meal in Mandarin.

"I'm impressed," I said. "Are you sure you're seven?"

"No big deal," she said. "Millions of kids my age can speak Chinese." Then she giggled. "But they all live in China."

After dinner, we took her home, where we spent another twenty minutes getting a tour of Sophie's room and a personal introduction to every one of her possessions. It would have gone on longer, but Carly pulled the plug.

"School tomorrow, young lady," she said. "Get ready for bed, and no arguments."

Sophie rolled her eyes at me. "You see what I have to go through?" she said. "Will you stay and tuck me in?"

I melted.

"Yes," I said.

Carly, Diana, and I waited in the living room while Sophie got ready for bed.

"Thank you," Carly said. "Sophie adores you guys,"

Diana smiled. "Especially Mike."

"She doesn't have a lot of male role models," Carly said. "Her father left when she was eight months old." And then the tears started coming. She buried her face in her hands.

"What's wrong?" Diana asked.

"Nothing. Sorry."

"Carly, tell us. What's the matter?"

Carly sniffled and wiped her eyes. "You know my mother has MS."

"I know," Diana said. "But I thought it was under control."

"She's been stable for years," Carly said, "but in the past few weeks she's been deteriorating. She's seventy-eight years old. It doesn't look good."

"Oh, Carly, I'm so sorry," Diana said. "Are you going to go back to China to see her?"

"As soon as I can get someone to take care of Sophie. I thought about pulling her out of school and taking her with me, but my mother lives in a cramped apartment, in a crowded city. Sophie would hate it."

Diana looked at me. I understood the look and nodded.

"Carly, what if Mike and I took care of her while you were away?" Diana said.

"Oh, God," Carly said. "You probably think I was fishing for that, but no. I think I have someone lined up. Thanks, I can't tell you how good it makes me feel that you would even offer."

She was about to start crying again, when Sophie came bounding in.

"Is this how you act when you're tired?" I asked. "It's a good thing I didn't give you any espresso."

"Sophie!" Carly said. "You asked for coffee?"

Sophie shrugged. "They didn't let me have any. They are totally responsible."

172

"Right," I said. "All we did was buy her a couple of beers."

Sophie kissed Carly and Diana good night, then took my hand and we walked to her bedroom.

"Thanks for the books, and for the museum, and for Chuck E. Cheese, and for everything," she said once she got into bed.

"You're welcome," I said. "You think you got enough material to write a story about it?"

"Just one chapter," she said. "I'm gonna have to do more research. We might have to do this again."

"Anytime," I said, kissing her on the forehead. "Sweet dreams."

I turned off the light, and stood outside her bedroom door. And then it hit me. The feeling I had been fighting off all day. Joanie and I desperately had wanted to have a baby. Eventually, we did what a lot of frustrated married couples do. We went to see a fertility specialist. He was the one who discovered the ovarian cancer. I stopped wanting kids after that. Even with Big Jim's meddling, I didn't think a baby was in the cards for me and Diana. But maybe I was wrong. Diana still had a few ticks left on her biological clock. Maybe we should consider it.

*A kid is a tremendous responsibility*, the little voice inside my head reminded me.

I thanked him for telling me something I already knew.

*On the other hand . . .*

On the other hand? The little voice inside my head was Mr. Cautious. Doctor Doom and Gloom. Always ready to point out the downside of anything.

*On the other hand*, what? I asked him.

*On the other hand, when was the last time you had a day as glorious as this one?*

# CHAPTER 43

**I GOT TO** the office at seven on Monday morning. Terry was at his desk.

"Thank you," I said.

"You are absolutely welcome," he said. He took a long sip of his coffee. "At the risk of having you retract the first nice thing anyone has said to me all morning, what the hell are you thanking me for?"

"For not calling me over the weekend."

"Mike, there's a long list of people who are grateful when I don't call them. Glad you could join."

"No, really," I said. "I needed to get away from being a cop for a couple of days."

"And did you?"

I told him about my weekend. Emphasis on Sophie.

"Prepubescent children have a unique ability to make the world a happier place," he said. "Emily, on the other hand is one of those teenage organisms that feeds off other living things, especially parents."

"What now?" I said.

"Remember Hilda Beck, affectionately known as Mercy Nurse or the Serial Scrapbook Killer?"

"Vaguely," I said. "I spent the entire weekend not being a cop. But it's starting to come back to me. She was ridding the world of evildoers by spreading scrapbook love and splenic hemorrhages."

"That's the lovable one-woman death squad I'm talking about," he said. "She has a fan club on Facebook."

"Par for the course," I said. "There's always a handful of people who glorify mass murderers."

"As of last night, the handful was up to sixty thousand people," he said.

"You're kidding."

"Mike, there are something like half a billion people on Facebook. It's not a problem finding sixty thousand to drink the Kool-Aid. I'm just pissed that my darling daughter Emily is one of them."

"Did you ask her why?"

"Oh yeah. Although I might have phrased it more like, where the hell did I go wrong. She said—and I quote—because 'by killing the wicked, Hilda Beck made the world a little bit better for all of us.'"

"And by implication, by hunting Hilda down, you and I made the world a little bit worse."

"She didn't mention you," Terry said. "Just me. 'Couldn't you at least have let her kill all the people she made scrapbooks for, Dad?'"

"Emily did not say that," I said.

"Maybe she didn't, but it sounded like it."

"She's a kid," I said. "I think you're overreacting."

"I guarantee you the other sixty thousand Mercy Nurse fans are not kids, and you're in a particularly forgiving mood after spending the day with a seven-year-old charmer. Why don't you take little Sophie to the mall ten years from now, and let me know how that works out for you."

"Good morning, boys. Can anyone jump into this fray?"

It was Wendy Burns.

"Good morning, Wendy," I said. "Terry is just a little pissed off because one of his daughters joined the Hilda Beck Admiration Society."

"Lighten up, Biggs," she said. "Weren't you ever a teenager?"

"He was," I said, "but he was a big fan of Mary Lou Retton and the 1984 girls Olympic gymnast team."

"You guys wrap up the paperwork on Hilda Beck?" Wendy asked.

"Autopsy and tox reports are due this afternoon," I said.

"I'd like the two eyewitnesses, Sonia Woo and Lori Gibson, to look at a photo lineup and see if they can give us a positive ID on Hilda Beck. I can send out a team, unless you guys need the legwork."

"No thanks," I said. "I had Chinese food last night."

"No problem," Wendy said. "I'll send the Shellys."

"Tell them Sonia Woo is a waste of time," Terry said. "She's convinced that Betty White did it."

At nine o' clock, Karen Winters showed up.

"I saw Gladys yesterday," she said. "She's glad she could help you close the case, but she feels terrible. She thinks she's responsible for Hilda's death."

"She's welcome to spend a few more years in the slammer repenting," Terry said.

Karen laughed politely. "The parole board meets next week."

"We'll have our letter of recommendation for you by tomorrow," I said.

"Would you consider making a personal appearance?" Karen asked. "You guys would make a big impression on the board. You're high profile, articulate, personable—"

"And snappy dressers," Terry said. "Parole boards love a cop who cuts a dashing figure."

"So is that a yes?" Karen said.

I looked at Terry and he nodded imperceptibly.

"We'll do it," I said.

"Thanks," Karen said. "I can't tell you how much having you

there in person will mean to Gladys."

"It means a lot to us, too," Terry said. "We've got this reputation for helping to put murderers in jail. It's time for us to start helping a few get out."

That afternoon, the LA Coroner's office ruled Hilda Beck's death a suicide.

"The tox report on Beck found small to moderate traces of alcohol, antihistamine, and benzodiazepine," I said.

"Booze, allergy meds, and Valium," Terry said. "This is LA. Half the population has that in their system. Get to the good part."

"Lethal dose of morphine sulfate."

"Just like the bottle said. Simone was right. It wasn't Heinz ketchup. I owe her an apology."

We called her.

"I have some good news myself," Simone said. "Our lab guys went over the scrapbooks we found in Hilda's studio. They match the ones left at the murder scenes. Cat hair and all."

"We agreed to make a personal appearance in front of the parole board for Gladys Wade," I said.

"Hey, she deserves it," Simone said. "I think Gladys got a raw deal to start with. She was defending a bunch of battered women from an abusive guy, and she shot him by accident. As far as I'm concerned, she did more than enough time. Once we close the books on this case, do you guys want to have a couple of beers to celebrate?"

"Sure," Terry said. "Can we invite Cody Wade? He's so damn cute, I can't get enough of him."

She hung up.

The Shellys showed up at three. Shelly Lawter and Shelly LeBlanc, a young detective team. They're both smart, but one of them is a real ballbuster.

"How'd it go?" I asked.

"We showed Lori Gibson the pictures and she ID'd Hilda

Beck," Shelly Lawter said. "She thought Beck looked younger in person, but I told her that mug shots usually add ten years. She was a solid witness."

"How about Sonia Woo?" Terry said.

"You were wrong about her," Shelly LeBlanc said.

"She ID'd Beck?" Terry asked.

"No," LeBlanc said. "We showed her six pictures and she picked out the actress, Betty White."

"That's what I told you she would do," Terry said. "How was I wrong?"

"You told us it would be a big waste of time to even bother asking her," LeBlanc said. "You were wrong. Lunch was fantastic."

Like I said, one of them is a ballbuster.

# CHAPTER 44

BY WEDNESDAY THE case was written up and being reviewed by the DA's office. By Thursday, Hilda Beck was in the ground, having attracted a gaggle of her newfound fans to her funeral. By Friday, it was murder as usual.

"You guys deserve an easy one," Wendy said. "Two cars going after the same parking space at a strip mall at Hollywood and Highland."

"Are you sure you need a homicide cop?" Terry asked. "It sounds like an episode of *Law and Order: Fender Bender Division*."

"It started that way," Wendy said. "But it ended with one driver shot to death, and the other explaining to the cops on the scene that the fat bastard was asking for it."

"As long as you've already got the shooter in custody," Terry said, "I think we can solve it."

The following week was just as easy. A stabbing at a bar where there were sixteen eyewitnesses, and a domestic dispute that turned into a murder-suicide. We spent two days testifying in court on an old case, and made our pitch to the parole board on behalf of Gladys Wade.

Two weeks later, she showed up in our office.

"I'm a free woman," she said, her eyes welling up.

"Congratulations," I said.

"I told myself I wasn't going to cry." She handed me a metal cookie tin. "I hope you don't consider homemade chocolate chip cookies a bribe."

"We do," Terry said, "and we accept."

"Karen said your appearance at the hearing made all the difference."

"It didn't hurt that you helped us catch Hilda," I said.

"I feel terrible that she took her own life."

"You and a hundred thousand of her fans," Terry said. "She's becoming a cult hero. The Scrapbook Vigilante."

"Oh, I know," Gladys said. "Some fellow from a production company contacted me the day I got out. They want to do a movie about her, and he asked if I'd be willing to consult. I told him no."

Terry was stunned. "No? You got a call from a Hollywood producer and you turned him down?"

She looked surprised. "I told him I'm not making any life decisions until I get adjusted."

"I'm adjusted," Terry said. "Tell him to call me."

"I didn't even write down his name," she said. "I have no desire to be part of the movie business. I need to get back to the real world."

"And when you say real world, do you mean the battered women's shelter?" Terry asked.

"Yes. In fact, I've decided not to ask Cody to move back to the studio," she said. "He can keep the house. My life has always been about helping other people, and I think I can get back to it faster if I live with my girls in the shelter."

"How many girls do you have?" I said.

"Fourteen. Most of them with small children."

"Who pays for all that?" I asked.

"Do you know the country-and-western singer, Amy Gray? She's our benefactor. She saw a lot of domestic abuse growing up."

"She has a song about it," I said. "Trailer Park Woman."

"Amy is the most wonderful, generous woman on the planet, but I wish she never recorded that song," Gladys said. "One in four women have experienced some kind of domestic abuse in their lifetime. Trailer Park Woman perpetuates the myth that it only happens to poor people."

"Maybe she can do a follow-up," Terry said. "Rodeo Drive Woman—about a plastic surgeon to the stars who comes home drunk to his Beverly Hills mansion one night and cuts up his old lady's Amex Platinum card."

"I know you think that's funny, Detective Biggs," she said, "but domestic abuse is not a joking matter. I think you should visit the shelter one of these days and learn what it's all about."

"I will," Terry said. "I'm sorry."

"He means well," I said. "It's just that the man has no off switch."

"Well, I could never stay mad at either of you," she said. "I'm too grateful for what you've done. Thank you." She leaned over, gave me a light kiss on the cheek, did the same for Terry, and left.

"Well, that's something I'd like a little taste of," Terry said.

I handed him the canister.

"Not the cookies. The movie. If they're doing a film about Hilda Beck, we should be involved. Maybe I could get a shot at writing the script."

"You?"

"In case you forgot, I'm a screenwriter."

"Does that mean you finished writing *Semi-Justice?*"

"No, but it means I've written the first eight pages and they are brilliant."

"What does Big Jim think about them?" I asked.

"He hasn't seen them yet. I'm not about to e-mail him a script. It's better if I lay it on him in person. I'm going over there on Sunday afternoon."

"So am I," I said. "Jim invited Diana and me to lunch. He never said anything about sitting through a movie script."

"Don't cancel," Terry said. "I need you to back me up. Your father doesn't know squat about how to write a screenplay."

"Well, you certainly offset his ignorance with your depth of knowledge," I said.

"Shut up and have a cookie." He opened the tin and handed me one.

I waved it off. "Do you trust her?" I asked.

"I trust her enough to eat the cookies," he said. "Do you think she poisoned them?"

"No."

"Well, there's one way to find out." He took a bite. "You mind telling me what's going on in that cop brain of yours?"

"I was just wondering why she brought us cookies."

"Gratitude," Terry said. "No big deal. It's not like it's a bag of hundred-dollar bills. What am I missing?"

"Something bothers me. We were so hungry for leads when she told us about Hilda that we never stopped to ask, how does she know so much?"

"She saw Hilda at the library."

"Yeah, but looking back on what she gave us, it feels more like insider information," I said. "The way Gladys told it, she made it sound like it was something she picked up as a casual observer."

"Well, we know she wasn't a casual observer," Terry said. "Not when it came to Hilda. They were close friends. When Hilda got out, Gladys let her stay in her house. You have to know somebody pretty well to do that."

"That's my point. She did know Hilda well. Hilda even confided in her that she'd like to kill Eleanor Bellingham-Crump," I said. "So that Sunday night Gladys was watching TV and heard that a woman named Eleanor Bellingham-Crump got murdered. She must have figured out it was Hilda the minute the news broke. Why didn't she blow the whistle right then? Why didn't she tell her lawyer to call us first thing Monday morning and try to make a deal?"

"Because you don't rat out a friend without thinking about it for a while," Terry said. "But even if her timing was off, she finally came around, did the right thing and gave us the killer."

"And we helped her get a parole," I said.

"From what I can tell she probably would have gotten paroled anyway. It was a stiff sentence, and she was a model prisoner. So what's the problem?"

"I don't know," I said. "But somehow I think Gladys Wade used us."

Terry reached into the tin and pulled out another chocolate chip cookie. "Well, if she's still using us," he said, chomping down on the cookie, "she's doing a damn tasty job of it."

# CHAPTER 45

**THE CALL CAME** at four on Sunday morning. Diana and I were naked—arms, legs, and souls blissfully intertwined in post-coital slumber.

"It's for you," she said, tightening her arms around me so I couldn't move. Middle-of-the-night calls are always for me.

The phone rang a second time.

She ground her pelvis into my butt, so that even if I could have moved, I no longer wanted to. "You're making this hard for me," I said.

"Mmmm, that's my goal. Hard is good. Especially when you're naked."

The phone rang a third time.

"I don't understand why people can't kill each other during civilized hours. Homicide should be a nine-to-five job," she said.

"I'll talk to my union rep and see if we can get that worked into our next contract," I said, prying loose from her grip. I grabbed the phone just before the machine picked it up.

"Lomax," I said.

"Mike, it's Carly Tan." Her voice was breathy, pained. "God, I am so sorry to call you at such a wretched hour. And on a Sunday."

"Carly, I'm a cop. I'm used to it. What's the matter? Is Sophie okay?"

"She's fine. She's asleep. My brother called me from China. They had to put my mother on a ventilator. I was planning to go in two weeks, but I can't wait that long."

"When do you want to leave?"

"Today."

"Do you need someone to take care of Sophie?"

"I worked it out with my cousin Kiki to stay with Sophie till I get back, but Kiki is a la-di-dah production assistant, and she's somewhere in the middle of the Mojave desert shooting a movie—a zombie western of all stupid things. I texted her, but—"

"Carly, your cousin can't tear herself away from her job," I said, "and you're not shipping Sophie off to the middle of the Mojave with a bunch of zombies. Diana and I offered to take her till you get back."

Diana wrapped her arms around my neck and leaned into the phone. "Carly, the offer is still good," she said.

"Tell Diana I feel terrible," Carly said. "You both work. I don't know how you'll be able to manage to get Sophie to school in the morning, pick her up every—"

"You're a single mom. You work and you manage," I said. "We'll do fine. What time do you want to leave for China?"

"There's a flight at eleven this morning, if I can make it."

"You'll make it. Diana and I will come over. She can help you and Sophie pack, and I'll give you a police escort to LAX."

Diana pressed her breasts against my shoulders, nuzzled her face into my free ear and started making circles with her tongue.

"Are you sure?" Carly asked. "Mike, I feel so—"

"Carly, stop talking and start packing. Diana and I will head over to your place in ten . . ."

Diana's tongue was finished with my ear and began working its way south.

"We'll leave in about thirty minutes," I said.

It took forty.

Six hours later, Diana and I had a kid living with us.

"This is cool," the kid said.

"Cool for who?" I asked her.

She giggled and I got a rush just being on the receiving end. "For me," she said. "And I think it's cool for you and Diana. My mom said you didn't mind."

"Mind?" I said. "We invited you weeks ago. What took you so long?"

"What are we doing today?"

"One of us is doing her homework. Your mom said you're supposed to read two chapters of something."

"My mom likes to nag me about stuff," she said. "I read it already."

"Good, because this afternoon we're going to my father's house in Riverside."

"Why?"

"For a barbecue and to give him lots of time to nag me about stuff."

"What's your father's name?"

"Big Jim."

"That's cool. What's your mom's name?"

"Tess. She died about eight years ago."

"Who else is coming to the barbecue?"

"My partner, Terry, and his wife, Marilyn. Terry and you have something in common," I said. "You both want to be writers."

"What does he write?"

"He's trying to write a movie, but I don't know if he's going to be any good at it."

"Maybe I can help him," she said.

I laughed. "Somebody should."

"I'm sorry about your mom," she said.

"Thanks," I said. "Big Jim got remarried to an absolutely wonderful woman named Angel. She's a great cook and a very nice lady. You'll like her, and I know she'll love you."

"What about Big Jim? What is he like?"

"Big."

"Duh-uh," she said.

"He's got a bunch of dogs, and about fifty cars and trucks that he rents out to companies who make movies. I think you'll like him, too."

"You think he'll like me?"

"I don't know, Sophie," I said. "Has anyone in your life ever *not* liked you?"

She pursed her lips, squinched up her face, rested her chin in her hand, and pretended to think real hard.

"You're right, Detective," she finally said. "Big Jim will like me."

# CHAPTER 46

**BIG JIM DIDN'T** just like Sophie. He adored her. And the feeling was mutual.

Given the chance to help the women fix lunch, Sophie opted to hang with Jim. The first thing they did was what any guy in his sixties would do on first meeting a super-precocious seven-year-old girl. He taught her how to drive an eighteen-wheel, forty-ton semi.

Granted Sophie couldn't reach the pedals, but that didn't stop Big Jim from giving her a tutorial on gauges, gears, and air brakes.

"Did you have fun?" Marilyn asked when we sat down to lunch.

"Yes, ma'am," Sophie said. "As soon as I'm tall enough, Big Jim is going to let me drive the big red one."

I looked at Jim. "Tall enough? Don't you mean old enough?"

He shrugged. "Whatever. It's not like I'm going to take her out on the freeway."

"When my girls were your age, they preferred Barbie dolls," Marilyn said.

"I have dolls," Sophie said, "but I like to learn how stuff works, so I can write about it."

"Sophie is quite a talented writer," Diana said.

"After lunch, Mike said I could help Terry with his script,"

Sophie said.

Terry's head snapped around and his eyes bugged.

Marilyn almost spit out a mouthful of food. "That would be excellent," she said. "Right Terry?"

"Well, it's still a rough draft," Terry said. "I was only planning to show it to Big Jim and Mike."

"Show it to Sophie, too," Jim said. "That way she'll be eligible for our generous dental plan."

"Cool," Sophie said.

"And a child shall lead them," Angel said.

"A child," Marilyn repeated. "So keep it rated PG."

After lunch, the women cleaned up while Sophie and the guys headed for Big Jim's office. It's a jumble of mismatched furniture, buckling shelves, and a lifetime of dust-crusted trucker memories. Ever since I was a kid it's been my favorite room in the house.

Jim plopped down on the only chair wide enough to accommodate him, and Sophie hopped on his lap. I rested my butt on the desktop, and Terry stood center stage, looking more nervous than he did when we busted through the front door of a coke cartel in Compton.

"Let's hear it," Jim said.

Terry pulled a handful of pages from his back pocket and unfolded them. "*Semi-Justice*," he said. "Scene one. We open on a long, dusty dirt road."

"Why?" Jim asked.

Terry looked at him. "You're interrupting already?"

"I just asked why?"

"Why what?"

"Why are we opening on a long, dusty dirt road? I thought Tim and Jerry are going to show up in Pittsburgh."

"Trust me," Terry said. "You need something more cinematic than Pittsburgh. Anyway, this big sixteen-wheeler comes barreling down—

"Eighteen," Jim said.

"What?"

"There are no sixteen-wheelers. They're eighteen."

"Sorry, it was a typo," Terry said. "Nobody in the movie theater is going to be sitting there counting the wheels. Anyway, the truck is hauling ass down the road, and something darts out in front of it."

"What?" Jim said.

"I don't know yet," Terry said, lowering the pages. "A deer, maybe."

"A deer? In the desert?" Jim said. "I don't think so."

"It doesn't matter. A dog . . . some kind of a desert dog, or a kid chasing a ball, or an old lady in a wheelchair—*it doesn't matter*. What matters is that *something* darts in front of the truck, and Dirk . . ."

"Who in God's name is Dirk?" Jim demanded.

"Dirk is the young cop," Terry said. "He's me. I'm driving."

"Your name was supposed to be Tim. I'm Jerry. We're Tim and Jerry."

"I hate Tim and Jerry. They sound like two guys who should be driving an ice cream truck. You want to be Jerry? Fine. We can be Dirk and Jerry."

"That's lame," Jim said. "No rhythm. The names should play off one another."

"Okay, then. We can be Dirk and Jerk. I'm Dirk."

Sophie laughed.

Terry kept going. "Anyway, something darts out in front of all *eighteen* wheels, and Dirk slams his foot down hard on the brake."

"Uh-oh," Sophie said.

"Now the kid is a critic?" Terry said. "What's your problem, little lady?"

"You never slam your foot down hard on the brake. The trailer could jackknife," she said, sounding like she crammed for the

190

oral exam and aced it.

"And we'd both be killed," Big Jim said. "Who's the jerk now, Dirk?" He turned to Sophie. "Tell him how to stop a big rig, kiddo."

"You feather the brake," she said. "Nice and gentle."

"Fine," Terry said, handing her the sheaf of papers. "You write it."

"I think we're witnessing our first case of creative differences," I said.

"I think it's more like the screenwriter has turned into a prima donna," Jim said. "Don't get your undies in a bunch."

That one got a big laugh from the kid.

"It's none of my business," I said, "but I think Dirk should do a little more research into how to actually drive one of these big monsters before he tries to write this trucking movie."

"Mike is right," Jim said. "If I could teach Sophie the basics in an hour, I can probably teach you in a couple of days."

"And your feet can reach the pedals," she said.

"Some night after work, I'll take you out in the Peterbilt," Jim said. "We'll hook up a trailer. You gotta learn to drive one of these semis if you expect the script to be believable."

My cell phone rang. Big Jim knew what it meant.

"Again?" he said. "We didn't have dessert yet. There's pie, and brownies . . ."

I stepped out of the room to take the call. It was Kilcullen.

"I thought Terry and I had the weekend off," I said.

"This one's huge. It's screaming for you and Biggs."

"Give it to the Shellys," I said. "Or Langer and Sutula. Those guys have solved homicides before."

"This is different," Kilcullen said.

"A homicide victim is a homicide victim," I said. "What's different about this one?"

"The killer left behind a scrapbook."

# CHAPTER 47

"TELL ME AGAIN how you wound up with this kid," Terry said as we were speeding back toward LA and the crime scene.

"Sophie must really have gotten to you, if you'd rather talk about her than the fact that we have another scrapbook killing."

"I'd rather talk about anything than the fact that somebody *thinks* there might be another scrapbook killing. We closed that case."

"Denial is a wonderful crutch, isn't it?"

"Crutch, hell. It's the cornerstone of my existence. If it weren't for denial I'd have quit after three bad marriages, but I kept at it until I found Marilyn. Denial is like alcohol. It helps you cope with the fact that you screwed up."

"So you're saying we screwed up," I said.

"No. I'm saying Hilda Beck killed those people and then she killed herself. If we made one mistake, it's not thinking that she would attract disciples."

"Copycats," I said.

"Why not?" he said. "She went from obscurity to America's most beloved vigilante. There must be at least one nut job out there hoping to be the next Internet cult hero. How many gun massacres have we had since Columbine? But I'll bet you a hundred bucks this scrapbook murder won't look anything like the others. We haven't given out enough information for a copycat to copy."

I should have taken the bet.

The crime scene was a Laundromat on Highland Avenue. If the place had a name, they didn't care to divulge it. The big red, white, and blue sign out front simply said Coin Laundry.

The storefront was fifty feet in length—all glass. But the windows were painted white, so it didn't matter if somebody on the inside were folding their underwear or committing murder, no one on the street could see what was going on.

By the time we showed up, the place was crawling with cops, crime scene techs, and one very angry FBI agent.

"This is a disaster," Simone said as soon as we came through the door.

"Great to see you, too," Terry said. "Who else is coming to the reunion?"

"Jessica Keating is over by the dryers with the body."

She handed us shoe covers and gloves and the three of us walked to the rear of the store. I stopped cold when I saw the victim.

She was a teenager—pretty, blond, and pregnant. A pair of scissors was protruding from between her ribs.

"She's a kid," Terry said.

"She's older than she looks," Jessica said. "Her name is Velinda Toohey. Her driver's license puts her at twenty-seven."

"How pregnant was she?"

"According to the scrapbook the killer left behind," Simone said, "she's been pregnant for about seven years."

"You mean months."

"No. I mean years," Simone said. She bent down and lifted the young woman's maternity top.

The lump that appeared to be an unborn child was a prop—a prosthetic, like the pregnant bellies they use in movies.

"What the fuck is that?" I said.

"She's a scam artist. She preys on young couples who are

trying to have children but can't. They run ads looking for unwed mothers who want to put their babies up for adoption. This girl would answer the ad, meet with the couple and tell them they were her first choice. They would then cough up money for medical expenses, and a month later she would call to say she fell down the stairs and lost the baby. She usually took the marks for about ten to fifteen grand."

"How do you know all this?"

"She has a rap sheet dating back to when she was a juvey," Simone said. "But she never did any serious time. Some victims never even knew they were hosed. The others were either too embarrassed or too grief stricken to press charges. For many of them, the pregnancy was real, and they were mourning their dead child."

My stomach knotted up. Joanie and I had desperately tried to conceive. We lit candles to the fertility gods, and spent thousands on the fertility doctors, who act like they're gods. We even ran ads in the hopes of being able to adopt from a young unwed mother, but we never got a response. I had always regretted that. Until now.

"Those scissors look incredibly familiar," I said, looking over at Terry.

"So does the scrapbook," Jessica said. "I've seen copycats, but whoever did this was spot on."

"That's impossible," Terry said. "Nobody knows enough of the details to copy it exactly."

"Bullshit," Simone said. "I know the details. Gladys Wade knows the details."

"In that case," Terry said, "you have the right to remain silent. Anything you say, can and will be held against you."

"Why don't you think it's possible that Gladys could have done this?" Simone asked.

"Two reasons," Terry said. "First of all, Gladys was in jail when the other murders took place."

"I'm not saying she did the others," Simone said. "I'm saying she's out now, and she might want to pick up where her old prison-mate left off. What's the second reason?"

"You, me, and Mike helped get her paroled. She wouldn't pay us back by picking up where Hilda left off."

"Terry's right," I said. "Gladys Wade would probably pay us back by coming to our office with a tin of homemade cookies."

"Is that what she did?" Simone said.

"Chocolate chip," Terry said. "And damn tasty, too. We set some aside to share with you, but you know what happens to cookies in a police station."

"Cookies!" Simone said. "That bitch. You know what this means don't you? Gladys Wade is not just a suspect. She's at the top of my list."

"You know what else it means?" Terry said. "If Gladys murdered this girl, we just might be the three dumbest cops in America."

# CHAPTER 48

**I FOUND A** semi-quiet spot in the Laundromat and called my father.

"It's going to be a long, long day," I said. "Terry took Marilyn's car, so make sure that she, Diana, and Sophie all get home."

"No problem," he said. "What did you think of Terry's script?"

"Dad, this is so the wrong time to ask that."

"I didn't ask you to freaking critique it," he said. "In the amount of time it took you to blow off my question, you could have said it's good or it sucks."

"Fine," I said. "It sucks."

"Why? Where do you think he went wrong with it? Did I make a mistake asking Terry in the first—"

"Dad! Shut up!"

One of the forensic evidence techs who works for Jessica Keating stopped dusting for prints and looked up at me. She shook her head and laughed.

"Sorry," I said to her.

Jim heard me, and decided the apology was meant for him. "No problem," he said. "You've been touchy all day. How long do you think you're going to be tied up?"

"Long," I said. "That's why I asked you to please make sure the girls get home."

"I got that covered," he said. "I was just thinking about Sophie."

196

"What about her?"

"You've been her father for less than a day, and you're already paying more attention to your job than to her."

"Dad, where is your head? I'm not her father. I'm her babysitter."

"Babysitting is for a few hours," he said. "Sophie will be living with you for weeks, so you're like a foster father. I'm just wondering how she's going to feel about you ignoring her."

"I don't know," I said, "but I can't begin to tell you how good I would feel if my father would start ignoring me. Good-bye."

I snapped my cell phone shut.

The forensic tech had been watching me the entire time. She had dark hair, dark eyes, and a body that men notice, even when it's shrouded by a county-issue jumpsuit.

"You sound like me talking to my mother," she said. "She is constantly meddling in my life."

"Same with my father," I said. "I don't suppose they have a support group for that."

"Actually they do," she said. "They meet around five o'clock every night at the bar. Want to take in a meeting after we're done here?"

It had been a while since I was hit on, and I stalled. "Umm . . . thanks. But umm . . . I've got to get home to my daughter."

"I thought you told your father she wasn't your daughter." She winked. "I'm Kelly Cummings. I collect evidence."

"And you seem to be collecting it very well," I said. "I appreciate the invitation, but I have a date with a dead woman tonight."

"That's not what I had in mind for you," she said. "But if you change your . . ."

"Mike. Over here."

It was Jessica.

"Nice to meet you, Kelly," I said, and headed back to the others. Quickly.

"I see you met Wonder Woman," Jessica said.

"Who?"

"Kelly. She hits on a lot of guys. The ones who have taken her up on it said something about a Wonder Woman costume."

"That's the last thing I need," I said. "Thanks for bailing me out."

"Oh, the three of us were enjoying watching her work on you. Sorry to interrupt, but something came up I thought you should know about. Take a look at the scrapbook," Jessica said. "She's back to her old form. I thought the one she did for Jock Noonan wasn't up to her standards, but this one is really well done."

"Do you know how bizarre that sounds?" I said. "I feel like we're judging the scrapbook entries at the County Fair. And when you say *she's* back to her old form, may I remind you that Hilda is dead. Just show me what we've got."

The scrapbook was resting on a countertop usually reserved for folding clothes. It looked exactly like the others. But as Jessica slowly turned the pages, I could see that she was right. This was the best one yet. There were far fewer newspaper clippings, because Velinda Toohey didn't get the kind of press coverage that Eleanor Bellingham-Crump or Father Fleming got. But what it lacked in newsprint, it made up for with well-crafted graphics. The most chilling among them was a beautiful pink-and-white scene of a baby's nursery. Turn the page, and the same page was reproduced, only this time the colors were black and dark purple.

Velinda was a con artist, but her con was so cruel, and the victims so hurt, that by the time you got to the last page in the scrapbook you thought of her as a villain who not only stole money, but crushed the hopes and dreams of desperate couples who wanted nothing more than to start a family.

"I can see why she was a target," I said.

"There's something you can't see," Jessica said. "I could make it out with a magnifying glass, but I have to take this back to the lab to make a positive ID."

"What is it?" I asked.

"You're not going to like hearing this," Jessica said.

"Try me."

"Cat hair."

# CHAPTER 49

**"ARE YOU SURE** it's cat hair?" Terry asked.

"Not a thousand percent," Jessica said. "I'll check it out in the lab, but what else could it be?"

Terry grinned. "Copycat hair."

He paused and waited for the laugh. He got it handily from me and Jessica, but Simone threw up both arms in disgust. "Damn it, Biggs! Don't you ever give it a rest? Do you always have to crack wise?"

"I've been working this homicide gig for a while, sweetie," Terry said. "If you lose your sense of humor, you're doomed."

"I'll tell you what's doomed," she said. "My career. You might not be worried about yours, but if Gladys Wade had anything to do with this murder—and I'm betting she did—I'll be the dumbass FBI agent who helped spring her from prison."

"Take it easy," I said. "Why do you think Gladys Wade had anything to do with this?"

"Why not?" Simone said. "She's already a convicted murderer. She either did it on her own or she had one of her battered women do it."

I took a few seconds to process the thought. Simone was hardly a dumbass FBI agent. It sounded plausible. "You could be right," I said. "Gladys also has an overriding sense of justice. Maybe she decided to pick up where Hilda left off."

"I have a better theory," Simone said.

"Which is?"

"Gladys Wade is the mastermind. Hilda Beck is the disciple. It's fucking brilliant. Think about it. Gladys is in prison and she gets friendly with Mercy Nurse, who is already doing time for developing exit strategies for people she feels no longer belong on the planet. Hilda is about to be released, and Gladys figures she's going to get a job at some hospital, and go back to turning up the morphine drip on patients who refuse to die on their own. So what does Gladys do?"

"You're on a roll," I said. "You tell us."

"She convinces Hilda to let the dying die on their own and turn her talents to a more noble form of killing. Get rid of Eleanor Bellingham-Crump, and Tavo Maldonado, and Johnny Walmark, and this little bitch down here on the Laundromat floor. She tells Hilda that the world is a better place without them. And you know what, I find it hard to disagree."

"Take a deep breath, Simone," I said. "Repeat if necessary."

She inhaled and let it out slowly. "Sorry," she said. "I hate having to white out the Case Closed stamp on a file."

"One question," Jessica said. "If you're right, and Gladys got Hilda to kill people, what are the scrapbooks for?"

Jessica is a techie who only looks at hard evidence. Terry, Simone, and I are detectives who don't always need cold hard facts to leap to conclusions.

"My guess," I said, "is that Hilda's MO has always been to kill her victims in silence. Most of them were presumed to have died of natural causes. Gladys needed Hilda to become a high profile serial killer, so she could turn her in. The scrapbooks did that. And by having Hilda mail a scrapbook page to Cody, Gladys was able to step into the picture, help the cops catch the killer, and buy our support to get her out of prison."

Simone gave me a hint of a smile. "Are you agreeing with my theory?"

"I'm not sure what I agree with," I said. "Until a few minutes ago I thought Hilda Beck was behind it all. But this murder is too close to the others, and Hilda is dead. Gladys Wade sounds like the most logical piece of the puzzle. I think we should pay her a visit."

"No," Simone said. "Why not just tail her? Why let her know that we're on to her?"

"Because she led us to Hilda," I said. "Basic cop logic dictates that Gladys should be the first person we talk to. If we *don't* pay her a visit, then she'll really know we're on to her."

Simone nodded. "You don't think she'll figure out she's a suspect?"

"Not if we don't treat her like one. We'll just go, pretend to pick her brain, and see what she feeds us."

"Then what?"

"Then we'll tail her," I said.

Simone looked at her watch. "Should we go talk to her now?"

"I don't want to come off as too anxious and rush right over there," I said. "I'd rather wait till tomorrow morning. Plus let's see what Jessica comes up with in the lab."

"Garet Church is flying back from D.C. tonight," Simone said. "He expects me at a meeting tomorrow that will probably take most of the day. Can you guys handle it and fill me in later?"

"No problem," I said.

"In fact," Terry said, "if we're going to pay Gladys Wade a visit, I'd prefer to do it without you."

It was the first thing he said to her since their little blowup. Simone's jaw clenched and she glared at him. "And why is that?" she asked.

Terry stared back at her, his face completely deadpan. "More cookies for me and Mike."

Simone's face relaxed and she laughed into her hand. When she finished laughing she pointed the hand in his direction and wagged a finger at him. "Y'know, Biggs, I can see why your first three wives divorced you."

Terry shrugged.

And then Simone smiled. "But I can also see why the fourth one stuck around."

# CHAPTER 50

IT WAS 8 P.M. and we were hungry and cranky.

"I don't understand why you can't get a pizza delivered to a crime lab on a Sunday night," Terry said.

Jessica was peering into a microscope. "The local pizza guy cut off our supply," she said without looking up. "It's punishment."

"For what?"

Jessica lifted her head from the scope and shook her curly blond hair. "Some idiot lab assistant ordered a sausage pizza, didn't like the way it tasted, and ran an analysis on the meat. He found traces of E. coli. Nothing lethal, but when he complained to the pizza place, they blew him off, so he posted the whole story in the restaurant review section of *yelp.com*. Now Sal's Pizzeria is at war with us. Somebody from HR went down and worked out a deal with Sal. We retracted the review, but no pizza for us for ninety days. It's a matter of honor."

"So call another pizza joint," Terry said.

"They're all backing Sal," she said, burying her face in the scope again.

"What about Chinese?"

"Trust me," she said, "we've analyzed that. I'd rather buy a sandwich from the vending machine."

"Where's that?"

"It's on the third floor, but they don't stock it on weekends, so whatever's in there might be a little gamey. I may have some yogurt in the fridge."

"Forget it," Terry said.

She looked up again. "More bad news," she said. "It's a perfect match. The cat hair in Velinda Toohey's scrapbook is the same as the samples we found in the others."

"How is that possible?" Terry asked. "We arrested those two little feline accomplices and threw them in the pound. Maybe they escaped. Or maybe they got some fat cat to post bail for them."

"Or maybe Hilda made this scrapbook before she died," I said, "and somebody else carried out her mission."

"I don't think so," Simone said. "Look at this."

She was at a table looking at Velinda's scrapbook. It was opened to a page of newspaper clippings. Classified ads, all posted by young couples in search of birth mothers. Most of them had toll-free numbers.

"I called a few of these to try to get some insight into the victim," Simone said. "One called me back immediately. This was the first time she and her husband have advertised."

"So?"

"So their ad ran for the first time last Sunday. Which means that by the time somebody put Velinda Toohey's scrapbook together, Hilda's scrapbooking days were over. She was dead."

The room went silent as we all let it soak in. Terry finally broke the ice. "Shit," he said. "This is worse than no pizza."

The implications were clear. The latest scrapbook had traces of cat hair, but it wasn't created until after Hilda's cats were in the pound. And since the new cat hair matched the old cat hair, Hilda's cats were never near any of the scrapbooks. Ever.

"Oops," Terry said. "I think we locked up the wrong kitties."

"Did you bother to check their DNA against the cat hair from the previous crime scenes?" Simone asked.

Terry shot back at her. "Did *I* bother to check? Since when is that LAPD's job? I thought the FBI checked those kinds of things. Isn't that the first rule they drum into your head at Quantico? The case is never wrapped up till you analyze every freaking piece of cat dander."

"Don't try to pass the buck," Simone said. Her eyes were smiling. She loved sparring with Terry. "You locked up two innocent cats—young, happy, in the prime of their nine lives."

"I'll make a donation to their legal defense fund," Terry said. "But if Hilda's cats are innocent, where are the pussies who were in the room when these fucking scrapbooks were being made?"

"I have an educated guess," I said. "The battered women's shelter. I know we found a lot of scrapbook paraphernalia in Hilda's studio, but maybe she did some of her cutting and pasting at the shelter. Maybe she and Gladys were teaching the girls how to scrapbook. And I'll bet you they have a couple of cats roaming around."

"This is turning out to be one hell of a bad day," Terry said. "First some seven-year-old kid craps all over my screenplay, then a case that I thought was solved turns out to be totally unsolved, and now I find out that the sweet lady who baked cookies for us could be training a houseful of battered women to become cold-blooded sociopaths."

"You left out the fact that two innocent cats are rotting away in the California prison system because you denied them due process," Simone added.

"I'm more interested in getting some DNA from the cats who live in the shelter," Terry said. "And we should do a background check on the women who live there."

"Good luck getting their names," Simone said. "These women are all victims. Everything about the shelter is protected by the system—the address, the phone number, and details about the residents."

"Protected from the cops?" Terry asked.

"You never heard of a cop who beat the shit out of his old

lady? They are protected from everybody."

"We have the address," I said. "And the names of a few women who live there. They signed in when they visited her in prison."

"The population turns over on a regular basis, so you won't have too many of the current residents," Simone said.

"It doesn't matter," I said. "If any of them are involved they're just foot soldiers. We need to know more about Gladys. Muller got the background on the shooting that landed her in jail, but now we need him to dig deeper."

"I'm sorry I can't go with you guys tomorrow," Simone said. "I don't imagine she'll be very cooperative."

"Maybe she'll cooperate if we threaten to throw her back in the slammer," Terry said.

"Why don't you just threaten to turn her into a pumpkin?" Simone said. "Either way, she'll laugh you out of the room. Gladys knows we can't put her back in jail. We didn't spring her. The parole board let her out. We're just the gullible cops who fell for her bullshit and held the door open."

We talked for another half hour, then Terry drove me home. I called Diana from the car.

"You hungry?" she asked.

"No, I was hungry four hours ago," I said. "Now I'm desperate."

"I'll fix something for you. What do you want?"

"Anything but Sal's pizza. It's rumored to be contaminated."

"I can have a bowl of mac and cheese in ten minutes."

"Two bowls," I said.

"I already ate," she said.

"They're both for me."

They were ready and piping hot when I got home. I gave Diana a quick kiss and attacked my dinner.

After I devoured the first bowl, I slowed down and began to eat like a human being.

"This is for you," Diana said, handing me a sheet of typing paper.

It was a drawing of a big fat man and a small girl. Behind them was an enormously large truck.

"You're pretty good," I said. "You should consider moving up from crayons into oils."

"Sophie worked very hard on it," Diana said. "That was her fifth try. She wanted to get it perfect. Count the wheels on the truck."

I did. "There are eighteen," I said. "And amazingly you can see them all from this angle."

"Can you tear yourself away from the pasta for a minute?" she asked. "I want to show you something."

She took my hand and walked me to the guest bedroom. She opened the door, and enough light poured in so I could see Sophie, lying on her right side, one arm under the pillow, the other dangling off the side of the bed.

"I work with sick kids every day," Diana whispered. "I can't tell you how wonderful it feels to be with a child like this. She's a dream."

I didn't say anything. I just put my arm around Diana and thought about all the young couples who dream of having children—myself and Joanie included.

And then I thought about the dead woman in the Laundromat. My job is to put the person who killed her in jail. But what I really wanted to do was say thank you.

# CHAPTER 51

**I GOT TO** the office at seven-fifteen the next morning. Terry was already at his desk.

"Hey, partner," he said. "How was your weekend?"

"Do we really need sarcasm this early in the morning?" I said.

"My weekend was fantastic," he said. "Saturday I got together with Clooney, Travolta, and a couple of my movie buds, then Sunday, I drove up to the cabin and worked on my screenplay."

I decided to play along. "My weekend was even better," I said. "I got a middle-of-the-night phone call letting me know that I'm suddenly responsible for a seven-year-old girl, got called out to a brutal murder in a Laundromat, and I nearly died of starvation in a crime lab."

"Sounds like fun," Terry said. "Sorry I couldn't be with you."

Muller showed up at seven-thirty and we asked him to dig down as far as possible into Gladys's past.

"How far, dudes?" he said.

"We'd like to know what her parents ate for dinner the night she was conceived," Terry said.

By 8 A.M. we were on the road. Simone Trotter was right. The battered women's shelter was well protected. Even the address we had turned out to be bogus. It wasn't on Nichols Canyon Road. It was off. Way off.

Just a few blocks north of the glitz and grit of Hollywood

Boulevard there is a completely different world. Hundreds of undeveloped acres of wild chaparral, drought-resistant evergreen trees, and hiking trails. Most people who live in LA never venture near it. Nature has that effect on a lot of Angelinos.

The Department of Parks and Recreation manages some of it, but the rest is private property. Amy Gray owned some of that land and built the shelter on it for Gladys Wade to run.

We didn't want to call Gladys and give her a heads-up that we were coming, so we got directions from a 911 operator.

There was a hairpin turn on Nichols Canyon Road that had two outlets. One was Bantam Place. The other was a dirt road that had no name. We turned onto it. We had only gone a few hundred yards when Terry stopped the car.

"Oh my God," he said.

"What's the matter, country boy? Did you see a jackrabbit? This wildlife must be pretty scary to a guy who grew up in the Bronx," I said.

"Mike, I can't believe it. This is it," he said, spreading both arms to encompass the vista outside the windshield. "This is the road."

"What road?"

"This is the road I was thinking of when I was writing the movie," he said. "It's all brown with shrubs and trees and . . . oh shit . . . look over there—a prairie dog."

"It's a chipmunk," I said. "I'm guessing you don't spend too much time in the great outdoors."

"We have a pool," he said. "That's outdoors."

"Is it heated?" I asked.

"No."

"Okay, in LA that's considered roughing it."

"Would you shut up and just look at this fantastic stretch of dirt road," Terry said. "It's so damn filmic."

"I guess the only thing left for you to do is write the script," I said. "And maybe learn what the inside of an eighteen-wheeler looks like. Anything else? Oh yeah, get Dr. Untermeyer to cough up a couple of million bucks."

"I'm inspired," he said. "I feel like calling up your father."

"If you do, I'll get out and walk."

"Okay, okay, but one of these days I want to bring him back here."

"Good idea," I said. "Why don't you show up around twilight?"

"You have a camera phone, don't you?" he said. "Why don't you take it out and snap some pictures of the landscape."

"Terry, if I take out my phone I'm calling dispatch and asking if they've got a real detective to replace the starstruck wannabe screenwriter I wound up with as a partner."

"You're just jealous," he said.

"You're right," I said. "I always wanted to go into show business with a three-hundred-pound teamster and a dentist."

He gunned the car and raced down the road, burning rubber and kicking up dust.

"Act one, scene one, take one," he yelled, laughing maniacally. "Dirk and Jerry barreling down a country road in Kansas in their big-ass semi."

I have no idea how other homicide detectives go about their day, but I'm willing to venture a guess that none of them handle it like Lomax and Biggs.

# CHAPTER 52

ALL WE SAW for the first quarter of a mile were signs. *Private Road. No Trespassing. No Outlet. This Property Protected By Video Surveillance. This Property Patrolled By Guard Dogs.*

"I think they've made their point," I said.

"Yeah, but when we shoot the movie, those signs are going to have to come down," Terry said.

It wasn't a typical Terry wisecrack. I'd swear he was serious.

It was a mile before we saw the house. It was a large two-story gray wooden building with a wide front porch. To the right of it was a garage. The door was open and I could see it was stacked up with beds, chairs, a small tractor, and assorted junk. Two vehicles—a white Chevy pickup and a green Honda—were relegated to a patch of brown dirt that sat next to a small playground area with swings, a jungle gym, and a paved area with a basketball hoop. To the left was a fenced-in vegetable garden that was well cared for and seemed to be flourishing.

The sign that warned us about video surveillance wasn't kidding. I could see at least four cameras. And two dogs. German shepherds. Big ones. The kind that might convince a wife beater to make a hasty U-turn. Terry stopped the car about fifty feet from the house. The dogs didn't bark. They just walked toward us. One approached the driver's side; the other came up to mine.

"Hop out and see if they're friendly," Terry said.

"I think they might be trained to be unfriendly. Especially with strangers. Especially if the strangers are men," I said.

"They're police dogs. I'll let them know we're cops," Terry said.

He rolled down his window and the dog on his side bared its teeth and barked. Terry snapped the window back up in a hurry.

"We're on video," I said. "I'm sure someone will show up."

Thirty seconds later, the front door of the house opened and Gladys walked out, followed by two women. One white. One black. Both large. Gladys smiled and waved when she recognized us. She yelled something at the dogs, both of which backed off from our doors and sat down about five feet away.

Gladys opened Terry's door. "It's okay to come out now," she said. "Zanna and Hera never attack anyone who helped me get out of jail."

"Are Zanna and Hera the dogs," Terry asked, "or those two bodyguards behind you?"

Gladys smiled. "The girls are Desiree and Ronice. We have a policy. When anyone shows up, we like to greet them with a welcoming committee. What brings you gentlemen here? Are you out of cookies already?"

"We have a few questions," I said. "Can we go somewhere and talk?"

"My office. You want something to drink?"

"No thanks."

She clucked to the dogs and they lumbered along behind us.

"Those are pretty intimidating dogs," Terry said.

"They keep the crazy husbands and coked-up boyfriends away," she said. "It's a lot easier than having me shoot any more of those bastards."

"I'll bet the cats around here are scared when those two puppies show up," Terry said.

"You mean the mountain lions?" Gladys said. "I've only seen one in all the time I've been here."

"I meant house cats."

"Oh, we don't have cats," she said, laughing. "Zanna has a bad habit of eating them. I think she must have some coyote blood in her somewhere."

Terry hung back and let Gladys get a few steps ahead of us. Then he shrugged and mouthed two words. "No cats."

We walked to the back of the house. "There's a private entrance to my office," Gladys said. "I'd rather not have you walk through the living room. Some of these girls get spooked whenever they see a man on the property."

Ronice and Desiree peeled off and went around to the front. Gladys unlocked the rear door and we stepped into her office. It was small and cozy. She sat down behind her desk and Terry and I sat across from her.

"Something's wrong," she said. "I can tell."

"There was another murder yesterday," I said.

She raised her hand to her mouth. "Oh dear. Someone I know?"

"Her name was Velinda Toohey," I said.

Gladys looked relieved. "I was afraid it might be one of our girls," she said, "but it's not. They're supposed to steer clear of men—especially the ones from their past, but some of them just can't. Most of these women don't have jobs yet, so the opportunity to get into an abusive relationship is even greater. I try to drive into the city and check on our recent graduates as often as possible, but I can only do so much."

"Did you ever hear the name Velinda Toohey?" I said.

"No. Is that all you came to ask about? If I knew her? You could have called."

"Did Hilda Beck ever mention her?"

Gladys sat back in her chair and held both hands up. I know a little about body language and that said *get these cops out of here*.

"What does this have to do with Hilda?" Gladys asked.

"Velinda was stabbed with a pair of scissors," I said.

"When?"

"Yesterday. The killer left a black scrapbook behind. Same make and model as the ones Hilda was using."

If Gladys Wade was faking shock and surprise, she was a damn good actress. She was stunned. "Someone is imitating Hilda?"

"More than imitating," I said. "Duplicating."

"This is why I don't want to help make a movie about Hilda," Gladys said. "It's only going to glorify what she—" And then it dawned on her. "Why are you here?"

"We thought you might be able to help," I lied.

"I already helped. I led you to Hilda. But now that there's another murder, you think . . . what the hell do you think, anyway?" She stood up. "Never mind. I can imagine. I'm not saying anything else to you unless Karen is in the room."

"What do you need a lawyer for? You're not under arrest."

"But I'll bet I'm under suspicion," she said. "I have the right to remain silent, and I will. Please leave. Ronice will walk you back to your car."

She left the room through the door that led inside the house.

"I guess we're back to buying supermarket cookies," Terry said.

The black woman came back into the room. She crossed to the back door and opened it for us.

We followed her into the yard. One of the dogs stood up, but Ronice turned and said, "Zanna, sit, stay." The dog lowered herself back to the ground.

Terry and I got into the car, but before I could close my door, Ronice blocked it and stuck her head in. "You upset Mrs. Wade," she said.

"She did seem kind of upset, didn't she?" Terry said.

"Please don't harass her. The woman is a saint," Ronice said.

She stepped away from the car door, and I pulled it shut.

Terry started the car, then turned to me. "I guess they're giving out sainthood to people who did time for murder," he said.

"Involuntary manslaughter," I reminded him.

# CHAPTER 53

HELEN TOOK A long slow sip of her chai tea and reflected on how things had changed. "The best laid plans of mice and men . . ." she said to Dizzy, who was curled up in her lap.

The cat responded to her voice by looking up at her.

"Mice and men," she repeated. "Don't you get it? Cat joke."

Dizzy did not seem to be amused.

"I don't know why I bother," she said. "I guess if I wanted a pet who laughed at my jokes I should have gotten a hyena."

She lifted the tabby off her lap, set it down on the floor, stood up, and swept the cat hair from her skirt with the back of her hand.

She went to the kitchen cabinet and opened the door. Dizzy perked up. Wayne, who had been snoozing on the sofa, heard the door and eyed it carefully.

Helen stared at the Tupperware bowl on the shelf. There were fourteen Ping-Pong balls left. The priest, the dog guy, the diplomat's wife, the slumlord, the porn potato stuntman, and the adoption scammer all had won the lottery. The world was a better place without them.

She wanted to reach for the bowl and choose another winner, but now was not the time. She closed the cabinet door.

Dizzy and Wayne were sitting up, waiting for the Ping-Pong balls to be released. "Sorry, kids," Helen said. "Mama's expecting company."

She busied herself with her scrapbooking.

An hour later the doorbell rang, and she picked up the intercom.

"Helen," the voice on the other end said. "I'm downstairs. Buzz me in."

She buzzed the lobby door, then did a quick turn around the apartment, collecting scrapbook paraphernalia. There was no time to open the fire safe, so she tucked it neatly into a drawer.

The elevator was slow and she waited patiently for the knock on the door. Finally it came, and she opened it.

Gladys Wade stood there. "Hello, Helen," she said.

"Welcome to my humble abode," Helen said. "How do you like it?"

Gladys entered the apartment, closed the door, and looked around. "Very nice," she said. "You've always had a flair for these things."

Helen responded with a modest smile. But inside she felt warm and good all over.

"I'm here because those two detectives, Lomax and Biggs, came to see me," Gladys said. "There's been another scrapbook killing."

"Velinda Toohey," Helen said proudly. "She deserved to die."

"And Hilda wasn't around to help, so you took care of it, didn't you?"

Gladys sounded angry now. This didn't feel warm and good at all. Helen lowered her head and curled her lips in a pout.

"Shame, shame, shame, shame," Gladys said, getting louder on every word.

Helen's head snapped up. "They all had it coming," she said. "Especially Hilda. How many of her so-called killings do you think were really assisted suicides?"

"All of them," Gladys said. "Hilda told me. These were people who didn't want to wither away in bed, or be a drain on their families. They asked her to help. Some of them begged her.

"She lied," Helen said. "Hilda Beck got off murdering old people."

"And you?" Gladys asked.

"I don't kill innocent people like Hilda did," Helen shouted back. "I avenge the atrocities committed against others. That's why I make the scrapbooks. Every killing is documented."

"Documenting a murder doesn't change the facts. You killed six people. No, seven," Gladys said. "Because Hilda didn't kill herself."

"Don't be so quick to judge," Helen said. "You killed a man."

"Yes," Gladys said, lowering her voice to a near whisper. "And I went to jail for it."

"They were wrong to put you in jail," Helen said. "That's why I had to get you out."

"And you did," Gladys said. "Thank you."

"Ha! You don't sound very grateful."

"I am incredibly grateful," Gladys said. "Or at least I was until the police showed up this morning. But I'm out of prison now, and you're still killing people. Why?"

Helen looked at Dizzy, then at Wayne, her two partners in crime. But Wayne had gone back to catnapping, and Dizzy was licking herself. She was on her own.

"I thought I would stop once you got out, but there are so many bad, bad people out there," Helen said. "Nobody else is punishing them. Somebody has to stand up for justice. They can't get away with being bad, bad, bad."

Gladys put her arms around Helen. "Sweetheart, you have to stop. You have to. The police will surely catch you, and then you'll not only destroy your life, you'll ruin mine and Cody's. Do you want that?"

"No," Helen said, pulling away. "I just want the three of us to be back together."

"Helen, you've had a . . . a hard life. You grew up surrounded by women who were victims of terrible abuse."

"Yes, and every time I *jam* those scissors into an evil person,

I think, this is for you, ladies." She didn't just say the words. She acted them out, her right hand deftly striking upward and twisting a phantom pair of scissors.

"I fight for the helpless," Helen said. "I have a God-given ability and I use it for good, not for evil. The Lord says 'what thou doest to the least of my creatures thou doest for me.'" She smiled. "You want some tea? It's chai."

"No, thank you," Gladys said. "Helen, you've done the Lord's work, and now you're finished. It's time for you to go."

"Where?"

"It doesn't matter," Gladys said. "Just go. Vanish. I know you. You can disappear without a trace. Now hurry, before the police find you."

Helen's face froze. "The police . . ." She shook her head. "Promise you won't tell them about me."

"I won't. But they're smart. If you kill any more people, they *will* catch you," Gladys said. "And what will happen then?"

Helen lowered her head again. "They'll take me to the police station."

"Yes," Gladys said. "And they will grill you, harass you, and keep asking you questions until the truth comes out."

"No," Helen said. "That can't . . . no."

"Then go," Gladys said. "Run away. Never come back. Can you promise me that? Can you promise me that you'll never come back?"

A tear streamed down Helen's cheek. "Go away?"

"Please," Gladys said. "Go far, far away, and don't come back. I don't want them to catch you."

Helen was crying openly now. "I'll go," she sobbed. "Will you miss me?"

"Sweetheart," Gladys said, putting her arms around Helen one final time. "I will always miss you. I love you, Helen."

Helen pulled Gladys close and hugged her. "I love you, too, Mother."

# CHAPTER 54

AFTER TERRY AND I left the shelter we drove back to the hairpin turn on Nichols Canyon Road, found an inconspicuous place to park, and waited for Gladys.

"I say she'll be on the road in forty-five minutes," I said. "You want over or under?"

"Under," Terry said. "I've never been on saint surveillance before. Do you think she'll take the Chevy pickup, the Honda, or rise up and transport herself through the heavens on sheer divinity power?"

Gladys opted for the Honda. She only kept us waiting twenty-six minutes.

We followed her to a dilapidated apartment house on Wadsworth. She parked, went to the lobby, rang a bell, and entered.

We called the address in to Muller. "Check the tenant rolls with the Housing Department," I said. "Then cross-check the list for rap sheets. She might be with a woman who recently got out of the shelter, so don't just look at criminals, look at victims."

Muller called back in fifteen minutes. "Not the classiest place in LA to raise a family. Four of the tenants have records—all male. But there's one woman who filed several TRO's against a boyfriend. She was referred to a shelter by the court. It doesn't say which facility, but she was one of the women who visited

220

Gladys in Corona."

A few minutes later, Gladys came out and drove to another rundown building, this time on East Sixth Street.

"Looks like she's on the *Architectural Digest* tour of Los Angeles," Terry said.

We called Muller with the second address. Once again, he zeroed in on a single tenant, a woman who had filed domestic abuse charges against her husband.

By the time Gladys hit the third dump, Terry and I were starting to think we pegged her wrong.

"It looks like she's doing a field check of women who just got out of the shelter," I said.

"Normally, I would say that's very noble of her," Terry said, "but I was kind of hoping she'd either race to her lawyer's office or lay one of those trademark splenic hemorrhages on someone. Doesn't she realize that we're trying to catch a killer here?"

The pattern continued for two more stops. Gladys would drive to one of LA's countless low-end neighborhoods, enter a building, and come out about twenty minutes later. In each case Muller could pinpoint a probable battered woman among the tenants.

But the sixth stop was a nice change of scenery. It was a tree-lined block on De Longpre Avenue. The redbrick apartment building had a trim little patch of grass in front and a low border of yellow and white flowers.

"Somebody got lucky," Terry said. "This is a big step up from a battered women's shelter."

Gladys went to the lobby, rang a bell, and was buzzed in.

I called Muller, but I got his voice mail. I left a message with the address of Gladys's latest stop. She came out forty-five minutes later and headed to her car.

"She doesn't look very happy," I said.

"I was going to say she looks downright pissy," Terry said. "Something didn't go well."

We followed Gladys for another twenty minutes, until we realized she was headed back to Nichols Canyon Road.

"Damn," I said. "She's going back to the shelter. We practically accused her of being connected to the latest killing and she just drives around town doing bed checks and head counts. She doesn't even go to her lawyer."

"Or confession," Terry added.

When she got to the hairpin, she turned onto the dirt road. We drove past the turn and parked. A few minutes later my phone rang. It was Muller.

"You've been out of touch for an hour," I said. "Where've you been?"

"Busy."

"What have you got for us?"

"You're never going to believe this," Muller said.

"Try me."

"My grandmother just fell out of a hayloft."

"Are you serious?" I said.

"I don't joke around when it comes to Grandma," he said.

"We'll be right there," I said.

Terry heard my end of the conversation and started the car before I even hung up. "What's going on?" he said.

"Muller's grandmother fell out of a hayloft."

"Son of a bitch," he said, hitting the gas and peeling out.

We raced back to the station, lights and sirens all the way.

# CHAPTER 55

**MULLER DOESN'T HAVE** a grandmother. What he does have is a heaping dose of paranoia about the security of radio and cell phone transmissions. Which means that when he has a really big piece of news to tell us, he refuses to broadcast it all over the Southland.

Instead, he sends for us.

The code word is grandmother. The rest of the sentence depends on his mood.

So far Grandma Muller has been arrested for selling marijuana at a senior citizens' bake sale, kidnapped by a band of gypsy dwarves, and won a Pulitzer Prize for knitting. Whenever Terry and I get a Granny call, we drop everything, because we know Muller has dug up something that is going to help make us look good.

There's nobody like Muller in all of LAPD. Until recently, he led two lives—brilliant computer cop by day, incredibly talented jazz pianist at night. Then six months ago he gave up music. Cold turkey. Totally and completely.

His new passion—photography.

Those of us who know him thought he was nuts for trading in his keyboard for a top-of-the-line digital Canon SLR camera.

But then he surprised us all. His photographs turned out to be brilliant. Even more surprising was that people were buying them. At first it was just friends and family, but then he set up a Web site, *timefly.net*, and now he's getting orders from around the world.

"Great news," he said when we got back to the station.

"Lay it on us," Terry said.

"The couple in Houston who bought two pictures last month just bought two more. And a gallery in Japan wants to do a show of my stuff. An Asian Mullerpalooza."

"I'm thrilled for you, kid, and I'm really going to miss you when you make a zillion yen and leave LAPD," Terry said. "Till then, tell us about Grandma and the hayloft."

"Fine. Ignore my joy," Muller said. "I dug into Gladys Wade's past, and there's a lot more to her than meets the eye."

"We knew that," Terry said. "Give us some meat to chew on."

"I've got enough meat to choke a horse," Muller said. "But first you have to sit through two minutes of background."

Terry looked at his watch. "I'm putting a clock on you. Go."

"She was born Gladys Hollister in Logan, West Virginia," Muller said. "At the age of nineteen she married Hiram Wade, a coal miner, a drunk, and a wife beater, not necessarily in that order. He had a few arrests, but nothing stuck. Back then, men in rural West Virginia got away with a lot of shit. They had twins, Helen and Cody. Helen died when she was five years old. Drowned in the bathtub."

"Was the father implicated?"

"No, he was at work when it happened. Gladys took full responsibility. She said she put Helen in the tub, went to the kitchen, got distracted, and when she came back, the kid was dead. The coroner ruled it an accident. A month after Helen died, Gladys ran off with Cody. Never even filed for divorce. She just split."

"Some women just can't handle the glitz and glamour of being married to a drunken coal miner," Terry said.

"She moved to California," Muller said. "I picked Cody up in the LA school system fifteen days after he and Gladys left West Virginia."

"What about the husband?"

"He didn't follow them," Muller said. "From what I can tell, he couldn't have even if he wanted to. Gladys didn't leave any bread crumbs. He died in a house fire three years later."

"So far none of this is Grandma-fell-out-of-a-hayloft-worthy," Terry said.

"I know, but you needed some history," Muller said. "Now cut to this morning. Gladys visits six apartments. The first five each have a tenant who fits the profile of someone who spent time at a battered women's shelter. But the last building is filled with solid citizens. None of them have priors, so I go over the list of tenants. One name jumps out at me. The woman in apartment 5-E. Her name is Helen Wade. Same as the dead daughter."

"It's a pretty common name," Terry said.

"Right. So I searched the DMV files. The Helen Wade at that address has a driver's license," Muller said. "And here's what knocked Granny right out of the hayloft. The ID Helen used when she applied to the California DMV was a West Virginia birth certificate—Helen Ann Wade. Born in Logan County the same day as her brother Cody Lee Wade."

Muller pulled up a screenshot of Helen Wade's license on his computer.

"She looks like she could be Gladys's daughter," I said. "And Cody's sister."

"I'd be happier if she looked like Betty White," Terry said.

"So where do we net out?" I asked. "Is Helen Wade dead or alive?"

"According to the county records, she was in kindergarten until she was five years, eight months, two days old, and then she was issued a death certificate. The school board changed her status to deceased, and there's no record of her being enrolled in any school after that," Muller said.

"So the great state of West Virginia says she's dead, but California doesn't mind if she drives a car," Terry said. "What do the Feds say? If she's alive she should be paying taxes."

"That's what I thought," Muller said. "So I checked it out. Helen Wade has a social security number that her mother applied for when she was three weeks old. But Helen's retirement fund is a tad low. She never worked a day in her life, so she never paid a cent in taxes."

"So the Helen Wade that Gladys visited today is uneducated and unemployed," I said.

Muller nodded. "Both states agree on that."

"I'll tell you one thing," Terry said. "If she's trying to survive in LA with no education and no job, she might as well be dead."

# CHAPTER 56

**CULLIN HERWIG WAS** a deputy with the Logan County Sheriff's Office the day Helen Wade drowned in her bathtub. Thirty years later he was still on the job. Only now he was top dog. I dialed his office from a speakerphone, so Terry and Muller could listen.

It was almost seven o'clock in West Virginia. I didn't expect him to be in, but I was determined to track him down.

"Sheriff Herwig's office," the voice at the other end said.

"Is he there?" I asked.

"Gone for the night. Not reachable till seven tomorrow morning. What's this about?"

"This is Detective Mike Lomax from LAPD, Hollywood Station. I'm working a homicide."

"In that case, this is Cullin Herwig," the voice said. "My wife just called me for the third time to remind me that I'm late for dinner. I didn't want to get tied up on the phone with some cop from Boone County who's looking for a stolen tractor, but you said Hollywood and homicide, so I'm in. What can I do for you?"

"It happened a long time ago," I said. "You signed off on an accident report back when you were a deputy. A five-year-old girl drowned in her bathtub at home."

"Helen Wade," he said.

I was surprised. "You remember that?"

"Detective, Logan County ain't exactly a hotbed of rampant

227

criminal activity. But even if it was, trying to breathe life back into a little girl and failing—I won't forget that till my dying day."

"I'm going to ask you a real stupid question here, Sheriff," I said.

"Good. I got a department meeting tomorrow and it sure would be a hoot to tell my boys and girls that the Los Angeles Police Department is no smarter than your local redneck sheriff here in West Virginia. Lay it on me."

"Are you sure Helen Wade was dead?"

"Shit, boy, that *is* stupid," he said. "Of course she was dead. Which part of 'I won't forget it till my dying day' didn't you follow?"

"Sorry," I said. "We're investigating a woman who used Helen Wade's birth certificate to get a California driver's license. And what makes it more difficult is that she looks like she could be Gladys Wade's daughter."

"Don't matter if she looks like the Virgin Mary Herself," he said. "She's a fake. Little Helen was dead when I got to the scene, dead when I left, dead when I paid my respects at the wake, and dead when I watched them put her in the ground."

"What do you remember about Helen's mother, Gladys Wade?" I asked. "How did she behave that day?"

"Well, that's a much smarter question," he said. "Because there was something strange about her. My partner, Betsy Tuel, and me, we both noticed."

"Strange, like how?"

"You see people get killed all the time," he said. "Accidents, homicide, it don't matter. What's the very first reaction you get when you tell the next of kin that their loved one is dead?"

"Shock. Disbelief."

"Right," Herwig said. "They say stuff like, this can't be true. This can't be happening. They try to make it go away."

"They're in denial," I said.

"Exactly," he said. "But Gladys was different. She was wailing and carrying on, and saying how it was all her fault, and how she killed her daughter, and God should punish her."

"She was confessing," I said. "Taking the blame."

"More like trying to convince me and Deputy Tuel that she did it, and that we shouldn't look at anyone else."

"We were told her husband had an alibi," I said.

"That bag of shit? I'm not talking about him," Sheriff Herwig said. "I'm talking about the little boy."

"Cody Wade?" I said. "The five year old?"

"Betsy caught onto it first—one of them women's intuition things. The boy wouldn't look at us. Plus there was something else."

"What's that?"

"When we got there, his hair was all wet."

Muller, Terry, and I just stared at the speakerphone. None of us said a word.

The sheriff finally broke the silence. "I can tell by your reaction that your head is going to the same place as me and Betsy went."

"What do you think really happened?" I asked.

"The kids were in the tub together. Country folks would do that. No big deal about a brother and sister taking a bath together at that age. Saves time and water," he said. "The kids were playing. Maybe the boy pushed his sister under and held her down too long. He was only five. He wouldn't know any better."

"Did you talk to him?"

"We asked permission, but the mother said no. He'd been through enough."

"Did you try to pursue it? Investigate it any further?"

"Come on, Detective," Herwig said. "The woman just lost her daughter. What should we do? Arrest her son? We ruled it an accident and the Coroner's office agreed. Whatever happened in that bathtub I'm sure that boy is still carrying it with him. That's gotta be enough punishment for one lifetime."

"Thank you, Sheriff," I said. "This was a tremendous help. Anything you want to add?"

"No," he said. "Just that I think about that little girl a lot. Every cop's got one he can't shake loose. Helen Wade is mine. I tried to bring her back. I gave her CPR—we didn't have defibrillators or fancy equipment in those days. Just a bunch of country cops with some basic first aid training. But she was long gone when I got there. Poor little thing. God rest her soul."

I thanked him again and hung up.

"Well, we know one thing for sure," Terry said. "Helen Wade is dead."

"What we don't know is, who is the woman who's using her identity, and why did Gladys Wade visit her this morning?" I said.

"And did Cody drown his sister?" Terry said.

"Even if he did," Muller said, "nobody's going to put him in jail. He was a minor. Maybe you guys should talk to Gladys and see what you can get out of her."

Terry and I both shook our heads.

"Why not?" Muller said. "Why wouldn't you talk to her?"

"Because whatever happened, she covered it up and took the heat back then," Terry said. "She's not going to open up to the cops now."

"But there's something we can do," I said. "Something that Sheriff Herwig couldn't do thirty years ago."

"What's that?" Muller said.

"We can talk to her little boy, Cody."

# CHAPTER 57

**WE CALLED SIMONE** Trotter.

"I was wondering when you guys were going to get around to me," she said. "Did you go to the women's shelter and track down those two elusive felines we're looking for?"

"The shelter is a cat-free zone," I said. "But we think they might be holed up in an apartment on De Longpre with a woman by the name of Helen Wade."

"Any relation to Gladys?"

"That's what we're trying to figure out."

We filled Simone in on our day.

"Wow, I can't imagine how well you guys would have done if I were there to help you," she said. "Let me see what I can dig up on Helen in our database, and I'll get a search warrant for her apartment."

Terry and I headed for Cody's office. "Let's not come on too strong," I said. "We don't want to spook him."

"How about something like this," Terry said. "If your sister is dead, why doesn't your mother put her in the ground instead of an expensive apartment?"

"Great," I said. "That ought to put him at ease."

Cody seemed happy to see us. "Hey, this is a nice surprise," he said.

"Sorry to bother you," I said, "but your mom's parole officer is out sick and we got pulled in to check with the family and see how she's doing."

Two homicide cops filling in for a corrections officer is like a brain surgeon stepping in for a proctologist. Total bullshit, but Cody bought it.

"Mom is doing great," Cody said. "She's back at the shelter, working with her girls. She seems happy."

Terry took out a pad. "On a scale of one to ten," he said, "what should we put in our report?"

"Eleven," Cody said laughing.

"The CDC will like that," Terry said, writing in the pad. "They really like it if we get one more person to give us feedback. Do you think Helen would agree that your mom's doing well?"

"Helen?" Cody said. "Where did you get Helen's name from?"

Terry checked his pad. "The Department of Corrections. Oh man, it says here she's your twin sister. I've got twin daughters myself."

"Identical?" Cody said.

"Polar opposites," Terry said. "Those two girls are as different as my hat and a pair of socks. I always thought twins would be . . . I don't know . . ."

"A lot alike?" Cody said.

"Exactly," Terry said. "What's it like with you and Helen? Are you guys like two peas in a pod, or are you from two different planets like my kids?"

"Helen and I have always gone our own separate ways. Ever since we were little kids, we've had different interests."

"But you're still brother and sister," Terry said. "I mean, Sarah and Rebecca may be different, but they still hang out together."

"Not so much with me and Helen," Cody said. "At this point, I'd have to say we're kind of estranged."

"Listen to me," Terry said. "Yakking on about my two daughters when I'm getting paid to check on how your mom is doing."

"She's doing great," Cody said.

"That's all we need to know," Terry said, heading toward the front door and smiling like a used car salesman who had just unloaded a lemon and was in a hurry to put some distance between him and the sucker.

He kept smiling till we got in the car and back on the road.

"What the fuck just happened?" he said.

"For starters," I said, "you just gave the worst performance by a cop investigating a homicide since the last episode of *Columbo*. Could you have been any more nauseating?"

"At least he opened up about his sister."

"He didn't open up," I said. "He closed up. He lied through his teeth. He forgot to mention that his sister has been dead for thirty years."

Terry didn't say anything for at least a minute. He was processing something inside his brain, and I know him well enough not to interrupt him. He pulled the car over to the curb and turned off the engine.

"If Cody is lying to us," he said, "let's just give him plenty of rope and see if he hangs himself. But what if he isn't lying?"

"Of course he is. Sheriff Herwig made it clear that Helen died thirty years ago."

"Maybe Cody doesn't know that," Terry said.

"Terry, he was there. He was probably in the damn tub with her."

"He was five. He was traumatized. Maybe he blocked it out. Selective memory, or whatever the shrinks call it."

"Okay, Dr. Biggs," I said. "Let's just say that Cody doesn't remember Helen dying. But there is a real live Helen Wade who Gladys just visited, and who Cody says he never liked. Who the hell is she?"

"The replacement Helen."

I stared at him and repeated the words slowly. "The replacement Helen."

"Mike, I know it sounds bizarre . . ."

"No. You and my father thinking you can do a movie about a couple of trucker vigilantes—that's bizarre. This is way beyond that," I said. "But if I could humor you on that one, I can do it for this. Try me."

"Helen drowns," Terry said. "Gladys and Cody are both in shock. They move to LA, but Cody is miserable. He misses his sister. He feels guilty, maybe even responsible. Gladys is willing to do anything to help him snap out of it. So she finds someone to take Helen's place."

"*Finds someone?* Like she just picks up a random five-year-old girl and says, *we're changing your name to Helen; welcome to the family?*"

"She works with battered, homeless women," Terry said. "Most of them have kids. A lot of those kids are unwanted and get sent off to foster homes. How hard would it be for Gladys to just adopt one of those kids?"

"Legally?"

"No," Terry said. "That would leave a paper trail. Come on, Mike, you know the system. Dirt-poor teenage mothers, who are victims of abuse—they've been known to abandon their kids. What if Gladys just *absorbed* one, and instead of turning it over to the Child Welfare system, took it home and said to Cody, 'here's Helen. She's all better.'"

"And little Cody accepts it?"

"Why not? He's five, and it makes him feel better," Terry said. "Then he and new Helen are raised like brother and sister, but they don't get along that well because they really have nothing in common."

"How come the county has Cody's school records, but nothing for Helen?" I asked.

"Gladys would be afraid to enroll her. She could fool Cody into thinking the girl was his dead sister, but there's a death certificate on file in West Virginia. If the LA school system did a background check they could catch it."

My cell phone rang. Simone had the search warrant.

Terry pulled the car back into traffic and we headed for Helen Wade's apartment.

"Do you think the woman who became Helen Wade is behind any of the killings?"

"I think she did them all," Terry said. "I think she set it up to help get Gladys out of jail. Then she pinned it on Hilda, and gave the Mercy Nurse a taste of her own medicine. Assisted suicide."

"That almost makes sense," I said. "But once Gladys got out of jail and Hilda took the fall, why did Helen have to murder Velinda Toohey?"

"Serial Killer 101, Detective Lomax," Terry said. "Once they start killing, they can't stop."

# CHAPTER 58

**TERRY, SIMONE, AND** I were outside Helen Wade's apartment door, along with five more FBI agents. A dozen more surrounded the building, covering every possible exit.

"Do you realize we've got twenty people with guns to take down a woman who's been dead thirty years?" Terry said.

"It may be nineteen more people than we need," Simone said. "We've got images on the infrared. The bad news is Helen's not home. The good news is I think we found our missing cats."

The building manager supplied us with a key. I opened the door, and we barreled in.

It felt like déjà vu. Just a few weeks ago we were coming through another door ready to nail the first scrapbook killer.

The door slammed against the inside wall with a bang. A fat striped tabby scampered for safety. But the second cat, a black-and-white curled up in a chair, seemed completely unfazed by the intrusion.

"Check the coloring on those two cats," Simone said. "They look like they match the cat hair we found in the scrapbooks."

One of the agents came out of the bedroom. "The place is clear, Agent Trotter. Nobody here except for the cats."

"Grab onto them until the lab techs get here," Simone said. "They're both scheduled for a kitty DNA check."

"Offer the fat cat a deal," Terry said to Simone. "He tells me where Helen is, and I don't put him in the microwave."

"We'll find her," Simone said.

Two agents each picked up a cat, while Terry, Simone, and I began combing the apartment.

We started in the living room. We found one drawer with a small amount of scrapbook stuff in it.

"It looks like it's just the tip of the iceberg," Simone said. "A work in progress. We want the mother lode."

"Mother is in here," Terry said from the bedroom. "And I'll bet she's loaded."

There was a large fire safe with a combination lock. It looked like it could hold a lot of secrets.

"I'll bet there are some big pieces of the puzzle right in here," Simone said.

"Let's not even think about opening it," I said.

"We have a warrant," Simone said.

"I'd feel better if we had a bomb squad," I said.

"You think it's booby-trapped?"

"It might not blow up in our faces," I said, "but it could be rigged with acid packs or an incendiary. If we don't open it right, we'll have lost our evidence."

"Your bomb squad or mine?" Terry asked Simone.

"I'll call the Bureau," she said. "They'll jump in like it's a terror cell. Sometimes a little overkill can't hurt."

We checked the rest of the apartment.

"I can't find a computer," Terry said. "She's probably got a laptop that she took with her."

Without a computer there was no electronic trail to trace. It would make for a lot slower going.

We checked the kitchen.

"It looks lived in," I said. "Food in the fridge, fresh milk, fruit."

I opened a kitchen cabinet. I pulled out a big Tupperware bowl and put it down on the counter so I could get a better look at the shelf behind it.

"Shit!"

It was the agent who was holding the orange tabby.

"Sorry, the damn thing got away from me," the agent said.

The cat jumped onto the counter and began pawing at the bowl. The agent grabbed it by the back legs, and the cat scratched him.

"You're bleeding all over my crime scene," Simone said. She gently lifted the cat and held it in her arms. The cat settled down.

"Something good has got to be in this bowl," I said, popping open the cover. "Ping-Pong balls. Numbered. Like the lottery."

I lined them up on the counter. They went from one to twenty, but six of them were missing from the sequence.

"What a coincidence," Terry said. "We have six murders. There are seven, counting Hilda, but hers was supposed to look like a suicide."

"You think Helen was pulling Ping-Pong balls out of the bowl to see who she would kill next?" Simone asked.

"There's an easy way to find out," I said. I swept my arm across the counter and the Ping-Pong balls clattered to the floor. Both cats broke loose and dove at the balls, trying to corner one.

Terry, Simone, and I looked at each other and the three of us started laughing. It wasn't hard to figure out what was happening.

"I guess the cat's out of the bag now," Terry said.

# CHAPTER 59

**JESSICA KEATING CONFIRMED** what we had already figured out.

"These cats are guilty as charged," she said. "They shed over every square inch of the apartment, which means they've been living here for a while. I would guess all the scrapbooks were made here."

"Not at Hilda's place?" I said.

Jess shook her head.

"Then Hilda's cats were framed," Terry said.

"I think we were all set up," Jessica said. "I was convinced Hilda was the mastermind."

"Everybody was convinced," I said. "That's how Gladys got out of jail."

"You mean Helen Wade killed all those people just so her mother could rat out Hilda Beck and get an easy parole?" Jessica asked.

"Yes," I said. "And it worked."

"Wouldn't one have been enough? Why did she have to kill six?"

"I'm not so sure one would have been enough," I said. "I think Helen had to create a case of major proportions that was baffling to the cops. Gladys was able to give us some convincing information about the murders, which got our attention, but the icing on the cake was telling us about Johnny Walmark and Jock Noonan before we even knew about them. At that point she had everybody's attention, and we gave her our word that we'd go to bat for her with the parole board."

"In writing," Terry said.

"Damn," Jessica said. "Now that you know you were suckered, can you put Gladys back in prison?"

"For what?" I asked. "We can't prove she's involved in any of the murders. She was in jail for all but the last one."

"But she told you guys all those stories about Hilda collecting newspaper clippings, and learning how to scrapbook, and making plans to teach the victims a lesson. She was lying."

"She was a con trying to con a cop, and she pulled it off," I said. "Maybe she planned it with Helen. Or maybe Helen just told her what to say, and she followed orders. Either way, we took the bait. We can talk to the DA, but Karen Winters is one smart lawyer, and I can't think of anything we could say that would convince a judge to put Gladys back behind bars."

"It was the perfect crime," Jessica said. "Until Helen went out and murdered the girl in the Laundromat."

"I'm not a psychologist," Terry said, "but I'm starting to think that Helen may not be mentally stable enough to grasp the concept of quitting while you're ahead."

"You think she'll try to kill again?" Jessica said.

"Hopefully her scrapbooks are in the safe, and she doesn't plan on killing anyone unless she can leave behind a lasting tribute," Terry said. "But she's not coming back to feed her cats. I think she'll find a new place to hole up, stock up on art supplies, and start making more scrapbooks. That could buy us some time."

"This morning's paper is on the table," Jessica said. "It looks like she just moved out today. A few hour earlier and you'd have caught her."

"Our mistake," Terry said. "We went to see Gladys this morning and told her there was a new scrapbook murder. Even if she had no prior knowledge of it, I'm sure it didn't take long for her to figure out that Helen was the killer. Concerned mom that she is, Gladys came here and probably told her murdering daughter to vacate the premises."

Simone had been outside on the phone. She came back in. "Our best bomb squad team was working down in Orange County," she said. "They'll be here in an hour. It will probably take them at least another hour to open the safe. You guys game to stick around?"

Terry looked at his watch. "I've got a personal commitment to take care of. Why don't I come back in two hours?"

"In that case I'd rather go back to the office and work with Muller," I said. "Maybe we can dig into Helen's background and come up with a clue as to where she might run off to. I'll be back in a couple of hours, too."

My car was in the parking lot at the station, so Terry drove me there. "What kind of personal stuff are you doing at six-thirty on a Monday night?" I asked. "You're a cop. Who gave you permission to think you have a life?"

"I'm only a cop for now," Terry said. "One day, I'll be an internationally famous screenwriter. But before that can happen I have to learn how to drive a truck. I'm meeting Big Jim. He's going to give me a lesson."

"That's the *personal commitment* you have to take care of? My father is going to teach you how to drive an eighteen-wheeler?"

"I'm not going to turn in my badge and join the Teamster's Union," he said. "I'm just going to get the basics, so I don't embarrass myself when I read the next draft of my script to your little seven-year-old know-it-all friend."

We made the turn from Sunset onto Wilcox and Terry pulled up to the station.

"My car is here," I said. "I'll meet you back at Helen Wade's apartment about eight-thirty."

"Okay, but do me a favor and call Simone before you go back

there," he said. "If there *is* a bomb in that safe, you want to show up *after* it's diffused, not before."

"Is that why you wanted to get out of there?" I asked. "You afraid it's going to go off?"

"Hell no," he said. "Given the choice of being in a room that might explode at any minute or sitting in a big-ass hot truck with your crazy father, I'd much rather take my chances with the bomb."

"Then why didn't you?"

"Because I really don't have the heart to tell that to your father."

# CHAPTER 60

**"DID YOU ARREST** Helen Wade yet?" Muller asked when I got back to his office.

"No, but we're putting the rubber hose to her cats," I said. "I'm sure they'll crack any minute and tell us where she's hiding."

"Let's hope so, because I can't find her," Muller said.

"What are you talking about? You could find a piece of pocket lint in a room full of mirrors. You and all that magic Google stuff you do."

"Google? Mike, I've searched every imaginable government, medical, financial, and law enforcement database," Muller said. "This woman is a total ghost."

"Well, she's been dead for thirty years, but Terry thinks another Helen Wade took her place. That's the one we're looking for. She's got to be in your computer somewhere. Everyone in the world is in there. You don't actually have to find her. Just point me in the right direction."

"You don't get it," Muller said. "What's Diana's last name?"

"My Diana? Trantanella."

He started typing her name.

"What are you doing?" I said.

"I'm trying to prove a point. Give it a few seconds."

Diana's picture came up on the screen, followed by row after row of scrolling type.

"What's that?" I said.

"That's Diana's spending patterns," he said. "In the past month she used her Visa card four times at the same gas station, auto-paid her membership to a gym on Third Street, used her debit card at Target, and wrote a check for $117 to Victoria's Secret. This is more than enough information for you to track her down."

"And with any luck, when I find her she'll be wearing whatever she bought at Victoria's Secret."

"This took me ten seconds," Muller said. "But I can't track Helen Wade because she doesn't have any credit cards, any income, or any bank accounts. And I called the manager at her apartment building—she pays cash."

"If she doesn't have any visible means of support, how does she survive?"

"Survive? Mike, as far as I can tell, this woman doesn't even exist."

We took another approach. Based on Terry's theory, we tried to reconstruct Gladys's employment history from thirty years ago and track down the real mother of the fake Helen.

But it was a dead end. The same privacy laws that protect battered women today kept their private lives private thirty years ago.

My cell phone rang. I instinctively looked at my watch. It was too soon for either Simone or Terry to be calling.

I answered it. "Detective Lomax."

"Mike, it's Cody Wade." His voice was a whisper, but at the same time, desperately urgent.

"Cody, what's going on?"

"My sister is here."

"Where? Where are you?"

"The office. Mike, I should have listened to you. You were right. Helen is involved in these murders. She's here now."

"Can you keep her there?"

"I don't know. She wants me to go with her." The whisper

suddenly turned into a scream. "Helen, put that down. Put it down."

I yelled into the phone. "Put what down? Cody, what's going on? What does she have?"

"A pair of scissors. She said there are cops at her apartment and she can't go home. She thinks I sent them. She's really . . . this is the worst I've ever seen her."

I scribbled Cody's office address on a piece of paper and shoved it at Muller. "Helen Wade. She pulled a pair of scissors on her brother. Get some cars rolling."

Muller bolted from the office and headed for the Watch Commander's desk.

I went back to the phone. "Cody, help is on the way. Just keep her for two, three minutes."

He screamed. "Aaaaahhhh, you bitch."

"What happened?"

"Ahhh, shit, she cut me. It's just my hand, but I'm bleeding. Okay, okay, Helen, you win. I'll go with you."

"Cody, don't go anywhere with her," I yelled. "Stall. Two minutes."

"I don't know if I . . . ahhhh." Another scream, followed by scuffling. Finally, Cody came back on. "Mike, I'm sorry I called. Helen said we won't be needing your help anymore."

Then I heard a woman's voice. It was filled with venom and rage. "Put the phone down, you scumbag, and get in the fucking car."

Cody yelped in pain one more time. He was sobbing now. "Mike, I'm scared. She's going to kill me. Please do something. She's taking me to the—"

And then the phone went silent.

# CHAPTER 61

I YELLED CODY'S name into the phone two more times.

"Tell him the cavalry is coming," Muller said, racing back to his desk. "Sergeant Bethge has six units rolling, and one of them is less than a minute away. He's also putting out a call for a hostage negotiating team."

"We're too late," I said. "She took him."

"Where? Bethge can reroute them."

"I don't know where," I said, "but I have a good guess. I'm going now."

"I'm going with you," Muller said.

"You?" I said. "You're a computer geek."

"I'm a cop," Muller said. "I went to Cop University."

"This is dangerous. I've got to go out there and deal with a deranged woman."

"You think I can't handle that?" Muller said. "You obviously haven't seen my wife when she's in full-blown PMS. I'm going."

He grabbed a leather shoulder bag off his desk.

"I hope you have a gun inside that man purse of yours," I said as we ran for the parking lot.

"You mean that standard-issue semi-automatic Glock paperweight the department gave me? I'm sure it's in here somewhere."

We jumped in my car and barreled out onto Wilcox, siren

wailing.

"Where are we going?" Muller asked.

"Where do you think two siblings who have hated each other all their lives would go when they have a blowup this big?" I said.

"Mommy," he said.

"That's what I'm thinking. I'm betting Helen is taking Cody to the shelter. But I don't think she wants Gladys to sort this one out. Helen is beyond all rational reasoning. I think she's going there so she can kill her brother right in front of the woman who always loved him best."

"Should I call Bethge and have him send the troops?"

"No. I don't want a bunch of hothead rookies in uniforms storming the palace, waving guns, and screaming 'freeze motherfucker,'" I said. "That alone might put Helen over the top, not to mention freak out a house full of battered women. Besides, it's at the end of a narrow dirt road, and they'll look like the Keystone Cops trying to find the place."

"But we need backup."

"I'm calling for it right now."

I grabbed my phone and punched Terry's speed dial.

"Hey," he said. "I'm with Big Jim. Anything blow up yet?"

"Yeah. Helen. She took Cody hostage. She's threatening to kill him with a pair of scissors. I think she's heading for the battered women's shelter. Muller and I are on the way there now."

"Muller? What's the matter? Were there no Girl Scout troops available?"

"Shut up and meet me at the shelter. How fast can you be there?"

Terry hesitated. "Ah, shit, it'll take me at least . . . never mind, I'll be there in fifteen."

"Lights and sirens," I said. "Step on it."

Eight minutes later I was careening down Nichols Canyon Road. When I got to the hairpin turn I did a full-blown movie

247

skid just the way my father had taught me when I was twelve years old.

"You're a hell of a wheel man," Muller said.

"A stunt driver would make about five hundred bucks just for pulling off that skid," I said. "The director would have wet himself over that one."

I swung onto the dirt road.

"Jesus, look at that," Muller said. He unzipped his shoulder bag and began rummaging through it.

"Look at what?" I asked.

"Out your window. Talk about movies. Look at that sky. It's amazing."

It was. I could barely make out the women's shelter on the horizon. It was a tiny speck wrapped in brilliant reds, pinks, oranges, blues, and purples.

Muller had his Canon out and was clicking away.

I couldn't blame him. Timing is everything for a photographer. Sometimes you can wait for months and never see a shot this magnificent. The last vestiges of sunlight were cascading down from the heavens, catching particles of dust, scattering them through the atmosphere, and creating a breathtaking palette of color across the sky.

It's a spectacular sight you rarely get to witness, and only then, in that single magic moment between sunset and nightfall.

A cinematographer's dream.

Twilight.

# CHAPTER 62

**"NOW THAT THIS** is becoming a reality," Muller said as the big gray building quickly came into view, "I guess I should ask what you expect from me in this situation."

I began slowing down, taking a quick look in my rearview mirror at the dust storm I had kicked up. "Don't go all geek on me now, computer boy," I said. "Just follow my lead."

"Okay, but what exactly are you planning to do?" Muller asked.

I have no idea."

I stopped the car about fifty feet from the house. Helen was standing in the middle of the yard. She had on a simple yellow dress, cinched at the waist with a white belt, and matching white sandals. Her light brown hair fell to her shoulders.

Helen almost looked like the kind of woman you'd see in the mall or the supermarket. Except she was waving a pair of gleaming chrome dagger-point scissors in the air, so she looked more like the kind of woman you'd see in a mental institution. She was ranting at Gladys, who was standing twenty feet away.

I got out of the car so I could hear. Muller, camera in hand, got out on his side.

At least a dozen women and the two dogs were on the porch watching the scene. As soon as we got out of the car, the dogs started barking.

"Girls, get inside the house," Gladys yelled. "And take Zanna and Hera with you."

The porch cleared in a hurry, and heads immediately began popping up in windows.

Gladys began walking toward me.

Helen screamed. "Stay away from him, Mom."

Gladys slowed, but she kept edging toward me.

"Stop," Helen called out, "or I swear to God I will kill Cody."

She put the point of the scissors directly against her ribs.

Gladys stopped about ten feet from me.

Cody was nowhere to be seen.

"Helen," Gladys called out sweetly, "this is Detective Lomax. He's one of the nice men who helped me get out of prison. He's your friend."

"Fuck him," Helen shrieked. "He's not my friend. He's Cody's friend. He's the cop Cody ratted me out to."

I looked left, right, and behind me. I turned to Gladys. "Where's Cody?"

And then I heard Cody's voice. "Mike, I'm over here."

It came from the middle of the yard. I turned as Helen, with the scissors still in her right hand, whirled around and smacked herself in the head with her left. "Shut up, Cody," she growled.

And then came the pained reaction, "Ow, you bitch." It was Cody's voice. But it was coming from Helen's mouth.

"There's plenty more where that came from, asshole," Helen yelled at her brother.

"Go to hell," Cody yelled back.

I clearly heard two different voices, but I could only see one person. It took a few seconds, but my mind finally opened up to accepting the unacceptable.

I turned back to Gladys. "Is that Helen?" I asked.

Gladys nodded. "Yes."

"And is it also Cody?"

"Yes, they're twins. You may only see one, Detective," she

said, as the tears began streaming down her cheek, "but there are two completely different people standing there, and . . . and they hate each other."

Helen had both hands wrapped around the scissors now, and once again they were pointing at her ribs. Or maybe they were Cody's ribs. I was completely out of my element.

I took a step toward her. "Helen," I said, "don't hurt anybody. Please put the weapon down."

"Stop right there, cop," she screamed, "or I swear to God I will kill my brother."

"She'll do it, Detective Lomax." It was Cody speaking now. His voice was panicky. "Please don't let her kill me. She's already killed seven people."

Helen was armed with a pair of scissors. I had a gun. In theory I had the advantage. I've also had enough hostage training to know that if the hostage is in imminent danger, and you have a clean shot at the abductor, take it. I could have easily taken Helen down, but I'd wind up killing Cody in the process. This was something they never put into the handbook.

I decided that my gun was useless. But I was close enough to rush her. "Gladys," I said in a whisper, covering my mouth with one hand. "If I try to tackle her, do you think she would actually stab herself?"

"No," Gladys said, "but I'm afraid she'd kill Cody. The sibling rivalry is intense. They were such happy children, but ever since the accident they've been competing for my love and attention."

I remembered what Sheriff Herwig had told us. "Are you sure Helen drowned by accident?" I asked.

"Oh yes," Gladys said. "It was tragic, but I know Cody didn't mean it." She raised her voice so Cody could hear her. "Cody, tell Helen you didn't mean it—that day in the tub. It was an accident."

"I was only five," Cody yelled. "It *was* an accident."

Helen came right back at him. "Bullshit," she said. "You did it on purpose. You held my head under water so you could have Mom to yourself."

"But I brought you back," Cody said. "Why would I bring you back if I wanted Mom to myself?"

Gladys was smiling now. "He did bring her back," she said to me with a kind of motherly pride. "It was Easter Sunday, just a few weeks after Helen's funeral. I had bought her a brand-new Easter outfit, and it was so adorable I didn't have the heart to bury her in it, so I kept it laid out on her bed. Just before church, Cody came in, all dressed up in that little pink-and-white dress, with the Mary Janes, and the little bonnet. He looked just like her. I was so happy to have her back. I cried, and she cried. It was a wonderful reunion. I call it my Easter miracle."

Helen/Cody was certifiably nuts. And now I realized that the nut didn't fall far from the tree.

"After that, Cody would come back as Helen every few days," Gladys said. "Sometimes for dinner, sometimes he'd put on her nightgown and I'd tuck him into her bed. But after a while, I wanted more. I wanted to take her shopping and do all kinds of mother-daughter things with her. But I couldn't—not in the little town where everyone knew us. That's when I decided to move to a big city and start all over. Coming to Los Angeles was the best thing I ever did. I got to spend time with both of my children. The three of us have been together ever since."

This was beyond weird. And just when I thought it couldn't possibly get any weirder, a loud blast cut through the air and rattled my brain.

*Honnnnnnnnnnnnnnk.*

It was an air horn blowing in the distance. I shaded my eyes and looked out at the horizon, and I saw it.

From out of the twilight, a gleaming eighteen-wheeler came barreling down the dusty country road.

Big Jim Lomax and Terry Biggs were hauling in a truckload of semi justice.

# CHAPTER 63

**THE HOSTAGE DRAMA** in the middle of the yard suddenly took a backseat as we stared at the 35,000-pound behemoth that was bearing down hard on the shelter. The truck was going fast. Too fast.

Muller had his camera out. "That guy should definitely get a speeding ticket," he said. "How come there's never a cop around when you need one?"

"There may be a cop behind the wheel," I said. "Terry is learning how to drive one of those rigs."

"Let's hope he learned how to stop," Muller said.

"A seven-year-old girl gave him a lesson in braking just yesterday," I said.

"Then let's hope he paid attention," Muller said, "or that battered women's shelter is going to be battered beyond recognition."

The women looking out the window had already figured that out, and there were screams coming from inside the house. The dogs joined in, and I yelled at everyone to get the hell out.

The front door opened, the women scattered, and then I heard the earsplitting screech of the brakes. Eighteen tires kicked up a dust storm as the big red cab and the fifty-three-foot silver box behind it came to a perfect textbook stop, and the hydraulic system belched air. It was incredibly dramatic and utterly unnecessary.

I didn't have to look to know that my father was driving.

Terry was on the ground in seconds. Big Jim followed from the driver's side. Zanna and Hera came bounding out of the shelter.

The dogs raced across the yard, instinctively going for the biggest target. That was their mistake. Big Jim has owned and trained dogs all his life. He snapped one hand up and growled a single word at them.

"*Zetz!*"

I don't know if these particular German Shepherds spoke any German, but they knew an Alpha dog when they met one. They both sat in front of Jim and waited for him to tell them what to do next.

Jim gave me a thumbs-up. "How can I help?" he asked.

I snapped one hand up and growled a single word at him.

"*Stay!*"

He had the good sense to obey.

By now Terry was at my side. "What's going on?" he said.

"Nothing I say is going to make any sense," I said. "Just listen, accept it for what it is, and let's resolve it. We have a hostage situation."

He looked around the yard. "Where?"

"The woman in the middle of the yard holding the scissors to her ribs is Helen Wade," I said. "But if you remove the wig and the dress, underneath it all she is actually Cody Wade. Helen hates Cody and she is threatening to kill him."

Terry's eyes widened, and his head began nodding as he took it all in. "And you interrupted my driving lesson for this?"

"I figured as a cop you wouldn't give a shit," I said, "but as a screenwriter you could probably get a lot of mileage out of this."

"Can I talk to her?"

"She hates me," I said, "so it looks like you're elected Good Cop by acclamation."

"Not my strong suit, but I'll give it a whirl." He called out to her. "Hey, Helen."

"Who the fuck are you?" she said.

"My name is Terry Biggs. I'm the guy who's taking care of your cats."

"My cats?" she said. "How are they?"

"They're fine," he said. "That black-and-white one doesn't really seem to give a shit that you left. As long as someone feeds him, he's cool. But the tiger-striped cat—she misses you something fierce. I can tell."

She relaxed the hand with the scissors. "That's Dizzy," she said. "I hated to leave her."

"What's the other cat's name?"

"Wayne."

"Wayne looks like he can handle himself," Terry said. "That's probably why you like Dizzy best."

"Dizzy has codependency issues. She needs more love," Helen said.

"That's what I heard about you."

"What the hell is that supposed to mean?"

"Hey, I'm a friend of your mom's," Terry said. "She talks about you all the time."

"What does she say?"

"Come on, Helen, don't make me say it in front of your brother."

"Say it."

"She loves you a lot," Terry said. "A real lot, if you know what I mean."

"More than she loves Cody?"

Terry shook his head. "Damn it, Helen, you're really putting me on the spot here."

"Say it!" she screamed, jamming the scissors under her ribs again. "Say it! Say it! Say it!"

"Yes!" Terry screamed back at her. "And you know what else she said? That if you kill Cody, the worst part will be that you'll go to jail and she'll never be able to see you again without a prison wall between you."

"But she came to my apartment this afternoon and told me to disappear—forever," Helen said.

"Helen, I didn't mean it." It was Gladys. "I love you so much I didn't want you to get hurt. I was trying to protect you."

"Why do you think your mother has been running a women's shelter all these years?" Terry asked. "She's protecting women like you from men who hurt them."

"Men like Cody," Helen said.

"Fuck you!" Cody was back. "It was an accident. I wasn't trying to kill you. I was only five years old."

"So was I," Helen snapped back.

"Cody, let me talk to Helen," Gladys said.

"You always loved her best," Cody said. "She got a brand-new Easter outfit, and what did I get? Nothing. She was your favorite. Admit it."

Gladys buried her face in her hands. When she looked up, she was crying. "I can't talk to you now, Cody. I only want to talk to Helen."

Helen looked up at her mother. "Is it true?"

Gladys was sobbing. She nodded her head. "Yes. I love you, Helen. I lost you once, and I don't ever want to lose you again." She spread her arms out wide and took two steps toward her daughter.

Helen paused. She stood there in silent agony for a solid thirty seconds. Maybe there was an inner dialogue going on between her and Cody that we would never hear.

And then she let the scissors fall from her hand. They dropped, point down, and stuck in the dirt.

Gladys took another step forward, and Helen began to inch her way toward her mother.

Somebody on the porch started clapping slowly. Someone else chimed in, and the clapping grew louder and more enthusiastic as Helen opened her arms and headed toward Gladys.

I glanced over at Muller, who still had the camera to his eye.

The applause was joyful now as the women on the porch all waited for the mother and daughter to embrace. In hindsight, maybe I should have tried to stop it. Maybe I should have slapped a pair of handcuffs on Helen as soon as she released the weapon. But I didn't. I was too caught up in the emotion of the moment.

In a few seconds I would read Cody Wade his rights. After that, he would spend the rest of his life in a man's prison. Or a loony bin. Whatever the courts decided, I knew that Helen would soon be gone forever.

I decided to let Gladys hug her daughter one last time.

They were five feet away from one another when Helen stopped. Her body seemed to go into a total spasm. She twisted left, then right. Then she let out a loud shriek, grabbed at her hair, ripped it off her head, and threw it in the dirt.

Cody was back, and he was enraged. "You fucking no good bitch," he screamed. "I hate you."

I thought he was talking to Gladys, and I moved in to protect her.

But it wasn't Gladys he hated. It was Helen.

He whirled around and ran back to where the scissors were standing upright in the ground.

"I'm sorry I ever brought you back," he screamed, grabbing the scissors. "This time you're out of my life forever."

Then, using both hands, he drove the blade into his rib cage and up into his spleen.

Some blood oozed out onto the yellow dress, but I knew that inside he was hemorrhaging. He fell backward, his hands still clutching the scissors.

Gladys ran to him, stumbled to her knees, and began pounding his chest. She let out a soulful wail. "How could you? How could you murder her again?"

The only sound that came from the body on the ground was a

gurgle, as the blood bubbled up, making it impossible to speak.

The lips moved. And the mouth shaped the words, "Mom, I love you." But at this point I couldn't tell which one of them was talking. Cody or Helen.

And then they were dead. Both of them.

# CHAPTER 64

**BIG JIM WAS** still standing next to the truck with the dogs. He was surprisingly silent.

"I need a favor," I said.

"Name it."

"The residents here are all battered and abused women," I said. "I want you and Muller to get them calmed down and settled back in the house until help arrives."

He nodded.

I looked over at the body. Gladys was still on the ground singing a lullaby to her dead child.

"These things don't always end this badly," I said to Jim.

"I know, son," he said. "But for what it's worth, I think you and Terry did everything you could."

A dozen residents were still on the porch, crying and hugging one another. "This has to be their worst nightmare," I said. "They just witnessed a man stabbing a woman to death."

"Mike, that's not what happened," Jim said.

"Don't try to explain it," I said. "Just be gentle with them."

"I'll try to muster up every ounce of sensitivity training in my body," he said.

I called Sergeant Bethge at the Watch Commander's desk. "We've had a bad night here, Carl," I said. "We're going to need half a dozen units, crime scene investigators, a coroner's bus, Anna DeRoy from the DA's office, and a bunch of social workers from the Department of Children and Family Services."

"Sounds like New Year's Eve in my old neighborhood in the Bronx." Terry said.

The next call was to Simone Trotter.

"Perfect timing," she said. "The Bomb Squad just opened Helen's safe. It's filled with scrapbooks of her future victims. And guess who one of the books is meant for."

"Her brother, Cody," I said.

"It sounds like you may know something that I don't."

"I do." I told her what I knew.

"*Merde*," she said. "Pardon my French."

"As soon as we pass the torch to the crime scene people, Terry and I can meet you," I said. "We'd like to take a look at those scrapbooks."

"My office," she said. "Hey, Mike . . . do you think it's really over this time?"

"There's gonna be a lot of postmortems and sorting out to do," I said, "but this time I think we got our man. Or our woman."

An hour later Muller, Terry, and I were in my car headed for the FBI offices at 11000 Wilshire.

"What's with the camera?" Terry asked Muller. "Are you going to be selling crime scene photos to your fans in Japan?"

Muller laughed. "I only took a few shots of the sunset."

"I saw you clicking away after I got there," Terry said. "What about those?"

"Oh, those weren't stills," Muller said. "That was video."

"You're kidding," Terry said. "You got some of that stuff on film?"

"Not film. Digital."

Terry was as excited as he ever gets. "But you got some of the action?"

"I got all of the action." He held up his camera. "It's a Canon EOS 5D," he said. "It's an SLR with high-def video. Plus, I have a zoom lens on it. You want to see what I shot?"

"At least fifty times," Terry said. "I can't believe it. First I was right about Gladys finding someone to replace Helen, and now you've got a movie of me and Big Jim showing up in the truck."

"Back up a second, Biggs," I said. "Your theory was that Gladys adopted a little girl to take Helen's place. But that's not what happened. Cody took her place."

"It's the same thing," Terry said. "Helen was dead, just like that sheriff in West Virginia said. Somebody took her place, just like I said. End of story."

It was after 10 P.M. when we got to Simone's office. The first thing we did was look at the scrapbooks. There were fifteen. Fourteen of them were numbered, and as we suspected, they matched the numbers on the Ping-Pong balls. The last one had no number. The cover was a deep burgundy instead of black. And Cody's name was embossed in gold on the front.

"She was planning to kill him," I said. "But he beat her to it."

"Here's what I can't figure out," Terry said. "I understand that Helen wanted to kill her brother, but didn't she realize she would also be killing herself?"

"That's the nature of a split personality," Muller said. "Did you ever read *Dr. Jekyll and Mr. Hyde?*"

"No, but I saw *Me, Myself & Irene*. It's a movie with Jim Carrey," Terry said. "Same concept, only a hell of a lot funnier."

"Why don't we ask Dr. Donahue?" Simone said. "He's a profiler for the Bureau. I'll bring him in tomorrow to evaluate Gladys's mental competency. He can also give us some insight into how Helen and Cody coexisted."

"We can show him the video that Muller shot," Terry said. "That'll help him get some real insight."

"What video?" Simone asked.

"Muller shot everything that happened at the shelter tonight," Terry said.

"You're kidding," she said. "Run it."

Muller plugged his camera into a monitor and hit play.

"Open on an eighteen-wheeler as it comes barreling down a country road at twilight," Terry said. "How's that for a dramatic opening shot?"

"Who's in the truck?" Simone said.

"Detective Terry Biggs," I said. "The star of the movie, hero of the open highway, and a true champion of semi-justice."

"Go ahead, Lomax," Terry said. "Have your fun now. Just wait till you want an autograph."

"How did you wind up arriving at a crime scene in a trailer truck?" Simone said.

"The Batmobile was in the repair shop," Terry said.

We watched the movie, with Terry narrating from beginning to end. I can mute the commentary on a DVD, but Terry is unmutable.

"That was amazing," Simone said when it was over. "I'm only sorry it had such a tragic ending."

"It's *cinema verité*," Terry said. "I only wish I could put it on YouTube."

"Great idea," I said. "I, for one, would love the world to see how you talked a suicidal person into dropping her weapon, then instead of cuffing her, I stupidly gave her enough time to run back, pick it up, and stab herself."

"That's not your fault, Mike," Simone said. "Cody Wade was a homicidal psychopath, and you helped stop him from killing anyone else. In any cop's book that is a job well done."

"If that's the case," I said, "how come I still feel like *merde?*"

# CHAPTER 65

**JOE DONAHUE HAD** a degree in forensic psychology from John Jay College of Criminal Justice and had been with the FBI for fifteen years. Joe is a big guy, about six foot five, with an easy smile, intelligent eyes, and a calming, affable radio announcer's voice. At the moment, he was using the smile, the eyes, and the voice to win over Gladys Wade.

They were in a small interrogation room. Simone, Terry, and I were on the other side of the two-way mirror.

"They've been in there thirty minutes already," Terry said. "How long does it take him to declare a total whack job mentally incompetent?"

"If the state provided a box on the assessment form that said 'check here if the arresting officer thinks the subject is a total whack job,' he'd be done by now," Simone said. "But unfortunately, Dr. Donahue is bound by California law and basic medical ethics."

"Quiet," I said. "He's going someplace interesting."

"I think I understand," Donahue was saying to Gladys. "You had a relationship with both your children, but Cody was able to get around more freely and spend more time with you."

"It's been that way for years," Gladys said. "Helen didn't like being in public. She kept to herself."

"Did she ever visit you when you were in prison?"

Gladys smiled. "One time. It was my birthday. What a surprise that was. But she said it was very difficult to do, so mostly she sent me things with Cody."

Joe smiled. "Nice. What kinds of things?"

"Pictures of herself, letters, little watercolors that she made. She was quite the artist. Cody never could draw a straight line."

"So Helen must have made those beautiful scrapbooks," he said.

"No. Hilda made the scrapbooks. I told the detectives I saw her."

"I'm a little confused," Donahue said. "Wasn't Hilda out of prison when she made the scrapbooks? Are you sure Helen didn't see her?"

"No, no, no," Gladys said. "Helen didn't see anything. It was Cody who saw Hilda making the scrapbooks. He was going to call the police and turn her in, but he had this idea that if I told the police it would look good on my record."

"Oh, I get it," Donahue said. "As long as Cody had some information that would help the police, he might as well help his mom, too."

"He was a good son."

"But, of course, you did lie to the detectives, didn't you? You told them that you saw Hilda clipping out newspaper stories in the prison library."

"It wasn't a big lie," she said, "because Cody really did see Hilda making the scrapbooks. But it made more sense for me to say that *I* saw her. That gave me a better chance of getting out of prison."

"Thank you," Donahue said. "Now I'm clear. Will you excuse me for a few minutes."

"I have a question first," she said. "Can I go to Helen's funeral?"

"We can ask the DA," Donahue said.

"Tell him I have to go," she said. "I'm her mother."

"I'll tell him," he said. "I'm very sorry for your loss."

Dr. Donahue exited and walked around to the viewing room. I closed the curtain on the two-way mirror and turned on the light.

"Have you seen the video that was shot at the crime scene?" I asked.

"Yes, I watched it twice."

"What did you think?" I asked.

"My first reaction was that the guy driving the truck was a maniac," Donahue said.

"But a well-meaning maniac," I said.

"Helen and Cody are fascinating," Donahue said. "This is the kind of stuff you read about in graduate school, but you hardly ever get to experience in real life. I know a lot of shrinks who would sell their mothers to watch this film."

"The Oscar buzz begins," Terry said.

"What's the diagnosis?" I asked.

"Cody Wade had DID—Dissociative Identity Disorder," Donahue explained. "It used to be classified as Multiple Personality Disorder, or in layman's terms, split personality The patient creates an alter ego, and he accepts it as real. For Cody, it was his sister, Helen. The disorder often stems from early childhood trauma, and in Cody's case, because of Helen's drowning, the trauma was severe."

"And the two personalities can be different enough so that one would want to kill the other?" I said.

"Absolutely. The person doesn't just *think* he has two different identities, he actually *becomes* two different people," Donahue said. "Did you hear Gladys say that Helen had artistic talent and Cody didn't? That is entirely possible. And it just reinforces the fact to each of them that they can't possibly be the same person."

"So Cody thinks he's Helen," Terry said. "But what about Gladys? She *knows* Helen drowned. Why didn't she straighten him out?"

"She can't. Because Gladys has an even more uncommon disorder," Donahue said. "It's known as *folie à deux*."

"The folly of two," Simone said.

"Right. It's also called Shared Psychotic Disorder. It's quite rare. A seemingly healthy person—Gladys—shares the delusions of the person with the psychotic disorder. Although technically Cody was not psychotic, it's the best way to understand what happened here."

"You mean like a man having sympathy pains when a woman is in labor," Terry said.

"Not exactly, but it's a close enough analogy," Donahue said. "Except for the fact that she believed Helen and Cody were both alive, Gladys Wade could appear to be relatively normal."

"This is LA," Terry said. "There's no criteria for relatively normal."

Donahue laughed. "She bought into the fact that both her children were alive. The disorder usually occurs in long-term relationships where one person is dominant."

"So Cody was psycho and Gladys bought his act," Terry said.

Donahue, an easy audience, laughed again. "That's not exactly how I'll write it up in my report, but essentially, yes."

"If Cody lived, his defense would have been insanity, correct?" I said.

"Definitely," Donahue said. "The man was as crazy as a soup sandwich."

"What about Gladys?" I said.

"Does she have a good lawyer?" Donahue asked.

"Extremely."

"Then she'll probably walk," he said. "She's not certifiable. Her delusion all revolves around the loss of a child. A lawyer could easily convince a judge that it was just a defense mechanism— an acceptable form of denial that allowed her to live with the pain of Helen's death and go on with her own life."

"But she lied her way out of prison," Simone said.

"Did she kill anyone?" Donahue asked.

"No," Simone said.

"Can the Bureau prove beyond a reasonable doubt that she planned any of the murders? Or that she was involved in them in any way?"

"No."

"So what did she do that warrants jail time?" Donahue asked. "She gave the cops information that she believed to be true. They commended her, and the Parole Board agreed she was a model citizen and released her back into society. Why should she go back to prison for choices that you guys made?"

"If that's how the story plays out, that would really suck for us," Terry said.

"Hey, I could be wrong," Donahue said. "I'm not a lawyer, but I'm guessing that's what a smart one would say."

"Karen Winters is smart," I said.

"Very smart," Terry said.

"So, gentlemen, is this case closed?" Simone asked.

Neither of us answered.

"I didn't think so," she said.

"I hate loose ends," I said. "And this case still has a few that need tying up."

"I think the best place to start is with the scrapbooks that were in Helen's safe," Terry said.

"What about the ones we found at Hilda's place?" Simone said.

"I wouldn't rule them out," Terry said. "But Cody rigged everything to pin the murder on Hilda. There's a good chance the scrapbooks he left there were dummies that weren't as important as the fifteen Helen left behind. Let's go over those first."

We put the one dedicated to Cody aside and focused on the other fourteen.

"You know, when you go through these scrapbooks and you see some of the shit that people get away with, you understand why Cody wanted to kill them," I said.

"We should call up these fourteen assholes and tell them how lucky they are," Terry said. "It might freak them out to know that they're only alive because some cat didn't pick their Ping-Pong ball."

It took us about ninety minutes to go through every scrapbook. We didn't know what we were looking for, but we knew we'd know it if we found it.

"There's a big fat manila envelope filled with clippings and crap that didn't make it into the books," I said. "Let's go through those."

"Outtakes," Terry said. "Sometimes that's the best part of the whole movie."

Twenty minutes later, Terry said the magic word.

"Jackpot."

He handed me a black-and-white photo that had been buried in the scrap pile.

"Time to pay Karen Winters a visit," I said, "and find out just how smart she is."

# CHAPTER 66

**TERRY AND I** drove to Karen Winters's office.

She was wearing jeans and a JUSTICE FOR BRANDON T-shirt. She looked like shit. She didn't smell that great either.

"If you're here to inform me that you'd like to interrogate my client, you're too late," she said. "Some scumbag cops already violated her rights. Oh wait, you're the scumbags in question."

"She's on parole, counselor," I said. "We have the right to question her without an attorney present. The law is on our side this time."

"There are limits to that law," she said. "I have no doubt that you pushed them. I'll move to get every word suppressed."

"Do you know all the details of what happened last night?" I asked.

"I got there at eleven and spent two hours with Gladys," she answered. "Then I went home where I did a little crying and a lot of drinking."

"We know how much Cody meant to you," I said. "We're sorry for your loss."

"So am I," she said. "I had to make my own coffee this morning and I really suck at it."

"Were you able to get any sleep?"

"Twelve hours," she said. "Then I took a milk bath and anointed my body in aromatic oils. Is that why you're here? To check on my health?"

"We're holding Gladys Wade," I said. "We're going to charge her as an accessory to murder. We thought you might want to accompany us to the DA's office and cut a deal."

"Bullshit. Gladys is completely innocent," she said. "This was all Cody. Or Helen. Or whoever else he was dressing up as."

"Did you know Helen?" I asked.

"You mean did she and I ever go out and get a mani-pedi together? No, I never met her. Don't you think I'd have recognized Cody in drag? All I knew was that he and his sister were estranged. It was family shit. I stayed out of it."

"She had fourteen more scrapbooks, ready to go," I said. "Cody couldn't get justice through the courts, so he decided to become judge, jury, and executioner on his own. Then he teamed up with Gladys to frame Hilda Beck. It almost worked, except Helen had a screw loose that Cody couldn't tighten."

Karen pounded on the desk and jumped up. "Cody did not team up with Gladys! He duped her into thinking that Hilda was behind it all. Cody told his mother exactly what to say, and all Gladys did was feed it to the cops."

"And how long have you held back that little piece of the puzzle?" I asked.

"Ten minutes. I swear to God," Karen said. "I just got an e-mail from Cody."

"He's been dead since last night," Terry said. "He must have one hell of an Internet service provider."

"He wrote it yesterday and programmed it to be mailed to me. If he hadn't been killed I'm sure he would have deleted it in the morning. Read it."

She swiveled her computer monitor, and Terry and I leaned in and read it in silence.

*Dear Karen,*
*Do you remember the day Ted and Cindy Cooper came to see us? I was so furious that the Brit bitch could get away with murder I told you I ought to kill her myself as a public service. We laughed about it, but then I started thinking. Why not? I'm not connected to the case. Nobody would ever suspect me.*

*That night I told my sister Helen about it, and she had a better idea. She offered to kill Bellingham-Crump and a bunch of other people who really have it coming. After three or four killings, the cops would be going nuts trying to solve it. Then Mom could rat Helen out in exchange for an early parole.*

*I told Helen that Mom would never send her to jail, so we figured out how to pin it on Hilda. Helen had the scrapbook idea. She said we needed a big splashy signature. I thought it was too much work, but she said it would be fun.*

*It worked, except that after Mom got out of jail, Helen couldn't stop killing. So now the cops know it wasn't Hilda. Helen ruined everything. She always does. I think she wants to kill me next. If she does, you have to go to the cops and tell them what she did. And tell them Mom had no idea what we were doing. I made up the story about Hilda getting the clippings from the prison library. Then I helped Mom memorize it. Don't let them put Mom back in jail. The women in the shelter need her. And so does Helen.*

*Cody*

"The shrink at the FBI called it Dissociative Identity Disorder," I said. "Cody really did think he was two different people."

Karen slumped back down in her chair. "The one I knew was a beautiful, gentle, caring young man," she said.

"It's too bad you never met Helen," I said.

She shuddered visibly. "Thank God I didn't. It would have tainted my memory of Cody forever."

I reached into my jacket pocket and pulled out the black-and-white photo Terry found in the hodgepodge of Helen's leftover clippings. "So then I guess you won't want to press this in your own personal memory book."

I handed it to her.

"What is this?" she asked.

"It's a picture of Helen with her arm around you, counselor," I said.

"It's obviously been doctored," Karen said. "My ten-year-old nephew could do this with Photoshop. I'm sure it would be no problem for someone as proficient as Helen."

"You'd have to wonder why she would do something like that," I said.

"Helen was obviously jealous of the relationship I had with her brother," Karen said. "Oh shit, this is insane—talking about them like they're two different people. There was only one person—Cody. I had a glorious relationship with him. Why would I ever want to spend time with him when he dresses up and pretends to be his crazy dead sister?"

"Because his crazy dead sister would help you get the justice you couldn't get with your law degree," I said. "Helen got you the biblical version."

"So much for 'an eye for an eye making the whole world blind,'" Terry said.

"You took Gladys's place," I said. "You had Cody and Helen competing for your love and your approval. They would do anything for you. And they did."

"Do you know how outrageously ridiculous that sounds?" Karen said. "Nobody would give that an ounce of credibility."

"I think Deputy District Attorney Anna DeRoy would," I said.

"And then what will she do? Wave a phony picture of me and Cody Wade in a dress at a judge and try to throw me in jail? A prosecutor without a lick of evidence persecuting a defense lawyer? The judge will throw her out."

"Cody Wade is dead," I said. "His mother is devastated. And six people who deserved jail time have all been murdered in cold blood. And you want to know what the most ironic part of the whole ugly mess is? I know you're behind it all, but I can't prove it. Which means you're right. The American ideal of liberty and justice for all doesn't always work."

She stood up again. "Is there anything else you want to say before you leave, Detective?"

"Yeah. The first time we met him, Cody Wade reminded us that justice and revenge are not the same thing," I said. I dug into my pocket, pulled out a twenty-dollar bill and slapped it on her desk.

"What's that for?" she said.

"You already got revenge for Brandon Cooper," I said. "This might help get him some justice."

I turned around and, with Terry behind me, I headed for the front door. I stood tall, held my head up high, and tried to walk out looking like a winner.

But it's not easy when you know you've lost.

# CHAPTER 67

IT TOOK ANOTHER three days to do all the paperwork. Normally, we'd have wrapped it up sooner, but we were trying to link Karen Winters to the murders.

All we had was the photo. It was evidence that she had been with Cody when he was Helen, but there were no connections to any crimes.

We knew that Karen wrote the e-mail from Cody, but we suspected that the part about Gladys was true. She was clueless, and had obediently followed the script Cody and Karen had written for her.

Dr. Donahue wrote a seven-page opinion stating that Gladys was "essentially normal," meaning that other than her shared delusion with her son there was no other evidence of mental illness, and therefore not enough reason to try to have her institutionalized.

Terry's learned opinion on Gladys's mental state was much more concise. "Who gives a shit?"

On Friday afternoon Simone, Terry, Lt. Kilcullen, and I met with SAC Garet Church in his office.

"I heard that the three of you played real nice while I was in DC," Church said. "How did you like working with one another?"

"Agent Trotter is a total bitch," Terry said.

"Detective Biggs has absolutely no sense of humor," Simone said.

"I can't stand either of them," I said.

Church grinned broadly at Lt. Kilcullen. "Well, Brendan," he said. "It looks like we put together a stellar team."

"They closed the case on seven murders," Kilcullen said. "It's a true testimony to interdepartmental cooperation."

"And yet, none of them seem to be smiling," Church said.

"It's hard to smile when you know that the big one got away," Simone said. "Karen Winters orchestrated the whole thing. She knew every detail of Cody's tragic past, and she turned him into a serial killer, with total disregard for the consequences he would have to pay. He paid with his life, and she's still playing the role of dedicated storefront lawyer, champion of the poor and downtrodden. I hope she rots in hell."

"Can I give you the point of view of a much older, much more cynical FBI agent?" Church said.

"Sure, boss. Lay some wisdom on me," she said.

"Off the record," Church added.

"That's usually easier to swallow than the standard agency rap," she said.

"I've crossed paths with a lot of lawyers in my time," Church said. "Some of the smartest ones don't work on our side. They use their satanic skills to convince juries to turn loose murderers, rapists, and pedophiles. Some of the most evil dregs of our society are roaming the streets because some fast-talking attorney kept him out of jail. Those are the lawyers I would like to see rotting in hell. Compared to them, what did Karen Winters do? She said fuck the system and she started serving up her own brand of justice. Tell me something, did you mourn for any of her victims?"

"Just Cody Wade," Simone said.

"I figured as much," Church said. "And I'm not even sure Karen killed Cody. I think Gladys started that process thirty years ago."

"Well, you're right about one thing," Simone said. "You definitely are one hell of an old, cynical son of a bitch." Then she smiled. "That was off the record, too."

"I have a question," Terry said. "What's the status of the video that Detective Muller shot?"

"Muller works for LAPD," Kilcullen said. "He was on duty when he shot it. What do you think the status is? It belongs to the department."

"It was Muller's camera," Terry said.

"We didn't confiscate his camera," Kilcullen said. "We removed the memory stick and reimbursed him so he can buy a new one."

"Can I get a DVD of the video?" Terry asked.

"For what?"

"For my personal use."

"*Personal* use?" Kilcullen said. "This was a department hostage negotiation that ended in a fatality. And you want to submit it to *America's Funniest Home Videos?*"

"I'm not going to send it anywhere," Terry said. "I just might want to show it to a few people in the biz."

"What biz?"

"Movies. I want to give producers a taste of the script I'm writing. The dramatic shot of a semi barreling down the country road. The cop jumping from the cab and talking the hostage into dropping his weapon—"

"The hostage bleeding to death on camera," Kilcullen said.

"I'd edit that out," Terry said.

"No," Kilcullen said. "Absolutely not. All rights to that film belong to the Los Angeles Police Department."

"That totally sucks," Terry said.

Kilcullen threw both hands up in the air. "Welcome to Hollywood, baby."

My cell phone rang. It was Diana calling from home. I

answered. "Hi."

"Mike," she screamed, "Sophie's father is here, and he's trying to take her away. Come home now. Hurry. Hurry."

"Call 911," I said. "I'll be right there,"

"What is it?" Terry said.

"It's Diana," I said, racing out the door.

Terry was right behind me.

# CHAPTER 68

**THE FBI OFFICES** were only ten minutes from my house. Terry and I had planned to call it a day after our meeting, so both our cars were in the garage.

"I'll take the 405," I said to Terry. "You take Sepulveda."

At five on a Friday afternoon, they both could be jammed, but with lights, sirens, and a lead foot, I had a better shot on the freeway.

I called Diana back as I was ripping down the shoulder of the 405.

"Are the cops there yet?"

"You said you'd be right here, so I didn't call them," she said.

"Where's the guy now?"

"I told him to wait. He's sitting in his van in front of our house."

"Is Sophie okay?" I asked as I swung off the 405 to the 10.

"She's in her room playing on her computer. I picked her up about an hour ago. She doesn't even know he's looking for her."

"Don't tell her. And keep the door locked. I'll be there in three minutes."

I took the loop from the 10 to South Bundy at fifty-five, scattered the traffic on Ocean Park Boulevard, hung the left on 23rd Street on two wheels, and braked hard when I got to Hill.

A sun-bleached 1997 blue Ford Windstar was parked outside my house. I angled my car in front of it and got out. Diana was behind the living room window. I gave her a hand signal to stay put.

The man behind the wheel had been engrossed in tapping on his BlackBerry as I approached. He was Asian, early thirties, with a cheap haircut and a few wisps of chin hair that looked like he was either trying to grow a goatee or was in the middle of shaving one off.

He opened the car door, and I shoved it closed. "License and registration, please," I said, flashing my badge.

He rolled down the window. "Oh, you must be the cop who has my daughter," he said.

"I'm the cop who asked for your license and registration. Now."

"Okay, tough guy," he said, digging them out and handing them over. "Don't shoot."

The name on both said Jeremy Tan.

Terry's car pulled behind the Windstar, boxing it in. He got out and walked to the passenger side of the vehicle. Tan rolled it down and Terry flashed his badge.

"What's the matter?" Tan said. "One guy with a gun isn't enough?"

"What are you doing here, Mr. Tan?" I asked.

"I came for my daughter, Sophie," he said. "Carly has no right to take off and leave her with some total stranger. My daughter should be in my care."

"You think *I'm* a total stranger?" I said. "Would you even recognize Sophie if you saw her? From what I heard you walked out when she was six months old."

"I had life problems," Tan said, "and when I left town to straighten them out, Carly went running to some judge, screamed abandonment, and got custody. But now Carly's the one who hit the road. Tit for tat, baby. My turn to get the kid."

"Do you really think you can show up after seven years and claim Sophie, just because her mother is out of town?" I said.

"Hey, Carly isn't just *out of town*. She out of the entire freaking Western Hemisphere."

"She'll be back any day now," I lied.

"I have friends and relatives in China, and they tell me she's moved in with her mother."

"Her mother is dying," I said. "Carly will be back."

"Till then, Sophie can live with me," he said.

"Hey pal," Terry said. "You don't understand. The girl's mother left her with Detective Lomax."

"Just because Carly asked some cop to babysit my daughter doesn't give him any rights. I'm Sophie's biological father."

"Can you prove it?" Terry said.

"What kind of stupid question is that?" he said. "My name is on her birth certificate."

"That's your proof? Your name is on a piece of paper?" Terry said. "That might work on *The Jerry Springer Show*, but it won't fly with the State of California's legal justice system. So allow me to repeat the stupid question. Can you prove you're her biological father? Because if you can't, hit the road."

I handed Tan his license and registration back. "You heard him," I said.

Terry walked over to my car and moved it, unblocking the Windstar.

I rapped on the roof. "Drive carefully," I said. "And don't come back."

Tan gave me the finger and drove off.

Diana came running from the house. "What happened?" she said.

"That guy claims he's Sophie's father," Terry said.

"He is," Diana said. "I recognize him."

"Don't testify to that," I said. "It would only help his cause. He knows Carly is in China and he wants custody of Sophie."

"Oh, Mike . . . can he do that?"

"Not if we get custody first."

# CHAPTER 69

IF YOU'RE GOING to appear before a Family Court judge, you can't do better than Elizabeth Sneed White. Diana and I met in her chambers on Saturday morning. Sophie waited outside with a bailiff.

We gave the judge the background on Carly and how we wound up with Sophie. Then we told her about our run-in with Jeremy Tan.

"You say the mother and daughter are close and the father has been out of the picture," White said.

"Carly and Sophie adore one another," Diana said. "In fact, this is the first time they've ever been separated, and Jeremy never showed any interest in Sophie until now."

"I find that rather curious. All these years in absentia, and now, when the mother is out of town, he wants to claim her," the judge said.

"We spoke to Carly last night and she has a theory," Diana said.

Judge White smiled. "I prefer to base my judgment on hard facts, but go ahead. I promise it won't influence me one bit."

"Jeremy got remarried a year ago. His new wife wants a baby, but they're having trouble conceiving," Diana said. "Carly thinks Jeremy decided they wouldn't have to worry about getting pregnant if he can get his hands on the kid he already conceived."

"Delightfully creative theory," White said. "Much better than the standard 'he's doing it to hurt me, your Honor' rants I usually get. When is the mother coming back from China?"

"As of last night she doesn't know," I said. "She's waiting for her own mother to die, but she'll fly back immediately rather than take the chance of losing custody of Sophie."

"At the risk of sounding like a hard-ass, she should have thought of that before she jumped on a plane to China," White said. "Why would she take off and not leave a simple notarized document authorizing the two of you to be responsible for her daughter?"

"Your Honor, I kick myself for that one," I said. "Carly had a few hours to throw things together and race home to see her dying mother. But I'm a cop. I should have thought of it, and I didn't."

"I'll need a signed statement from Ms. Tan that she believes appointing the two of you as temporary guardians would be in the best interests of her daughter," the judge said.

"Will this help?" I said, reaching into my pocket. "Carly had a lawyer draw it up in China and she faxed it to me at six this morning."

The judge took the two pages and read it. "Well, it's obvious the two of you didn't write this," she said. "You never would have given yourselves such a glowing recommendation. If my kids weren't fully grown I'd be tempted to turn them over to you myself."

"So you agree we don't have to hand Sophie over to her father?" I asked.

"Whether or not you hand Sophie over to someone besides her mother is an issue for another time. The only thing I'm going to rule on now is whether or not I grant you temporary legal custody," the judge said. "You seem more than well suited for the responsibility, but I have to ask a few more questions before

I can rule on it."

"Ask away," I said.

"Not you," she said, smiling. She picked up the phone and pressed one digit. "Bring Sophie Tan to my chambers please."

A few seconds later, a bailiff escorted Sophie inside. She took in as much of her surroundings as she could in two seconds, then crossed the room, and sat on my lap.

The judge smiled and extended her hand. "Sophie, I'm Elizabeth."

Sophie took the hand and shook it lightly. "You're the judge. I never met a real judge before. Sometimes I see them on TV, but you're the first real one."

"Well, I'm happy to meet you," Judge White said. "I want to make sure that you have everything you need while your mom is in China. How do you feel about living with Mike and Diana?"

"Happy. They have a nice house, and I have my own room. And we can walk to the beach." She paused. "But I miss my mom. I talked to her last night. She doesn't know when she's coming back."

"I'll bet she misses you just as much as you miss her," the judge said, "and I'm sure she'll be back soon."

"Before she left, she asked me if I wanted to go to China with her, but I told her it sounded bor-r-r-ring, so I didn't go."

"Would you like to stay living with Mike and Diana till Mommy gets back?"

Sophie nodded her head. "Most definitely, your Honor," she said.

"What's the most fun about staying with them?" the judge asked.

"They're cool."

"They are. But what's the most *fun?*"

"We do a lot of things together. Like a family. That's the most fun."

"Well, I'm a Family Court judge, and I love hearing about

people who do family things," Judge White said. "My job is to make sure you get whatever you need while your mom is away, so I'm going to sign a piece of paper that makes Mike and Diana your temporary guardians. Does that make sense to you?"

"Is that like guardian angels?"

"That's a nice way to put it, Sophie. Yes, they'll protect you and take care of you like guardian angels."

"They do that now," Sophie said. "Why do you have to sign a piece of paper?"

"Suppose you got sick and had to go to the doctor," the judge said. "He might ask to speak to your mom. But this way Mike or Diana can take you to a doctor, and the piece of paper shows that they are your official guardians, and the doctor can tell them what medicines to give you, or whatever else he might tell your mother."

"Am I adopted?" Sophie asked.

"No, no, no, no, no," Judge White said. "You are still your mother's little girl. You are not adopted. Just protected until she gets back. How do you feel about that?"

"Fine."

The judge picked up her pen. "Any questions before I sign the piece of paper?"

"Yes," Sophie said. "Can I write a story about this?"

Judge White set down her pen, and stroked her chin. "Hmm, so many decisions for a judge to make." She paused for several seconds. Finally, she said, "Under one condition."

Sophie looked nervous. "What?"

"You make sure to send me an autographed copy of the story," the judge said. "Deal?"

Sophie's face lit up. The missing front tooth was halfway in by now. "Deal," she said.

The judge picked up her pen and signed the papers. She came around to the front of the desk, and walked us to the door. Sophie, Diana, and I each thanked her.

She handed me the papers, and said, "You're welcome."
Then she smiled and added, "Congratulations."

# CHAPTER 70

**AS LONG AS** we had been designated a fun family by Judge White, we decided to have some real family fun.

We went to Magic Mountain.

Seven hours, fifteen rides, six snacks, three souvenirs, and four hundred and thirty-five dollars later, we drove home.

Sophie took a bath, watched some TV, and was asleep by eight-thirty.

Diana and I were in bed by nine.

"This is going to be harder than I thought," Diana said, curling up next to me.

"Taking care of Sophie?" I asked.

"No. Giving her back."

The next day we had a commitment that we couldn't miss. We were going to Big Jim's house for a *"Three Strikes and You're Out Sunday Barbecue."*

"The first time, you got called to a homicide before lunch was even served," he had said when he invited me. "The second time, it was eat and run off to another homicide. This time you better check your cell phones at the door. No interruptions."

I called him Sunday morning.

"Don't tell me you're canceling," he said.

"No. I just thought you should know that Carly Tan won't be coming back from China for a while. Till then Diana and I have

286

legal custody of Sophie."

I told him the whole story. He listened without interrupting. No jokes. No wisecracks about having an instant granddaughter.

"Sometimes my father really understands the gravity of a situation," I told Diana later that morning.

"I think he always understands the gravity of the situation," she said. "But he likes being the guy who doesn't take it seriously."

"Maybe that's why he gets along so well with Terry," I said.

We got to Big Jim's place at noon. Terry and Marilyn were already there, along with their sixteen-year-old daughter, Emily, and her black Lab, Jett.

Sophie immediately fell in love with both of them, and Jett wasted no time flopping over and giving Sophie a belly to rub.

"She's a cool dog," Sophie said to Emily.

"She used to live here," Emily said. "Big Jim gave her to me."

Sophie looked over at me. "Big Jim gives kids dogs?" she said, and I could see the wheels spinning inside her head. "How come you never told me that part?"

We watched the girls and Jett play ball for a few minutes, then Sophie asked Jim if she and Emily could take a walk around the property.

"Don't let me catch you driving any of my eighteen-wheelers," Jim said.

"Don't worry," Sophie said. "I'll just kick the tires."

As soon as the two girls and Jett headed out to the yard, Big Jim stood up. "I have an announcement of major proportions to make," he said.

"Don't you always?" Marilyn asked.

"This one is really big, and it affects us all," he said. "You better sit down."

Angel, Terry, Marilyn, Diana, and I all dutifully followed orders.

"Your captive audience is seated," I said. "Let the Big Jim Show begin."

"Are you ready for this?" Jim asked. "Norman Untermeyer is banging his hygienist."

"Dr. Untermeyer, the dentist?" Marilyn said. "Our movie producer? The man hasn't even produced a single movie. Who cares who he's sleeping with? Jim, this is definitely not going to make the tabloids."

"Why is it an announcement of major proportions?" Terry said. "In fact, why do you think any of us give a shit?"

"You are such a babe in the woods, Detective Biggs," Jim said. "I would have thought a Hollywood screenwriter could figure out the rest of the scenario."

"Sorry," Terry said. "Clue me in."

"Mrs. Untermeyer caught the stupid bastard with his pants down," Jim said. "She's suing him for divorce."

"Uh-oh," Diana said.

"Uh-oh is right," Jim said. "Norman Untermeyer's movie days are over. By the time his wife is finished cleaning his clock, he won't have enough money left to buy a matinee ticket and a small bag of popcorn."

"Does this mean I'm not writing the script?" Terry said.

"Not unless you want to do it on total spec," Jim said.

Terry took it well. In fact, he looked relieved.

"Does this mean no more free dental work?" Marilyn said.

"Free? He'll probably have to double his prices to pay for the divorce," Jim said.

Marilyn looked pissed.

"Can we get to the important stuff here?" I said.

"What's that?" Jim said.

"Are we talking about the young redheaded hygienist with the fantastic knockers?" I said.

"That's the one," Jim said. "Apparently he's been giving her a good flossing for months."

"That is totally disgusting," Marilyn said. "She's young enough to be his daughter."

"Hey," Angel said. "I'm twenty years younger than Jim. Some of us prefer older men."

"Oh God, that came out stupid," Marilyn said. "I'm really sorry, Angel."

"No problem," Angel said.

Marilyn wiped her eyes. "I really am sorry," she said. "I've . . . I've had a rough day." She sniffed back the tears.

"Oh dear," Angel said. "What happened?"

"My husband's movie career just went down the freaking toilet," Marilyn screamed. Then she let out a howling laugh that was instantly infectious, and pretty soon we were all laughing and cracking jokes about Terry's failure to make it as a screenwriter.

Terry included. "I can't believe my screenwriting career is over," he said. "I gave it the best two weeks of my life."

Sophie, Emily, and Jett came back ten minutes later.

"When is lunch?" Sophie asked Jim.

"Half an hour," he said. "Can you wait?"

"Sure," she said. "Can you come out and do stuff?"

Jim looked at me, and I could see that he was in heaven. He turned to Sophie. "You bet I can," he said. "What kind of stuff would you like to do?"

She looked at him coyly. "Can we maybe do another driving lesson in the big red truck?"

"Absolutely, kiddo," Jim said. "You're going to have to learn sooner or later."

He stood up and she took his hand. He towered over her, this six-foot-four-inch, three-hundred-plus-pound gentle giant, and this tiny little gem of a child, whom God had suddenly, inexplicably entrusted to me and Diana.

Sophie called to the dog. "Come on, Jett."

Diana came up beside me, wrapped both arms around my waist, and pulled me close. We watched in blissful silence as the three of them walked toward the truck barn to bond among the eighteen-wheelers.

# ACKNOWLEDGEMENTS

When I showed an early draft of this book to Detective Wendi Berndt of the Los Angeles Police Department, she told me "if a cop ever did that at my crime scene I'd bring him up on charges." I rewrote the offending section. Thank you, Wendi. Once again you helped me keep the details of my make-believe crime believable.

Thanks to my fellow writer, Supervisory Special Agent George Q. Fong, assistant inspector at FBI Headquarters. I know it won't be long before you see George's name on the cover of his own crime fiction novel.

And to my friend and poker buddy, Undersheriff Frank P. Faluotico of the Ulster County Sheriff's office, thanks for being one smart, funny cop, and for making the best meat sauce in the Hudson Valley.

None of my books could have been written without the extensive help of a dedicated and brilliant shrink. That's especially true of this one. Thanks to Dr. Larry Dresdale who spent many hours teaching me just how nuts some people can get (not his words), so that even my most disturbed characters will ring true. If not to my readers, at least to the American Psychological Association.

Thanks also to Dr. Paul Pagnozzi for his medical advice (in fiction and in life), Ulster County Assistant District Attorney Lauren Swan for her in-depth knowledge of battered women's shelters, Graham Jaenicke (who actually owns two pairs of Nantucket Reds), Alex Marshall (my go-to guy on British diplomacy), Joe Drabyak (bookseller extraordinaire), Dennis Diamond (book buyer extraordinaire), the real Robert Muller (whose life is the blueprint for the fictional Muller), the Gibson family (Lori, Jim Sr., Jim Jr., and Melissa) for teaching me about scrapbooking and signing, Sophie Gilbert, the real-life seven-year-old aspiring writer who was the inspiration for Sophie Tan, and to the people who keep *lomaxand biggs.com* running smoothly and looking good: Dennis Woloch, Beth Fish, Chris Cactus, Mia, and Owen.

Thanks to the many booksellers, librarians, fan magazines, bloggers, and readers, who continue to go out of their way to support my life of crime.

Once again I am indebted to my good friend James Patterson, who got me started in this business, gave me guidance (and some killer blurbs) along the way, and who just asked me to coauthor my next book with him. They don't get any nicer than Jim.

As always, my love and appreciation to Emily, Adam, Lauren, Sarah, and Zach, who know the real me, and still keep coming back for more.

And finally, my gratitude to two men who have made a big difference in my professional life—my researcher and practically adopted son, Jason Wood, who helps bring out my craziness, and Mel Berger, my friend, my agent, my rabbi, who helps keep me sane.

Thank you for reading *Cut, Paste, Kill*. Shortly after it was finished, James Patterson called and asked if I'd coauthor a book with him. It was impossible to say "no," and a year later my name (alongside his) was in the #1 slot on the New York Times Bestseller List for *Kill Me If You Can*.

Pretty heady stuff for a writer. Even my wife had to admit it was kind of cool, and to this day she still pays homage to my achievements by saying things like, "Hey #1 bestselling author — take out the %$#@&! garbage."

I followed up my first Patterson co-venture with *NYPD Red*, and it spun out into a successful series. But I missed Mike, Terry, Marilyn, Diana, and Big Jim. And so, I'm happy to announce that I am finally working on the next installment. I can't give you a pub date, but as soon as it's finished it will be published by my friends at Amazon. For those of you who have been waiting for more Lomax and Biggs, I promise I will do my best to make your wait worthwhile.

— Marshall Karp

# ABOUT THE AUTHOR

**MARSHALL KARP** co-created and co-authored the first six books in the #1 bestselling *NYPD Red* series with James Patterson. Starting with *NYPD Red 7,* Marshall will become the sole author of the series, which features Detectives Kylie MacDonald and Zach Jordan as members of an elite task force dedicated to solving crimes committed against — and sometimes by — New York City's rich and famous.

He is also the author of the critically acclaimed *Lomax and Biggs Mysteries* featuring LAPD Detectives Mike Lomax and Terry Biggs, who work homicide out of the Hollywood Division.

After a successful career in advertising, Marshall's first mid-life crisis transported him from New York to LA, where he wrote and produced numerous TV sitcoms and a feature film, *Just Looking*, a coming-of-age comedy loosely based on his own embarrassing teenage years. It was during his time in Hollywood that Marshall met many of the people he kills off in his novels — a cathartic yet perfectly legal way for a writer to exorcise his demons.

Marshall lives and writes in the Mid-Hudson Valley of New York State. Since 2001, he has worked closely with Vitamin Angels, a non-profit organization that brings lifesaving supplements to millions of women and children in the US and around the world.

For more information, visit www.karpkills.com.

Ready for more Lomax and Biggs?

Read on for a sneak peek at

# TERMINAL

# AMATEUR HOUR

# ONE

**THE PRIUS IDLED** in total silence. The hybrid was so damn quiet that even when it was barreling down the road a pedestrian could barely hear it coming.

Which, of course, was part of the plan.

Bruce Bower angled the driver's seat so he could lean back and look through the moon roof. Not much moon to be looked at— just a sliver of white that did little to light the quiet suburban LA street. That too was part of the plan.

He stared heavenward and thought about his life—the fifty-one years that had gone by and the four to six weeks Dr. Spang said he had left. He smiled.

"What's so funny?" Claire asked.

He adjusted the seat so he could see her face in the faint glow that came through the windshield. Thirty-one years since he fell in love with her, and she was still beautiful, still sexy, still everything he ever desired.

"I was just thinking how I spent my entire career dispensing brilliant tax advice," Bruce said, "and now your entire financial future rests on where some dog decides to take a crap."

"Dogs are creatures of habit," Claire said. "Last night was a fluke. Tonight he'll get it right."

It all hinged on a five-year-old yellow Lab named Maverick.

Bruce and Claire had done three test runs. Every night

3

between ten and eleven, Wade Yancy would open the front door of his house at 476 Comstock Avenue, and Maverick would come bounding out, a flashing blue LED safety light hooked to his collar.

Three out of three times the dog headed for the opposite side of the street, stopped at the bend in the road, and did his business directly in front of somebody else's four-million-dollar home.

Yancy would follow with a glass of wine in one hand and a pooper-scooper bag in the other. He'd crouch down to pick up the shit, because that's the kind of thoughtful neighbor Wade Yancy was. But half-drunk and with his back to the oncoming traffic, he was an accident waiting to happen.

All Bruce had to do was put the car in gear, come around the blind turn doing forty, and the deadly silent Prius would do the rest.

Last night was supposed to be the night, but the dog never crossed the street. Maverick had opted to take a quick piss up against a tree on Yancy's property and went back into the house for the night.

That might be the kind of setback a professional killer could deal with, but not Claire. As soon as Yancy closed his front door, she started to cry. Bruce did his best to comfort her, but in the end, he cried along with her.

They went home, drank wine, made love, and did the only thing they could do. They pushed the murder off another day. Again, not much of a setback for a professional, but Bruce didn't have that many days left.

It was now twenty-four hours and fifteen minutes since the aborted attempt, and Bruce reached for the pack of Luckies sitting on the dashboard.

"Do you think that's such a good idea?" Claire said.

"I thought it was," he said, picking up the cigarettes, "but judging by the verbal topspin you put on the words *good* and *idea*, you think it's anything but."

"Very perceptive. I've got Nicorette gum in my purse. You want some?"

"Nicorette is for people who are trying to quit smoking. I'll quit for good soon enough. Until then, I have Dr. Spang's blessings to smoke like a Chevy Vega. I am no longer a gum chewer, Claire. I'm a Stage IV smoker."

"You're also a Stage IV asshole," Claire said. "Do you really think I'm trying to stop you from smoking? I'm only afraid that if you light up, somebody could see us sitting here."

"Oh," he said, putting the cigarettes back on the dash.

She reached into her purse and pulled out a square of Nicorette. "Chew this. You can smoke all you want when the cops get here."

"This reminds me of our third date," he said, chomping down on the mint-flavored wad of nicotine-infused rubber and resting a hand on her thigh.

She covered his hand with hers and kissed his cheek. "Don't get too horny, lover boy, because there are things I could do in the front seat of a car when I was twenty that I can't do now."

"I'm not talking about the sex," he said. "Third date was the first time you started bossing the shit out of me, and you haven't stopped since."

"Have I told you lately that you're an asshole?" she said, punching him gently on the shoulder.

"Stage IV," he said. He was about to return the kiss when she sat up straight.

"The door's opening," she said.

They watched as the flashing blue light loped across the street and headed for the curve in the road.

"Good doggie," Bruce said.

The light stopped moving, and the dog circled, looking for the perfect piece of Holmby Hills real estate to leave his mark.

"Poop is now in progress," Claire said in a mock robotic voice.

Bruce had one hand on the steering wheel, the other on the

5

gearshift. "Get your cell phone ready," he said.

Claire removed the phone from her purse, never taking her eyes off the flashing blue light that was the only insurance policy her dying husband had.

The dog finished and scampered off to piss in the bushes, leaving the pile of shit for his multimillionaire owner to deal with.

"Mr. Yancy has had a few," Claire said.

"More than a few," Bruce said as he watched his prey stumble off the curb and weave his way across the street.

As soon as Yancy squatted down, Bruce put the car in gear and hit the gas.

"Be careful you don't hit the dog," Claire warned.

"The dog doesn't deserve to die," Bruce said as the Prius accelerated from zero to forty in 5.3 seconds. "Yancy does."

They had done their research. Thirty was the speed limit on Comstock, but a pedestrian who might survive being hit at thirty would be roadkill at forty.

The headlights were out, but Bruce had no trouble honing in on the two-hundred-fifty-pound target. And then, as if God had decided that Claire and Bruce Bower had waited for closure long enough, Yancy stood up, and the front bumper of the Prius struck him at knee level, pummeling bones, blood vessels, and tissue.

As soon as he heard the thud, Bruce hit the brakes, but the laws of kinetic energy were still in control. The forward motion continued, and the hood of the car connected with Yancy's pelvis, and his body went airborne, landing on a lawn sixty feet away.

Bruce turned on the headlights before the Prius even came to a stop.

"Oh my God," he screamed. "Claire, I hit somebody, I hit somebody."

They had decided that scripting a story wasn't enough. Acting it out and living it in real time would make the lies much more believable.

Claire immediately went into character and dialed 911.

Bruce sat behind the wheel, dazed, numb. "I never saw him," he said. "He came out of nowhere."

"See if he's okay," Claire yelled. She turned to her phone. "My name is Claire Bower. We just hit someone with our car. I don't know—just a minute. Bruce, where the hell are we?"

"Comstock Avenue," he yelled. "Somewhere between Beverly Glen and Sunset, but closer to Beverly Glen. It wasn't my fault. He came out of nowhere."

Bruce threw the car door open and ran toward the body yelling, "I'm sorry. I'm sorry. I never saw you." He was immersed in the part now, and by the time the paramedics arrived, he was confident that his blood pressure would be through the roof.

The dog was on all fours, whimpering, nuzzling Yancy's face, trying to get a response.

Bruce knelt down in the grass next to the body. "I'm sorry," he said, first to the broken, bloodied man on the ground, and then again to the dog.

"The police will be here in three minutes," Claire yelled, getting out of the car and walking toward him. "Is he okay? Please tell me he's okay."

"I don't know," Bruce yelled back. "Hold on." He pulled his cell phone from his pocket and turned on the flashlight. Yancy's eyes were glazed over, locked in the thousand-yard stare.

Bruce made the official pronouncement. "He's dead."

"Are you sure?" Claire said, real tears streaming down her cheeks. "Maybe he's still breathing."

She dropped to her knees and pressed an ear to the dead man's chest.

A wet, gurgling moan erupted from Yancy's throat. Claire bolted backwards and screamed.

Yancy struggled to speak. "Call...nine...one...one," he implored.

She didn't have to. She could already hear the sirens in the distance.

# TWO

**"I CAN PRACTICALLY** hear the wheels turning inside that head of yours," Claire said. "What are you thinking about?"

"I was just doing the math," Bruce said.

They were sitting on the back step of LAFD Rescue Ambulance 71. The paramedics had taken their vitals, determined they were well enough to be detained at the scene, and had run down the road to join the cops and firefighters congregating around Wade Yancy.

Despite the fact that no one could possibly hear her, Claire whispered. "The math? Honey, there's fifty thousand in the bank in the Caymans, and by this time tomorrow, there'll be another four fifty. Even I can figure that out."

"Not that math," Bruce said. "I'm trying to calculate what it's costing the city of Los Angeles to respond to the accident. LAPD sent four patrol units and a T car; LAFD has two engines, an ALS and a BLS rescue ambulance; there's a team from SID taking pictures, the ME just arrived, plus the DOT has a crew detouring traffic at both ends of Comstock Avenue—all for one simple Vehicle versus Ped."

"For God's sake, Bruce," she said in a harsh whisper. "Lose the cop lingo, or somebody will hear you and figure out that you researched every inch of this investigation a week before the accident happened."

8

He shook his head. "This is why I love you. I was sitting here quietly, but you had to know what I was thinking. I tell you, and I get yelled at."

"I just don't want you to screw it up."

"I haven't screwed anything up yet—probably because I did all that research. And just a reminder—you're the one crashing the party here. You're not supposed to even know what I'm doing, much less be a part of it. It's totally against their rules."

"*Their* rules? What about Thou Shalt Not Kill? They have no problem if you break that rule. What are they going to do if they find out I was with you—ask me for their money back?"

Bruce shrugged. "I don't know what they'll do, but whatever it is, that'll be the new guy's problem."

"What new guy?"

"You're young, you're beautiful, you'll have a nice little nest egg—trust me, there's going to be a new guy."

"I don't think so, Bruce. Thirty-one years of living on the edge with a wild and crazy high-flying accountant is all the excitement I can handle in one lifetime."

He laughed. "Oh yeah—that's me—the Evel Knievel of CPAs."

"That cop is coming back," Claire said. "Try to act like you're in shock."

"I am in shock," Bruce said. "I can't believe I earned a half-million dollars for a couple of hours work."

Officer Matt McCormick had stepped out of the circle surrounding Wade Yancy and was walking up the road to the ambulance.

"How are you folks holding up?" he said gently. He was only three years on the job, but he had a natural gift for bringing calm to the chaos of a sudden and violent traffic accident.

Claire smiled. "Thank you, Officer McCormick. We're doing better."

"Mr. Bower," McCormick said, "the paramedic told me your

9

BP was high, but that's normal in situations like this. I'd like you to take me through the accident, but if you don't feel well, the ambulance can take you to UCLA Med."

"I'm okay for now," Bruce said. "But EMS has been here awhile, and he's still lying there, so I guess he's..."

"Yes sir, I'm sorry to tell you that the victim has expired. If it's any consolation, the coroner is pretty sure he never suffered. He died on impact."

"On impact," Bruce repeated. "I guess that's some kind of a blessing."

"Does he have a family?" Claire asked.

"A wife and two teenage daughters."

"I heard screaming," Claire said.

"That was one of the girls. She's in shock. They took her back to the house. One of the paramedics is with her now." He took out a pad. "Mr. Bower, why don't you tell me what happened."

"We were home and decided to drive out to Century City for some ice cream," Bruce said. "We always cut across Comstock from Sunset to Beverly Glen—it's faster. So I know the road. I wasn't speeding. And I didn't have anything to drink. You can test me."

"That's okay, sir," McCormick said. "I can tell."

"We're driving on Comstock, and out of the corner of my eye I see this flashing blue light on the other side of the street. Even so, I didn't look away. Then all of a sudden this man just stands up—he's right in front of the car, but his back is to me. I never saw him. He never saw me."

"He probably never heard you either," McCormick said. "The NHTSA is trying to get laws passed to make these hybrids noisier, but it's too late for Mr. Yancy."

"Is that his name?" Claire asked.

"Yes ma'am. Wade Yancy, forty-seven years old," McCormick said. "Finish your story, Mr. Bower. You say he just stood up in front of you?"

"I don't understand," Bruce said. "Where did he come from?"

"The way we pieced it together, it looks like he was squatting on the roadway picking up after his dog and stood up just as you came around the curve. There was an empty wineglass on the shoulder at the point of impact. He must have set it down when he was cleaning up after the dog. I have no doubt that the tox report will show he was drinking."

Bruce shook his head. "What happens next?" he asked.

"I'll write up a report stating that the primary collision factor was the pedestrian, probably impaired, in the roadway, and if it hadn't been for him, there would not have been a collision. A traffic detective will be out here shortly, and if he signs off on it, which I'm confident he will, you're free to go. Your car is damaged, but one of the uniforms checked it out. It'll get you home. Are you okay to drive?"

"I'm fine," Bruce said.

"He's fine," Claire said. "But I'm driving."

"Good call, Mrs. Bower," McCormick said, giving her a big smile. "Anything else I can do for you while we're waiting for the detective?"

"Just one question," she said. "How do you do it?"

"Do what, ma'am?"

"You must see tragedies like this every day. How do you manage to stay so positive, so upbeat?"

"I don't have a choice. When I get to a scene, people are hurting—physically, emotionally, psychologically. I'm not there to add more pain to the mix. My job is to sort things out and bring comfort wherever I can."

"Well, you have. I only hope you don't go home after work and cry yourself to sleep."

"Don't worry about that, Mrs. Bower. The one thing you learn on this job is to enjoy life as much you can, because you never know what's going to sneak up on you and pull the plug on the whole deal."

His cell phone rang. He checked the caller ID and smiled. "Speaking of fun, it's my fiancé. Excuse me."

"The kid's right," Bruce said as soon as the cop was out of earshot. "You never know what's going to sneak up on you and pull the plug on the whole deal." He paused and smiled. "Like a Stage IV asshole in a Prius."

PART ONE

# DIAGNOSIS

# CHAPTER 1

**I DID A** quick head count as soon as I walked into the waiting room. Eight people waiting for the doctor. I walked to the receptionist's desk and printed my name on the sign-in sheet. There were spaces for *Time of Appointment* and *Time of Arrival*. I left them blank.

The glass window slid open, and Nadine smiled up at me. She had blue eyes, silver hair, and a deep whiskey-coated voice. No matter how sick you were when you walked into Dr. Heller's office, Nadine immediately made you feel better.

"Hello, handsome," she said. "And how are you today?"

"Fashionably late."

She looked at her watch. "Honey, an hour and twenty minutes ain't fashionable—even in LA."

"I was stuck at a crime scene. I called and left a message with somebody—I didn't catch her name."

"I know. Somebody, whose name is Helen, told me you were out fighting crime, and you'd get here when you got here." She leaned close to the window and whispered. "I think you just didn't want to come back here for that prostate exam."

"Doug gave me a complete physical last week. Head to toe."

"Minus one part," she said, wiggling a finger in the air.

"Not my fault. He stepped out of the office, I got a call from my lieutenant, and I had to race back to the station. I'm sorry

I couldn't stick around for Doug to come back, grease up, and work me like a sock puppet."

She let loose with a lung-butter laugh that sounded like the Roto-Rooter man was unclogging her pipes. People in the waiting room looked up, half smiles on their faces, hoping to be let in on the fun.

"Nadine, serious question," I said. "How long a wait do I have?"

She put a finger to her lips. I shut up. She picked up a phone. "Brenda, I reserved a table for one—Detective Lomax. Yes, he just strolled in. Come and get him."

She waved me through the door to the inner sanctum, and I didn't look back, but I'm sure all eight of the people in the waiting room were thinking, *Who the hell is he?*

Brenda, Doug Heller's senior nurse, met me on the other side. "Hey, Mike, you bolted out of here in a big hurry last week," she said.

"It's all part of the glamour of being a cop. This way I get to live in dread of a prostate exam yet a second time."

She led me into an exam room, took my BP and my pulse, and handed me a gown. "Suit up," she said. "Dr. Heller will be right in."

I stripped down, hung up my clothes, set my gun on the counter next to a container of cotton balls, and put on a pale blue, one-size-fits-nobody hospital gown with the wide slit down the back.

There was a knock on the door, and Doug Heller walked in.

"Oh, hi," I said, struggling to tie the gown in the back. "I was just trying on prom dresses. Do you have anything in a pink taffeta?"

Doug and I have been friends for twenty years, so we start every session with the usual *how's your family* stuff, or at the very least, some guy banter.

Not this time. "So, Mike," he said, skipping the foreplay, "how are you feeling?"

16

"Fine."

"Fine is not a medical term. You tired? Run down?"

"Overworked. Does that count?"

"Hop on the table."

I did as told, and he put his fingers on my neck and started pressing. "How about dizzy spells? Shortness of breath?"

"None of the above. What's going on?"

"I got your blood results from last week, and your white blood count is a little off. That's why I called you back."

"I thought it was because I bailed on the prostate exam."

"You're forty-three years old. I could have easily let it slide till your next physical," he said. "But this can't wait."

"What is it?"

"Probably nothing, but I'm going to take some more blood and run it through the lab again. Lie down."

I stretched out, and he began poking my belly.

"What do you mean my white blood count is a little off?" I said.

"Out of range. Nothing to worry about, but it's worth looking at again."

"What if I get the same bad numbers on the next blood test?" I said. "Do you have a guess what it could be?"

"Mike, I don't guess," he said, still stabbing his finger into my gut. "If you want guesswork, go to the Internet and Google the word *health*. You'll have millions of choices. Don't make yourself crazy. If the blood work doesn't change, I'll run a few tests. And the best news is they're free—all paid for by the Los Angeles Police Department. Have you used any steroids recently?"

"Jesus, Doug."

"Your lymph nodes are good, but your spleen is enlarged. Sit up, and I'll send Brenda back to draw some blood."

"So no prostate exam?"

"Almost forgot. Like I said, I wouldn't have called you back for it, but now that you're here and dressed for the occasion, let's get it done."

He reached over to the counter, took a latex glove out of a dispenser, and popped the cap off a tube of KY jelly.

"I hate this," I said, getting on my knees and lowering my shoulders to the table.

"It's not exactly April in Paris for me either, sweetheart."

My ass was up in the air when I heard the first gunshot. Instinct kicked in, and I jumped off the table.

"Holy shit," Doug said. "Was that a gunshot?"

"Yes, get down on the floor and stay there. If you've got a cell in your pocket, call 911."

I dove for the counter and had my hand on my Glock when the second shot rang out. Shotgun blast. And judging from the sound, the shooter was close by, but not in the next room. Doug's office was one of dozens in the San Vicente Medical Arts Building. I had no idea which one the shots came from.

I opened the exam room door and peered out. Patients and nurses alike were screaming and running toward the waiting room. "LAPD," I yelled. "Get back to your rooms. They're safer. Do it. Now. Now."

A third blast rang out. I could tell by the spacing that it was a pump-action shotgun. My Glock in front of me, and my bare ass hanging out behind me, I ran through the waiting room and headed toward the sound.

# CHAPTER 2

**I STEPPED INTO** the communal hall. There were six other doctors' offices on that floor, and the door to every one of them was open. People were stampeding in my direction. Four-alarm panic. Whatever they were trying to get away from, I headed toward.

I can think of five other times in my career when I've had to run into a terrified crowd with my gun drawn. Three of those times I was in uniform, and twice in plain clothes with my badge on a chain around my neck. People were always relieved to see me, and the looks on their faces said it all. *Thank God—here comes the cavalry.*

Not this time. This time the reactions were more like, *oh shit—crazy man with a gun.* People either froze in their tracks, screamed, or both. Clearly, I'd have been a much more welcome sight if I had been wearing pants.

"LAPD. Get out, get out," I yelled, hoping that none of them were brave enough to try to tackle me.

I advanced down the hallway, barely looking at faces, just scanning the crowd for a weapon.

And then I saw him step through the center door at the far end of the corridor—white, middle-aged, balding, rimless glasses—hardly menacing, except for the Mossberg Pump-Action shotgun in his right hand.

19

"LAPD. Drop the gun," I bellowed.

He looked at me, dazed.

"LAPD," I shouted even louder. "Drop the gun. Now."

The gunman spooked, darted back into the office, and slammed the door behind him. I kicked it open, rolling to the floor as I came through the doorway.

Patients were huddled in corners, looking for protection behind fashionable teak side chairs that wouldn't protect them from a stiff kick, much less a 12-gauge shotgun blast.

"LAPD," I announced, jumping to my feet and looking in every direction.

A big beefy man closest to the door was acting as a human shield, his arms and body covering the woman beneath him. "In there," he said in a loud whisper, pointing toward an inside door.

I edged against the wall. All my training said, *wait for backup*. But my instincts said, *no time*. I dropped to a crouch and dove into the room.

The shooter was behind a desk in front of a window, the shotgun in his hand. But he wasn't pointing it at me. The barrel was tucked under his chin, and his right hand was extended all the way, his thumb on the trigger.

"Don't come any closer," he said.

I stopped cold. I'd had suicide prevention training, but I hadn't put it to use in years. Not only was I rusty, but I'm pretty sure the instructor never covered what to do if there's a dead man in a blood-soaked white coat lying on the floor only a few feet from the man whose life I was now obligated to save.

"I'm not moving," I said as slowly and calmly as I could. Meanwhile, my brain was racing back to the course material. *Introduce yourself. Give plenty of reassurance.*

"My name is Detective Mike Lomax," I said. "I'm with LAPD. I'm here to help."

"Too late, Mike."

"At least let's talk about it. What's your name?"

20

"Calvin Bernstein."

"Do you mind if I call you by your first name?" I asked.

"Cal. Call me Cal. Where the hell are your clothes?"

"Funny thing about that, Cal," I said. "I was at my doctor's office down the hall when—"

"I had no choice," he said. "I had to do it."

"Well that's definitely something we should sit down and talk about."

I could hear the sirens now. The building had been full of people. I could only imagine how many calls 911 logged since the first shot was fired. Cal heard them too.

"I'm sorry," he said, starting to sob. "I'm really sorry. I think you should leave now, Mike. You don't want to see this."

"Don't do it, Cal." I said. "We can work this out."

"Tell Janice I love her."

"I have a better idea, Cal. Why don't you pick up the phone on the desk, call Janice, and tell her yourself. I'm sure she'd much rather hear it from you."

"You're right. She would."

And then he pulled the trigger. Blood, bone and gray matter pelted the walls and the window behind him.

Nothing in my training prepared me for this. I'd only known Calvin Bernstein for the last two minutes of his life, but I took the loss personally. I stood there, stunned, shaking my head in disbelief. "Aww, Cal," I said. "I thought we were getting somewhere. I thought you were going to call Janice."

Cal didn't answer. If he could have, I'm sure it would have been something like, *It's not like I didn't warn you, Mike. I told you to leave. I told you that you don't want to see this.*

Whatever remained of Calvin Bernstein from the neck down had toppled to the floor. He was side by side with his victim, who was sprawled faceup on the rug, his frantic eyes staring blankly at the ceiling. I knelt down to get a closer look.

"Jesus," I said.

I knew him. His name was Kristian Kraus, and he was by far the best-known, most beloved fertility doctor in all of Los Angeles. Couples who desperately wanted to have a baby lined up at his door in the hopes that he could help them conceive one of Kristian's miracles.

Five years ago, my wife Joanie and I were one of those desperate couples. We tried every trick in the fertility handbook—stimulating ovulation, collecting sperm, screwing on a schedule. It cost a fortune, but nothing took.

And then, one day, about a year after we started, Dr. Kraus delivered the one thing we never expected—the news that Joanie had ovarian cancer.

Two years later, she died.

A voice came from behind me. It was young, female, and very shaky. "LAPD," she said. "Don't turn around. Just put the gun down nice and easy."

I didn't argue. I lowered my Glock to the floor. "I'm on the job, Officer," I said, not daring to turn around. "Detective Mike Lomax, Hollywood Division, Homicide Unit."

"I don't care who you are. Just stand up real slow, and put your hands in the air where I can see them."

I stood up. My hospital gown with the impossible-to-close slit down the back was embarrassing enough, but when I raised my arms high above my head, the gown hiked up, and the already immodest opening parted like the Red Sea.

I couldn't help myself. I started laughing.

"You think this is funny?" she said.

I looked down at the two bloody corpses on the floor. "Officer, from where I'm standing, nothing is funny, but I'll bet from your point of view, this little tableau has got to be a fucking laugh riot."

# CHAPTER 3

**AND THEN, A** familiar voice. "Don't shoot him, Officer. He's one of the good guys."

"Are you sure?" the cop asked. "You can't see his face."

"Are you kidding?" the voice drawled. "I'd recognize that asshole anywhere. He's my partner."

"Officer," I said, "if Detective Biggs has finished making a bad situation worse, can I put my hands down and lower my skirt? I'd like to show a little respect for the dead."

"Trust me," Biggs said. "The living will be even more grateful."

I dropped my arms and turned around. The cop was young, blond, and pretty—not an easy trifecta for a woman trying to get ahead in a male-dominated department. But to her credit, she was the one holding the gun on me.

"Detective Lomax," she said, holstering her weapon. "I'm sorry. I've never seen anything like this. You had a gun. There were two dead bodies. I just—"

"You did fine. What's your name, Officer?'

"Barclay, sir. Dawn Barclay."

"This building is about to be inundated with cops, Barclay. Before they come running and gunning, get on the radio and tell them the situation is contained."

"Yes, sir."

"And tell them nobody leaves. Get IDs and hold everyone who hasn't already bolted until we find out what happened here."

"Yes, sir," she said and backed out of the office.

"So," Biggs said, "apart from the body count, how'd that prostate exam go for you?"

"I managed to get out of it again. Meanwhile, you were parked in front of the building. I figured you'd come running when the first shot was fired. Where the hell were you, anyway?"

"Victoria's Secret, shopping for peignoirs."

Terry Biggs wants to be a stand-up comic after he retires from the force. So he's always on. The problem is, he doesn't know when to turn it off.

"For God's sake, Terry, look at this mess. Lighten up on the jokes, will you?"

"I'm not kidding. You said you'd be about thirty minutes. Next week is my anniversary, so I drove over to the mall. I was trying to decide between a lace camisole and a satin baby doll when I heard 'shots fired' over the radio. At least give me some credit—I got here in time to save your sorry ass. Not to change the subject, but is that your gun on the floor?"

"Yeah."

"Don't bend over. I'll get it." He reached down, picked up the Glock, and smelled it. "You didn't fire your weapon," he said.

"No. The man on the left is Calvin Bernstein. At least that's what he told me just before he gave himself a Mossberg Pump-Action facelift. But first he unloaded three rounds into the other guy. Him I know. His name is Kristian Kraus. He was Joanie's doctor."

"Holy shit. He was Joanie's oncologist?"

"No. He's a fertility specialist. He tried to help us get pregnant, but in the end, all he managed to do was be the one to deliver the bad news."

"Fertility doc," Terry said, handing me my gun. "Doesn't seem like the kind of profession that gets you peppered with a

12-gauge. You think it was personal?"

"I don't know. The last thing he said to me before he killed himself was 'Tell Janice I love her.'"

"Then let's go find Janice," Terry said.

"I have a better idea," I said. "Why don't you walk over to Heller's office and find my clothes?"

"Me? I'm a goddamn detective. Send a uniform. Tell Barclay to go get your stuff."

"Terry, there is no way in hell that I'm asking a hot blond cop to bring me back my pants and underwear," I said. "You get them."

"I can't believe it," he said. "It took less than ten minutes for me to go from fondling Victoria's gauzy thongs to retrieving Mike Lomax's ragtag skivvies."

He started to leave, stopped, and turned around. "Y'know, as long as you're dressed for it," he said, grinning, "are you sure you don't want to toddle on across the hall and get that pesky prostate exam over and done with?"

"Thanks, but I'll pass," I said. "And if you see a guy wearing a white coat and a latex glove with a glob full of K-Y jelly on one finger, tell him to—oh, hell, you'll think of something—you're the comedian."

# CHAPTER 4

**JESSICA KEATING KNELT** over the body of Kristian Kraus and shook her head. "Three shotgun blasts to the chest. Talk about overkill."

"Don't judge our shooter too harshly," Terry said. "It's still early in the investigation, but I think we've established that Mr. Bernstein was not exactly a professional."

Officer Barclay returned. "Nobody else was hurt," she reported, "although I'm sure several of the people I interviewed will be upping their Xanax intake for the next few days. Security cameras have the shooter's Volvo pulling into the parking lot at 1:14 p.m. He sat behind the wheel for eighteen minutes, finally got out, removed a four-foot-long canvas case from the trunk, and entered the building. Three minutes later, all hell broke loose."

"Any witnesses?" Terry asked.

"A long list, most of whom described a crazy man with a gun running down the hall half-naked, but the doctor's receptionist had a face-to-face with the shooter. Her name's Michele Melvin. She's waiting for you at the front desk."

I knew Michele. She'd worked for Kraus when Joanie was a patient, and despite the fact that she'd met thousands of infertile couples since then, she recognized me immediately.

"Detective Lomax," she said, offering me her hand. "I'm so sorry about your wife."

"You knew?"

"Dr. Kraus told me. He was very upset."

I nodded. My pants and my dignity had been restored, but I was still shaky after first staring down the barrel of a Mossberg, and then watching helplessly as Cal Bernstein blew his brains out. Bringing up my dead wife didn't help calm me down. "Can you tell us what happened?" I said.

"The man—the one who shot Dr. Kraus—came in. He was walking fast. He gets to my window and says, 'I'm meeting my wife, but I desperately need a bathroom before I sign in.' He's squirming all around like you do when you have to pee real bad, so I buzzed him in."

She closed her eyes and put her hand to her forehead. Cops see it all the time—an eyewitness reliving a moment of sheer horror that would stay with her for the rest of her life. We waited.

"And then I heard him yell Dr. Kraus's name," she said, opening her eyes. "Only it was more of a question, like he wanted to make sure he was talking to the right person. Then I heard the first shot, and I went on automatic pilot."

She looked at me and Terry to make sure we understood. We did, but we let her elaborate.

"I grew up in East LA. You hear gunfire; you take cover. You try to run, and you could wind up running into a bullet. I dove under the desk and prayed until I heard someone say, 'LAPD. Drop the gun.' That was you, wasn't it?"

I nodded.

She smiled. "You're the answer to my prayers."

"Did you know the man who shot him?" Terry asked.

"Never saw him before, but we get new patients all the time. It's the nature of the practice."

"His name is Calvin Bernstein. See if he's in your records."

She hesitated.

"What's the matter?" Terry said.

"Dr. Kraus is big on patient confidentiality, but I guess I'm allowed to break the HIPAA laws if my boss gets gunned down."

She searched her computer. "We've got six Bernsteins—no Calvins."

"Try Janice Bernstein," I said.

She went back to the computer. "Sorry. And nobody named Bernstein had an appointment today."

"Can you think of any reason anybody would want to kill Dr. Kraus?" I asked.

"No. You knew him, Mike. He dedicated his life to trying to give couples the one thing they wanted most in life." She pointed to a wall in the waiting room that was covered from floor to ceiling with baby pictures. "And even when they didn't conceive, he still gave them hope. People loved him."

"Somebody didn't," Terry said. "What can you tell us about his personal life?"

"Married, two kids in college."

"I'm looking for something a little more personal."

"You mean did he screw around? My last job, the doc had an affair. You can't keep that on the down low from the woman who answers your phone and opens your mail. But not Dr. Kraus. He was a good man."

"I'm sure he was," Terry said, "and we're very sorry for your loss."

She looked away. "Stupid, stupid, stupid," she said, pounding her desk with the flat of her fist. "I should never have buzzed him in."

"Michele," I said, "he came here to shoot Dr. Kraus. If you got in his way, he'd have shot you too."

She nodded. She knew I was right. It's just another one of those things you learn growing up on the streets of East LA.

# CHAPTER 5

**"YOU READY TO** go?" Terry asked when we'd finished talking to Michele.

"Almost," I said. "I've just got to make a quick stop at Doug Heller's office."

"Good idea. He probably can tell us a few things about the victim. I'll go with you, partner."

"Nice try," I said, "but I can handle this on my own... partner."

Terry shrugged and headed for the car, and I walked back down the same hallway I raced through an hour ago. Doug's waiting room was empty, but Nadine was still at the front desk.

She looked up at me, the radiant smile gone, her face drawn in pain. "Mike," she said, "I wasn't sure you'd come back. Dr. Heller is in his office."

Doug was sitting at his desk. When it comes to death, especially something as violent and senseless as the murder of Kristian Kraus, doctors are no different from the rest of us. Doug was shaken to the core.

I sat down across from him. "Was he a friend?" I asked.

"More of a colleague, but one I liked. Hell, everybody liked him. Most docs deal with pain and suffering. If we're any good, we can make you feel better. Kris helped people make babies."

"Can you think of any reason why anyone would want to kill him?" I asked for the second time in the space of a few minutes.

He shook his head. "I've been sitting here trying to come up with an answer, and the only thing I can come up with is that maybe the killer got the wrong doctor."

"He asked for Dr. Kraus by name before he shot him."

"Why, Mike, why?"

"I don't know, but I'm going to find out. I've got a long day ahead of me. I'm going to ask for a rain check on that prostate exam."

He smiled. "No problem," he said. "Especially now that I realize it's not your prostate that's going to kill you. You're more likely to die in a shootout at your doctor's office."

"Thanks." I stood up.

"Not so fast," he said. "I still want Brenda to draw some blood before you go."

"You mind telling me why?"

"I will, but as your primary physician, there's something I have to say first. Next time you hear gunshots, don't go running towards them."

"Sorry, Doc, but that's my job."

"And that, Detective Lomax, is exactly why I'm running these blood tests. Now if you don't tell me how to do my job, I won't tell you how to do yours."

Ten minutes later, I was back in the car with Terry.

It was unseasonably warm for the middle of October, and I had made the mistake of not wearing my jacket.

"What's going on?" he said, pointing to the telltale Band-Aid taped over the vein in my left arm.

"I don't want to talk about it," I said. "With anybody. So don't say anything to Diana about driving me to Doug's office."

"You never told her you were going back for a follow-up?"

"No."

"Why?"

"Because she'd start worrying, and there's nothing to worry about."

"Well, you better tell her soon, because it's going to be all over the news that LAPD Detective Mike Lomax was in the doctor's office with his ass hanging out when the shooting went down."

He was right. I had to talk to Diana. But first Terry and I had to break the news to two women that they were now widows.

Don't stop now.

The best is yet to come.

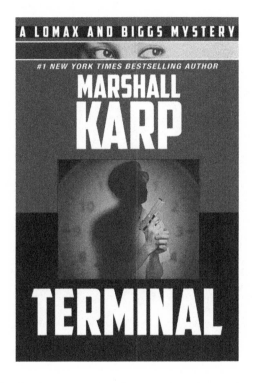

Available in paperback or e-book on Amazon

Thank you for supporting my life of crime.

— Marshall Karp

Made in the USA
Coppell, TX
15 March 2023

14296182R00194